# Research Methodologies for Auto/biography Studies

This collection of short essays provides a rigorous, rich, collaborative space in which scholars and practitioners debate the value of different methodological approaches to the study of life narratives and explore a diverse range of interdisciplinary methods. Auto/biography studies has been one of the most vibrant sub-disciplines to emerge in the humanities and social sciences in the past decade, providing significant links between disciplines including literary studies, languages, linguistics, digital humanities, medical humanities, creative writing, history, gender studies, education, sociology, and anthropology.

The essays in this collection position auto/biography as a key discipline for modelling interdisciplinary approaches to methodology and ask: what original and important thinking can auto/biography studies bring to discussions of methodology for literary studies and beyond? And how does the diversity of methodological interventions in auto/biography studies build a strong and diverse research discipline? In including some of auto/biography's leading international scholars alongside emerging scholars, and exploring key subgenres and practices, this collection showcases knowledge about what we do when engaging in auto/ biographical research. *Research Methodologies for Auto/biography Studies* offers a series of case studies that explore the research practices, reflective behaviours, and ethical considerations that inform auto/biographical research.

**Kate Douglas** is Professor in the College of Humanities, Arts, and Social Sciences at Flinders University. She is the author of *Contesting Childhood: Autobiography, Trauma and Memory* (Rutgers, 2010) and the co-author of *Life Narratives and Youth Culture: Representation, Agency and Participation* (Palgrave, 2016; with Anna Poletti). She is the co-editor (with Laurie McNeill) of *Teaching Lives: Contemporary Pedagogies of Life Narratives* (Routledge 2017); (with Kylie Cardell) of *Trauma Tales: Auto/biographies of Childhood and Youth* (Routledge 2014); and (with Gillian Whitlock) *Trauma Texts* (Routledge, 2009).

**Ashley Barnwell** is Lecturer in Sociology in the School of Social and Political Sciences at the University of Melbourne. Her research focuses on memory, emotion, and family storytelling. Her work has been published in journals such as *Life Writing*, *a/b: Auto/Biography Studies*, *Memory Studies*, *Cultural Sociology*, and *Emotion, Space & Society*. Her co-authored book (with Joseph Cummins), *Reckoning with the Past: Family Historiographies in Postcolonial Australian Literature* (2019), is published in Routledge's Memory Studies series.

# Research Methodologies for Auto/biography Studies

Edited by Kate Douglas and
Ashley Barnwell

Routledge
Taylor & Francis Group

NEW YORK AND LONDON

First published 2019
by Routledge
605 Third Avenue, New York, NY 10017

and by Routledge
2 Park Square, Milton Park, Abingdon, Oxon, OX14 4RN

First issued in paperback 2021

*Routledge is an imprint of the Taylor & Francis Group, an informa business*

*Library of Congress Cataloging-in-Publication Data*
Names: Douglas, Kate, 1974- editor. | Barnwell, Ashley, editor.
Title: Research methodologies for auto/biography studies / edited by Kate Douglas and Ashley Barnwell.
Description: New York, NY : Routledge, 2019. | Includes bibliographical references and index. |
Identifiers: LCCN 2019013726 (print) | LCCN 2019014988 (ebook) | ISBN 9780429288432 (Master) | ISBN 9781000005004 (pdf) | ISBN 9781000011845 (ePub) | ISBN 9781000018363 (Mobi) | ISBN 9780367255688 (hardback : alk. paper)
Subjects: LCSH: Biography—Research—Methodology. | Biography as a literary form—Study and teaching. | Autobiography—Social aspects.
Classification: LCC CT22 (ebook) | LCC CT22 .R47 2019 (print) | DDC 809/.93592—dc23
LC record available at https://lccn.loc.gov/2019013726

ISBN 13: 978-1-03-209211-9 (pbk)
ISBN 13: 978-0-367-25568-8 (hbk)

Typeset in Sabon
by Apex CoVantage, LLC

# Contents

*List of Illustrations*                                                    ix
*List of Contributors*                                                     x
*Acknowledgements*                                                       xvii

**What We Do When We Do Life Writing: Methodologies
for Auto/Biography Now**                                                   1
ASHLEY BARNWELL AND KATE DOUGLAS

Forms                                                                      11

1   **Writing Memoir**                                                     13
    CLAIRE LYNCH

2   **Archival Methods in Auto/Biographical Research**                     19
    MARIA TAMBOUKOU

3   **Zines**                                                              26
    ANNA POLETTI

4   **Objects and Things**                                                 34
    GILLIAN WHITLOCK

5   **Social, Media, Life Writing: Online Lives at Scale,
    Up Close, and In Context**                                            41
    AIMÉE MORRISON

6   **Studying Visual Autobiographies in the Post-Digital Era**           49
    SARAH BROPHY

 7  Biography                                                           61
    W. CRAIG HOWES

 8  Research Methods for Studying Graphic Biography                     68
    CANDIDA RIFKIND

 9  Working With Family Histories                                       76
    ASHLEY BARNWELL

10  Tracing Emotional Bonds in Family Letters: A Pursuit
    of an Epistolary Melody                                             83
    LEENA KURVET-KÄOSAAR

11  Life Narrative Methods for Working With Diaries                     90
    KYLIE CARDELL

12  Autoethnographic Life Writing: Reaching Beyond,
    Crossing Over                                                       96
    SALLY ANN MURRAY

13  Telling Life Stories Using Creative Methods in
    Qualitative Interviews                                             103
    SIGNE RAVN

14  Performing and Broadcasting Lives: Auto/Biographical
    Testimonies in Theatre and Radio                                   109
    GUNN GUDMUNDSDOTTIR

15  Big Data and Self-Tracking: Research Trajectories                  116
    JULIE RAK

Frameworks                                                             123

16  Another Story                                                      125
    JEANINE LEANE

17  Reading Digital Lives Generously                                   132
    LAURIE MCNEILL AND JOHN DAVID ZUERN

18  Reading the Life Narratives of Children and Youth                  140
    KATE DOUGLAS

19 Negotiated Truths and Iterative Practice in Action:
The Women in Conflict Expressive Life Writing Project 149
MEG JENSEN AND SIOBHAN CAMPBELL

20 Researching Online Biographical Media and Death
Narratives After the Digital Turn 161
PAMELA GRAHAM

21 An Epistemological Approach to Trans* Autobiography 169
SARAH RAY RONDOT

22 Genetics and Auto/Biography 179
PRAMOD K. NAYAR

23 Doing Disability Autobiography: Introducing Reading
Group Methodology as Feminist Disability Praxis 186
ALLY DAY

24 Sanctioning Subjectivity: Navigating Low-Risk
Human Ethics Approval 193
PHILLIP KAVANAGH AND KATE DOUGLAS

25 Girls' Auto/Biographical Media: The Importance of Audience
Reception in Studying Undervalued Life Narrative 200
EMMA MAGUIRE

26 Locating Diasporic Lives: Beyond Textual Boundaries 207
RICIA A. CHANSKY

27 The Diary as a Life Story: Working With Documents
of Family and Migration 213
ANNE HEIMO

28 Between Forced Confession and Ethnic Autobiography 220
Y-DANG TROEUNG

29 Autobiographical Research With Children 228
MARIA DA CONCEIÇÃO PASSEGGI AND ECLEIDE CUNICO
FURLANETTO

30 Ecocriticism and Life Narrative 236
ALFRED HORNUNG

Afterword                                                                       245

31  The Box in the Attic: Memoir, Methodology, and
    Family Archives                                                             247
    G. THOMAS COUSER

    *Index*                                                                     254

# Illustrations

6.1   Instagram post by @agotoronto tagged #infinitekusama          52
6.2   Google "Art Selfie" app result                                53

# Contributors

**Ashley Barnwell** is Lecturer in Sociology at the University of Melbourne, Australia. Her research focuses on memory, emotion, and family storytelling. She is currently working on a project about intergenerational family secrets and is co-author of *Reckoning with the Past: Family Historiographies in Postcolonial Australian Literature* (2018, with Joseph Cummins).

**Sarah Brophy** is Professor in the Department of English and Cultural Studies at McMaster University, Canada. She is the author of *Witnessing AIDS: Writing, Testimony, and the Work of Mourning* (University of Toronto Press, 2004), co-editor with Janice Hladki of *Embodied Politics in Visual Autobiography* (University of Toronto Press, 2014), and contributor to journals such as *PMLA*, *Literature and Medicine*, *Contemporary Women's Writing*, *a/b: Auto/Biography Studies*, and *Cultural Critique* (forthcoming 2019). Her current SSHRC-funded research examines the convergence of visual self-portraiture, installation art, digital labour, and activism.

**Siobhan Campbell** investigates how creative writing interventions can interact with other activism in ways that contest the borders of exclusion in post-conflict and recovering cultures. Author of five books of poetry and editor of *Stories and Poems by Combat Veterans* (CSUK), she is also co-author of *The Expressive Life Writing Handbook*, and wrote the UNDP SIRI report "Expressive Writing for Social Cohesion" (2017).

**Kylie Cardell** is Senior Lecturer in English and Creative Writing at Flinders University, South Australia. She is the author of *Dear World: Contemporary Uses of the Diary* (2014) and editor (with Kate Douglas) of *Telling Tales: Autobiographies of Childhood and Youth* (2015). Kylie is an executive member for the International Auto/Biography Association (IABA) Asia–Pacific, co-directs the Flinders Life Narrative Research Group (Flinders University), and is the essays editor for *Life Writing*.

**Ricia A. Chansky** is Professor of Literature at the University of Puerto Rico at Mayagüez. She is co-editor of the scholarly journal *a/b: Auto/*

*Biography Studies* and editor of the new Routledge Auto/Biography Studies book series. She co-edited *The Routledge Auto/Biography Studies Reader* (2015) and edited two volumes, *Auto/Biography in the Americas: Relational Lives* (2016) and *Auto/Biography Across the Americas: Transnational Themes in Life Writing* (2016). In the 2018–2019 academic year she led a large-scale public humanities project on Hurricane María in conjunction with the Voice of Witness program and the Humanities Action Lab. She has previous and forthcoming publications on auto/biography studies, diaspora studies, disaster studies, feminist rhetorics and gender studies, new American studies, pedagogy, social justice, transnational studies, and visual culture.

**G. Thomas Couser** is retired from Hofstra University, USA, where he taught English and founded a Disability Studies Program. His books include *Vulnerable Subjects: Ethics and Life Writing* (Cornell, 2004), *Signifying Bodies: Disability in Contemporary Life Writing* (Michigan 2009), and *Memoir: An Introduction* (Oxford, 2012). His most recent book is *Letter to My Father: A Memoir* (Hamilton Books, 2017).

**Ally Day** is Assistant Professor of Disability Studies at the University of Toledo, USA. She has published articles in *a/b: Auto/biography Studies*, *Canadian Journal of Disability Studies*, *Journal of Literary and Cultural Disability Studies*, and *Feminist Formations*, among others. She is currently finishing her book project, *The Political Economy of Stigma*, and continues to work as co-editor of *Disability Studies Quarterly*.

**Kate Douglas** is Professor in the College of Humanities, Arts, and Social Sciences at Flinders University (South Australia). She is the author of *Contesting Childhood: Autobiography, Trauma and Memory* (Rutgers, 2010) and the co-author of *Life Narratives and Youth Culture: Representation, Agency and Participation* (Palgrave, 2016; with Anna Poletti). She is the co-editor (with Laurie McNeill) of *Teaching Lives: Contemporary Pedagogies of Life Narratives* (Routledge 2017); (with Kylie Cardell) of *Trauma Tales: Auto/biographies of Childhood and Youth* (Routledge, 2014); and (with Gillian Whitlock) *Trauma Texts* (Routledge, 2009). Kate is Head of the Steering Committee for the International Auto/Biography Association's Asia–Pacific chapter.

**Ecleide Cunico Furlanetto** has a PhD in education. She is the coordinator advisor of Post Graduate Education at the University City of São Paulo, Brazil. She is Director of the Research Group NARRAR (UNICID-CNPq) and President of the 8th Conference International of Research (Auto) Biographical (VIII CIPA, UNICID 2018). Her research thematises autobiographical narratives as a research method and teacher training.

**Pamela Graham** is Lecturer in Cultural Studies at the University of South Australia. Her research focuses on the social uses of biographical media, especially in relation to processes of remembrance, cultural memory, and public history. Her work has been published in *Biography*, *Prose Studies*, and *Media International Australia* journals.

**Gunn Gudmundsdottir** received her PhD from the University of London in 2000 and is now Professor of Comparative Literature at the University of Iceland in the Faculty of Icelandic and Comparative Cultural Studies. Her research interests include life writing, memory studies, and contemporary literature. She focuses in particular on the politics of public and private memory in literature and culture. She has published widely on these issues, including her two books, *Borderlines: Autobiography and Fiction in Postmodern and Life Writing* (Rodopi, 2003) and *Representations of Forgetting in Life Writing and Fiction* (Palgrave Macmillan, 2017).

**Anne Heimo** is Acting Professor of Folkloristics at the University of Turku, Finland. Her research interests include the study of everyday memory practices and the creation of non-institutional cultural heritage. In her work she combines methodological approaches from ethnography, oral history, life writing, and memory studies.

**Alfred Hornung** is Research Professor of American Studies at the Johannes Gutenberg University of Mainz, Germany, and Director of the Obama Institute for Transnational American Studies. He is a founding member of IABA and of IABA-Europe and is on the editorial board of *Life Writing in Europe, Journal of Life Writing*, and *a/b: Auto/Biography Studies*. In 2013, he received the Carl Bode–Norman Holmes Pearson Prize of the American Studies Association. In 2014, he was elected a member of Academia Europaea and in 2017 a member of the Advisory Board of the Institute of World Literature (Harvard). His latest life writing publications are: with Zhao Baisheng, *Ecology and Life Writing* (2013)— Chinese translation (2016); *American Lives* (2013); with Carsten Heinze, *Medialisierungsformen des (Auto-) Biographischen* [*Media and (Auto-)Biographical Expressions*] (2013); "Life Sciences and Life Writing", *Anglia* 133.1 (2015): 1–16; *Jack London: Abenteuer des Lebens* (Darmstadt: Lambert Schneider, 2016); and "North American Autobiography", *Handbook Autobiography/Autofiction*, ed. Martina Wagner-Egelhaaf, 3 vols. (Berlin: de Gruyter, 2018), vol. 2., 1205–1259.

**W. Craig Howes** is Director of the Center for Biographical Research, Co-Editor of *Biography: An Interdisciplinary Quarterly*, and Professor of English at the University of Hawai'i at Mānoa, USA. He has published on life writing, nineteenth century literature, and literary theory and has managed the International Auto/Biography Association List since 1999.

**Meg Jensen** is Associate Professor of English Literature and Creative Writing at Kingston University, UK, where she is also Director of the

Life Narrative Research Group. Her most recent monograph, *The Art and Science of Trauma and the Autobiographical*, will be published in 2019 by the Palgrave Studies in Life Writing Series.

**Phillip Kavanagh** is a writer from Adelaide, Australia. He is a PhD candidate at Flinders University and has been awarded the Patrick White Playwrights' Award and Jill Blewett Playwright's Award. His plays have been produced by State Theatre Company of South Australia, Brink Productions, Griffin Theatre, and Adelaide Festival.

**Leena Kurvet-Käosaar** is Associate Professor of Cultural Theory at the University of Tartu, Estonia, as well as Senior Researcher at the Estonian Literary Museum. She is also the leader of the research group on migration and diaspora studies of the Center of Excellence of Estonian Studies at the Estonian Literary Museum. She has published widely in life writing studies, specialising in particular on post-Soviet life writing, personal narratives of Soviet deportations and the Gulag, and trauma studies.

**Jeanine Leane** is a Wiradjuri writer, poet, and academic from south-west New South Wales, Australia. Her first volume of poetry, *Dark Secrets After Dreaming: A.D. 1887–1961* (Presspress, 2010), won the Scanlon Prize for Indigenous Poetry, 2010, and her first novel, *Purple Threads* (UQP), won the David Unaipon Award for an unpublished Indigenous writer in 2010. Her poetry and short stories have been published in *Hecate: An Interdisciplinary Journal of Women's Liberation*, *The Journal for the Association of European Studies of Australia*, *Australian Poetry Journal*, *Antipodes*, *Overland*, and the *Australian Book Review*. She teaches creative writing and Aboriginal literature at the University of Melbourne.

**Claire Lynch** is Reader in English and Irish Literature at Brunel University London, UK. She is author of several chapters and articles on life writing topics and two books, *Irish Autobiography* (2009) and *Cyber Ireland: Text, Image, Culture* (2014).

**Emma Maguire** is a scholar of life writing, digital media, and feminist media studies. Lecturer in English and Creative Writing at James Cook University (Australia), her book *Girls, Autobiography, Media: Gender and Self-Mediation in Digital Economies* (Palgrave Macmillan, 2018) investigates autobiographical strategies employed by girls and young women in contemporary digital media and considers how such self-representations of youthful femininity are received and critiqued.

**Laurie McNeill** is Senior Instructor in English at the University of British Columbia, Canada. Her research in auto/biography studies focuses on digital and archival lives (including *Online Lives 2.0*, with John David Zuern) and pedagogies of life narrative (including *Teaching Lives*, with Kate Douglas). She also leads a research project on curriculum design and academic integrity.

**Aimée Morrison** is Associate Professor in the Department of Language and Literature at the University of Waterloo, Canada. Her work focuses on popular reception and remediation of computer technologies, as well as on design for digital media.

**Sally Ann Murray** is Professor and Chair of English at Stellenbosch University, South Africa. She has been creating academic autoethnographies since the mid-1990s, after abandoning a perfectly good doctoral study on the short story to risk a PhD that imaginatively storied possible links between "English Studies", magazines, malls, and sites of themed leisure (University of Natal). She is the recipient of numerous literary awards for poetry and fiction, most notably for her autobiographical novel *Small Moving Parts* (Kwela, 2009). In 2017, with colleague Dr Tilla Slabbert, she co-founded the Africa chapter of IABA, the International Auto/Biography Association.

**Pramod K. Nayar** teaches in the Department of English at the University of Hyderabad, India. Among his newest books are *Human Rights and Literature*, *The Indian Graphic Novel*, and *The Extreme in Contemporary Culture*. His essays have, most recently, appeared in *Biography*, *South Asia*, *a/b: Auto/Biography Studies*, *Journal of Postcolonial Writing*, *Image and Text*, and other journals. Forthcoming are essays on graphic novels, posthumanism, and the postcolonial literary celebrity, among others, and two books: *Brand Postcolonial: The "Third World" Text and the Global* and *Ecoprecarity: Vulnerable Lives in Contemporary Literature and Culture*.

**Maria da Conceição Passeggi** has a PhD in linguistics and is a CNPq Researcher. She is a master's and doctoral advisor of Post Graduate Education at the Federal University of Rio Grande do Norte Program and University Cidade de São Paulo, Brazil. She is Director of the Interdisciplinary Research Group Training, Autobiography, and Representations and Subjectivities (GRIFARS-UFRN-CNPq) and President of the Brazilian Association of Research (Auto) Biographical (2014–2016). Her research thematises autobiographical narratives as a research method and training device and focuses on autobiographical reflexivity as a promoter of human disposition and permanent reinvention of representations of the self and the other.

**Anna Poletti** is Associate Professor of English at Utrecht University, the Netherlands, and Senior Research Fellow at Monash University, Australia. Her research examines autobiography beyond the book, the importance of materiality and media in autobiographical acts, and life writing in youth cultures. She is a co-editor of the journal *Biography: An Interdisciplinary Quarterly.*

**Julie Rak** is Professor in the Department of English and Film Studies at the University of Alberta, Canada. She is the author of *Boom! Manufacturing Memoir for the Popular Market* (2013) and *Negotiated Memory: Doukhobor Autobiographical Discourse* (2004). She is the editor of many collections and the author of many articles about life writing, popular culture, and automedia. Julie is completing her third monograph, *Social Climbing: Gender in Mountaineering Writing*, for McGill-Queens University Press. Her latest collection, edited with Hannah McGregor and Erin Wunker, is the forthcoming *Refuse: CanLit in Ruins.*

**Signe Ravn** is Senior Lecturer in Sociology in the School of Social and Political Sciences at the University of Melbourne, Australia. Signe's research centres on the sociology of youth with a particular focus on risk, gender, and processes of marginalisation. She is a qualitative researcher and has extensive experience with innovative and creative research methods.

**Candida Rifkind** is Associate Professor in the Department of English at the University of Winnipeg, Canada, where she specialises in comics and graphic narratives and Canadian literature and culture. In addition to numerous journal articles and book chapters in Canadian studies and comics studies, she is the author of *Comrades and Critics: Women, Literature, and the Left in 1930s Canada* (University of Toronto Press, 2009) and co-editor of *Canadian Graphic: Picturing Life Narratives* (Wilfrid Laurier University Press, 2016). She serves on the Executive of the Comics Studies Society, the advisory board for the journal *INKS*, and is co-editor of the Wilfrid Laurier University Press book series *Crossing the Lines: Transcultural/Transnational Comics Studies.*

**Sarah Ray Rondot** is Director of the Women's, Gender, and Sexuality Studies program at the University of Central Missouri, USA, where she teaches courses in feminist theory, violence, masculinity, disability, and LGBTQ studies.

**Maria Tamboukou** (BA, MA, PhD) is Professor of Feminist Studies at the University of East London, UK, and a Leverhulme Research Fellow in 2018–2019. She has held visiting research positions in a number of institutions and is currently Affiliated Professor in Gender Studies at Linnaeus University Sweden and Adjunct Professor at the Institute for Educational Research at Griffith University, Australia. Maria's research activity develops in the areas of philosophies and epistemologies in the social sciences, feminist theories, narrative analytics, and archival research. Writing histories of the present is the central focus of her work, currently configured as an assemblage of feminist genealogies. Recent publications include the monographs *Sewing, Writing and Fighting, Gendering the Memory of Work,* and *Women Workers' Education,* as well as the co-authored book *The Archive Project.*

**Y-Dang Troeung** is Assistant Professor in the Department of English at the University of British Columbia, Canada. Her areas of teaching and research interests include transnational Asian literatures, critical refugee studies, and global south studies. She is completing a book project on the afterlife of the Cold War in Cambodia.

**Gillian Whitlock** is Emeritus Professor in Communication and Arts at the University of Queensland, Australia. She is author of *The Intimate Empire, Soft Weapons. Autobiography in Transit,* and *Postcolonial Life Narrative: Testimonial Transactions,* as well as numerous chapters and articles on life writing. She is currently working on *The Testimony of Things,* focusing on archives of refugee testimony from the Nauru camp.

**John David Zuern** is Professor in the Department of English at the University of Hawai'i at Mānoa, USA. His writing and teaching focuses on literary criticism and theory, fiction, life writing, and electronic literature. With Cynthia Franklin and W. Craig Howes, he co-edits the journal *Biography: An Interdisciplinary Quarterly.*

# Acknowledgements

Thank you to our Series Editor, Ricia Chansky, for your belief in this project. Your excellent communication, hard work, energy, and generosity have significantly enhanced this project at all stages of its development. Wonderful things always stem from our conversations at conferences and we are very thankful for this.

We are fortunate to have the most outstanding contributors for this project—incredible academics, wonderful writers. This Table of Contents was our dream. So, thank you to our contributors for their excellent, innovative, thoughtful, and rigorous analyses.

Thank you to the editors and production teams at Routledge.

Ashley: I am grateful for my dear colleagues @unimelbsoc whose comradery keeps me thinking and laughing each day, especially Signe Ravn, Brendan Churchill, and Geoffrey Mead. Big thanks to my co-editor Kate Douglas, for being the creative, determined, and collegial academic that we all aspire to be. Your hard work and intellectual generosity inspire me and working with you is a joy. A special mention must also go to the Land & Sea Brewery at Noosa, Queensland, where our stores were memorably replenished for the home-run. And finally, an extra special thank you to Joe Cummins for his daily care and love.

Kate: Enduring thanks to Ashley Barnwell for being such an exceptional collaborator. Your creative approaches, excellent communication, and diligent work made this project highly enjoyable and super rewarding. I am looking forward to our future collaborations!

I would like to thank my colleagues at the Life Narrative Research Group at Flinders University for their ongoing encouragement and support. In particular, thank you to Kylie Cardell and Lisa Bennett for listening to my ideas, problems, and questions on a daily basis, and for always having sensible solutions. Thank you to the Flinders University Return-to-Work Fellowship scheme. This funding created time for me to work on this project.

Lastly, thank you to Danni, Ella, Josh, and Darcy, whose love and support makes smart and creative work possible.

# What We Do When We Do Life Writing

## Methodologies for Auto/Biography Now

*Ashley Barnwell and Kate Douglas*

This book began before we two editors met: in conversations at International Auto/Biography Association conferences throughout the 2000s, but perhaps most urgently during the 2012 IABA conference "Framing Lives" in Canberra, in discussions during and after the conference. It seemed everyone was talking about method but was unsure about how or where this conversation might progress. Reflections on methodology were ever-present in informal discussions, conference papers, and published work in the field. There was a clear sense that our methods were diverse, interdisciplinary, creative, and agile. But to this point, there had been no extended work on methods for auto/biographical research. Though auto/biographical research shared many methods with its (arguably) primary parent, English literary studies, when it comes to methods, auto/biography has grown, even rebelled, from its disciplinary origins.

Our project here draws on lively conversations we two, as collaborators and co-editors, have had about how the humanities and social sciences frame their methods differently. In the social sciences, there is an exhaustive requirement to detail methods in very technical terms, whereas in the humanities, methods—or exactly how we read and approach texts—is often unstated. Humanities researchers too often default to statements like "I engage in close reading", or "I offer a theoretical reading", which tells us very little about how we might replicate this method should we like the results of the research. But within the humanities, we are increasingly finding ourselves much more accountable to methodology. For instance, articulations of methodology are routinely required in thesis proposals, grant applications, briefs for industry partners, and in other collaborative activities.

So, we need to be better at talking about methods, and the ever-burgeoning interdisciplinary spaces of life narrative studies deserve some focused attention. There have been some excellent books on methodology from the disciplines within which we work (most notably sociology, English, and creative writing). We are inspired by these works and we seek to explicitly extend on these studies in our book. For instance, Gabriele Griffin's collection *Research Methods for English* published a second edition in 2013 and forms part of the "Research Methods for Arts and the Humanities" series. This series was pioneering in terms of making humanities methodologies more visible. Griffin's collection covers important terrain, including chapters on archival methods, oral history, discourse analysis, ethnographic methods, textual analysis, interviewing, creative writing, and digital humanities. There is a recognition, in this collection, that researchers in the humanities are keen to articulate, and to access knowledge about, method and that particular skills and ideas are becoming particularly pertinent. We hope to expand on the important work in this collection, but also to take discussions of textual analysis, interviewing, and archival methods (for instance) into new subgenres of literature, through the examination of previously unexamined texts such as particular family archives, podcasts, visual texts, trauma narratives, and ethnographic research.

In the social sciences, there are rich collections that guide scholars toward deeper skills and knowledge in the collection and analysis of life histories, auto/biographies, and narratives via a range of methods. Despite the dominance of interview, survey, and ethnographic methods, leaders such as Liz Stanley have anchored auto/biography as a key source for the social sciences, beginning with Florian Znaniecki and William I. Thomas' classic *The Polish Peasant in Europe and America* (1958 [1918]), a study of migration based on the analysis of diaries and letters. Much more recently, Rachel Thomson and Julie McLeod's *Researching Social Change* (2009), Janet Wolff and Jackie Stacey's *Writing Otherwise* (2013), and Mona Livholts and Maria Tamboukou's *Discourse and Narrative Methods* (2015) (along with Smith and Watson, we have a pattern of stellar feminist double-acts here) all offer chapters on how to approach life writing through the frames of memory work, narrative analysis, and feminist genealogies.

Creative writing scholars have been leading the way on method; for instance, Donna Lee Brien and Quinn Eades' excellent recent collection *Offshoot: Contemporary Life Writing Methodologies and Practice* starts a much-needed conversation about methodologies for life writing practitioners. Brien and Eades rightly argue that when it comes to thinking about life writing methodologies, there are *many* potential areas for investigation. Because there is so much interest and work in this discipline, resources are needed: resources that will guide and support the work of writers, researchers, archivists, teachers, and students. Brien and Eades' text focuses on hybrid and experimental forms of life writing and offers some fascinating, important, and timely insights into why articulations of methodology are so important. Similarly, in our project, we want to give life writing scholars and practitioners from across disciplines a space to reflect upon and draw out exactly how they work with life stories and to address how methods crossover or transform both traditional forms, like letters and diaries, and new forms, like Instagram, podcasts, and vlogs.

In 2001, Sidonie Smith and Julia Watson published what has subsequently become the most influential book in the field of auto/biography studies: *Reading Autobiography: A Guide to Interpreting Life Narratives* (the book was re-published in 2010). It is an outstanding, accessible, theoretical book. But what sets it apart from other books concerned with life narrative theory is its attention to the "how" of auto/biographical work—seeking to make explicit the questions that scholars will have when reading life narrative texts. Chapter Nine of *Reading Autobiography* offered a section titled "A Toolkit: Twenty-Four Strategies for Reading Life Narratives", and for the first time scholars had an accessible and wide-ranging source for exploring and articulating methodological questions with peers, in their own studies, and with students. Smith and Watson explain,

> we present you with a "tool kit" for approaching and engaging self-referential texts. The sets of questions in twenty-four categories in alphabetical order offer entering points and strategies for addressing the burgeoning array of life narratives available today. They might also generate points of departure for writing your own autobiographical narrative.
>
> (235)

(Smith and Watson's comments here about the organising principles for their Toolkit were comments we took on board as we structured our collection, a point we return to further on in this discussion.)

The Toolkit is primarily a supportive reading strategy, "things to look for when reading" different types of life narrative. The reading prompts (for instance, "agency", "body and embodiment", "online lives", "trauma and scriptotherapy") point to ethical, generous, and diverse reading practices that recognise the dynamic, multi-generic, and political nature of life narrative nexts. The prompts also point strongly back to the literary studies origins of life narrative ("audience an addressee"; "authorship and historical moment"; "history of reading publics"; "narrative plotting", for instance) and remind us that life narrative texts can be read using some of the same methods we might use to read fiction, for instance.

However, Smith and Watson's final introductory comment to their Toolkit acknowledges a need to develop these strategies further—beyond reading and interpretation towards practice, whether writing life narrative or working practically through non-traditional texts or modes of life narratives. Method must be dynamic to respond to the emergence of different types of life narrative texts. And this comment provides some inspiration for our work in this collection.

Working in the field ourselves—but from different disciplinary perspectives (Kate in English literary studies, Ashley in sociology)—we see important and diverse work being done to explore methodological questions, although not always under the banner of "methods". For instance, in 2018, the journal *Biography: An Interdisciplinary Quarterly* offered a special issue on "Interviewing as Creative Practice"; in 2017, *a/b: Auto/Biography Studies* published a special issue on teaching life narrative in which each paper negotiated methodological questions; in 2017 and 2018, both *a/b* and *Biography* had special issues focusing on Indigenous life narrative. These special issues reflect some of the key preoccupations of the time, but also a desire to "lean in" and offer concentrated examinations of particular types of life narrative texts.

## Our Method

We imagined an edited collection that could offer rich insights into what happens when scholars approach and work with different subgenres of auto/biographical texts, but also how they devise methods for addressing the myriad themes that have become so central to life narrative disciplines. When we consider auto/biography as an inter/discipline, we see this work as making vital contributions to conversations about methodology across the humanities, social sciences, and well beyond. For instance, Meg Jensen and Siobhan Campbell's chapter in this collection points to the utility of life narrative methods for human rights work; and Phillip Kavanagh and Kate Douglas' reflection on creative life narrative practice engages directly with university ethics policies.

We wanted to create a collection that people could *use*; that they could take down from their shelves with each new project or to find inspiration for current work. We hope that the chapters will help scholars to articulate their existing methods and approaches, as well as to find new ways to work with auto/biographical texts as genres develop and new theoretical concerns emerge. A scholar encountering zines for the first time will find Anna Poletti's reflections directive; a would-be family historian wondering where to commence work with their own family documents could look at Leena Kurvet-Käosaar or Anne Heimo's thoughtful discussions working through their own intergenerational archive and could seek theoretical inspiration from Ashley Barnwell and Kylie Cardell's excellent chapters.

In building this book, we canvassed leading scholars in the field, both at conferences and over email. Our plan was to represent the most significant forms and themes impacting upon life narrative scholarship. We asked these scholars to think practically about how they design and execute their research. Beyond simple notions of "reading" and "researching"—what practical steps characterise their approaches? Importantly, how are their research methods for auto/biographical research unique, for example, how do they differ from research with fictional texts? What methodological issues or questions have inspired and troubled those doing auto/biographical research?

As a consequence, the chapters offer rich and experience-driven accounts of how we do life writing. The authors introduce a range of approaches to discussing and presenting methodological work. But it is worth noting that no chapter is exhaustive of the methods that can be used to analyse that form. Each chapter offers just one approach or account of using a method and provides a jumping off point for further inquiry. The collection does not offer the final word. We aim to start a conversation here that will extend well beyond this volume. For instance, we are keen to know more about what characterises research methodologies in auto/biographical research across the globe, and in more diverse interdisciplinary settings. We acknowledge that our collection has some geographical gaps (and this does not reflect a lack of effort on our part). The difficulty of securing and supporting authors from all corners of the globe to contribute chapters raised important methodological questions for us as editors. These important questions of how we can become more inclusive and de-centred from the "intellectual metropoles" remains foremost in our minds. Neither do we cover all the possible texts or genres of life writing that scholars currently work on. Hopefully we will have an opportunity to build on what we have laid as foundations here as the conversations around methods grow and articulate unseen or new avenues for attention.

## How to Use This Book

The book is designed for use by life writing scholars from across the humanities and social sciences, but also creative writers and practitioners, professional and non-professional family historians and biographers, qualitative and narrative researchers, and undergraduate and graduate students in life writing and creative writing. We hope various chapters will be used by scholars looking to be inspired to learn and try new methods; scholars looking for ways to articulate what they want to do or already do; and by students learning how to design research or creative projects. We also hope the collection will encourage people to be adventurous and that it will be "sticky". You will pick it up to inform your current project on youth and social media, stay on for Poletti on zines and Tamboukou on archives, and then walk away with a buzzing new idea.

Divided into forms and frameworks, the volume offers at least two entry points into thinking about methods. Reading through *forms*, you can start with the "object" of analysis, for example memoir, and read about how Claire Lynch, a scholar and author of memoir, has employed a methodology and to what effects. Reading through *frameworks*, you can start with an interest in new materialism and read about how Pramod K. Nayar works with genetics and biology as life writing texts. By opening multiple paths, we hope the book will be a useful text for teachers and supervisors seeking to give their students confidence to articulate their

methodology and the practical methods they may use to collect and analyse life narratives.

The chapters can be read individually, but can also be read across and
through one another. As a researcher you might begin by asking, how do
I work on diaries written by people with disabilities? And then read Kylie
Cardell on diaries through Ally Day on disability narratives. You might
ask, how do I apply for ethics to work with family letters? And then
read Leena Kurvet-Käosaar on family letters through Phillip Kavanagh
and Kate Douglas' refreshingly candid chapter on navigating the ethics
process. Given the diversity of inter/disciplinary perspectives, readers can
also use the volume to create a single project that knits together multiple
methodological and disciplinary approaches. We encourage readers to
seek out these connections between and across the chapters.

While each chapter deals with a specific methodological approach, several major themes run through multiple chapters. Authors are concerned
with ethics, project design, collecting and composing life narratives, analysing life narratives, selection and decision-making, and various modes
of collaboration. Across the chapters, scholars also demonstrate the
inventiveness of the field by working with both old and new forms. They
ask: how do we adapt tried and true methods, and how do we devise and
develop new methods? Similarly, our authors bring their methodologies
to a diverse range of texts, ranging from the most popular to the most
high-brow, the most classic to the most cutting-edge.

The chapters we collect here are written by both established and emerging scholars. This book therefore gives us a snapshot of methodological
work within auto/biography studies now, as well as a view toward the
future of the field. Read as a collection, the chapters help us to ask "big
picture" questions about methodological innovation: what methods will
we need? How will we find and apply them, and to what? Some questions are a constant, particularly those around ethics, authority, and
representation, or the political economy of how, why, and where texts
are produced. But as the forms of life narratives change, we need to be
nimble in developing approaches that can tackle nuanced shifts in how
these enduring issues are expressed. For instance, what approach might
we need to face the unique ethical issues presented by life narratives that
emerge out of big data or the monetised platforms that host blogs, vlogs,
and SNS profiles? How will we draw on our existing toolkit and the ethical discussions that have taken place in the field so far, and how can we
adapt and extend these conversations into the present? By reflecting more
explicitly on what we do and *how* we do it, we hope that this collection
will also help to further these conversations within the field.

## The Chapters

What characterises the chapters we present here are a series of prescient
issues for auto/biography scholars: devising a language and set of terms to

describe *exactly how* we work with a variety of texts; balancing responsibilities to critical, academic, and creative standards with our emotional/ethical responsibilities to those whose lives we narrate; and translating and reimagining the methods of reading developed for print materials to be useful for reading new media texts. The chapters also give us pause to consider how the ethical codes and practices that guide life writing scholarship are changing in response to the increasingly public nature of life writing, growing concerns about data privacy, and issues of access, ownership, and sovereignty within archives and museums.

In the first half of the book, "Forms", we collect chapters where authors anchor their methodological discussions around a particular genre or kind of text. This section covers the most established forms of the field, with Claire Lynch on memoir; Maria Tamboukou on archives; Leena Kurvet-Käosaar on letters; Kylie Cardell on diaries; W. Craig Howes on biography; and Ashley Barnwell on family histories. Here key life writing scholars also map out ways for working with forms that have taken centre stage in auto/biography studies in recent decades: Anna Poletti writes on zines; Gillian Whitlock on objects and things; Sarah Brophy on visual autobiographies; and Candida Rifkind on graphic biography.

We have also collected chapters on forms that cross over with disciplines like sociology and anthropology but are becoming increasingly popular in auto/biography studies, such as Sally Ann Murray on autoethnography and Signe Ravn on creative interviews. Giving us much-needed insight into how to work with emerging texts, Gunn Gudmundsdottir talks about her approach to analysing the creation of contemporary performance and podcasts, Julie Rak offers an insightful reflection on big data and tracking technologies, and Aimée Morrison sets out instructive guidelines for working ethically and rigorously with social media.

In the second half of the book, "Frameworks", we collect chapters where authors reflect how their methodological approach/es shape how their creative and/or critical practices. These chapters, like Smith and Watson's Toolkit, are driven by some of the central issues affecting life narrative scholarship and practice now and offer strategies for approaching life narrative texts that are sensitive, just, and ethical. Though this might also seem an appropriate description for many of the chapters in our "Forms" section, the work in this second section is most commonly driven by questions of social justice and life narrative practice, seeking means for finding the most appropriate frameworks for writing, reading, or interpreting diverse and often challenging life narrative texts.

For instance, Jeanine Leane explores methods for writing voices "through spaces and silences", and working with collective memories in her discussion of Indigenous Australian life narratives. Laurie McNeill and John David Zuern offer a "generous reading" method for thinking about texts that might be culturally marginalised; and, similarly, Kate Douglas draws on the scholarship of childhood and youth to argue for interdisciplinary approaches when reading life narratives by young authors. Meg Jensen and Siobhan Campbell ask us to consider storytelling as a methodology for human rights activism, but more particularly, they want to interrogate best practice around interviewing as a means for gaining testimony in human rights contexts. Pamela Graham's chapter asks how we might work with biographical media, more particularly death narratives at the digital turn; and Sarah Ray Rondot considers how diverse readings might respond to the wealth of trans* life narratives in cultural circulation. Pramod K. Nayar develops frames for reading the genomic autobiography; Ally Day looks at reading group methodology as a mode of feminist disability praxis for reading life narrative; and Phillip Kavanagh and Kate Douglas explore university ethics committee reviews as a productive site for thinking about life writing practice. Emma Maguire asks questions about audience reception as an emerging and significant method; Ricia A. Chansky considers how we might best engage with diasporic lives that are so often difficult to locate: these are "lives in motion"; and Anne Heimo thinks about sensitive methods for exploring family and migration narratives. Each of these authors is concerned with how to approach texts appropriately where varied cultural politics must be attended to, and with sensitivity. Y-Dang Troeung explores the diverse approaches required for working with diasporic life narratives of ethnicity and forced confessions; Maria da Conceição Passeggi and Ecleide Cunico Furlanetto consider best practices for working with children's life narratives in institutional contexts; and Alfred Hornung navigates the important methodological interstices of ecocriticism and life narrative. These chapters remind us that there is a "why now?" element to this collection. As we have previously suggested, the field has evolved to the point that it is a necessary and right step forward to explore and reflect transparently on methodology. However, there is also a timeliness in terms of current affairs and world politics: the need to understand and approach others and their life stories in very specific and careful ways.

Tying it all together, G. Thomas Couser kindly agreed to write an afterword for us. His piece captures how, when we set out to do auto/biographical research, we delve into layers of lives. Couser looks back on his life and career, the inheritance of ideas and methods, and how this shapes his efforts to look back on the lives of his forebears. His afterword beautifully entangles what it is to live and to read and to create life narrative. Couser's contribution to this volume is significant, not only because he is one of the leading and most influential scholars in the field of auto/biography studies, but because he is (to quote one of the volume's contributors, Ricia Chansky) the "accidental methodologist" that many scholars have turned to in the absence of something more planned (personal communication). In his chapter, Couser suggests that he doesn't consider himself a methodologist. However, his influence is obvious in that so many of the chapters in this collection cite his work.

Many of the chapters in this collection ask questions about the ways in which the field of auto/biography studies is evolving: is interdisciplinary, impacted by personal experience, and—foundationally—fraught with ethical implications regarding the life in the narrative. Therefore, our text also becomes a register of the field as well as a "how to". The chapters, individually and collectively, represent a great variety of methodologies, including generous and ethical reading practices, archival work, interviewing, and methods for reviewing particular life narrative forms such as social media texts, letters, and diaries. But embedded within the chapters are a myriad of lives; these are "studied" lives. And thus, our curation involves a particular ethics of representation as we seek to understand and represent what is, for many scholars in the collection, a life's work. It turns out that questions about method can become a very personal and reflexive inquiry, and this is something that is very particular to auto/biography studies where working with the lives of others often brings our own lives—and questions of what "a life" means—into view. Many of the chapters, including those of Couser, Leane, Lynch, Poletti, and Tamboukou, invite us into a very reflexive analysis of the author's own practices as researchers and writers. We see this as one of the strongest features of this book—that so many authors blur the boundaries between practitioner and scholar. This interweaving is also something that autobiography scholars seems to do more often, and arguably more distinctly, than scholars in other fields. This is a side of academic work we rarely get to glimpse, and so the chapters, in their candour, inspire us to be reflexive, rigorous, and creative in how we design research projects, and to think about how our methods—on a day-to-day level—shape what we can know.

## Works Cited

Beard, Laura J. "Indigenous Auto/Biographical Writings in the Americas." *a/b: Auto/Biography Studies*, vol. 31, no. 3, 2016.

Brien, Donna Lee, and Quinn Eades. *Offshoot: Contemporary Life Writing Methodologies and Practice*. Perth: UWA P, 2018.

Chansky, Ricia. Email to the editors, 24 Dec. 2018.

Griffin, Gabriele, editor. *Research Methods for English*. Edinburgh UP, 2013.

Masschelein, Anneleen, and Rebecca Roach, editors. "Interviewing as Creative Practice." *Biography: An Interdisciplinary Quarterly*, vol. 41, no. 2, 2018.

McNeill, Laurie, and Kate Douglas. "Teaching Lives: Contemporary Pedagogies of Life Narratives." *a/b: Auto/Biography Studies*, vol. 32, no. 1, 2017.

Smith, Sidonie, and Julia Watson. *Reading Autobiography: A Guide to Reading Life Narratives*. Minneapolis, MN: U of Minnesota P, 2010.

Stacey, Jackie, and Janet Wolff, editors. *Writing Otherwise: Experiments in Cultural Criticism*. Manchester UP, 2013.

Tamboukou, Maria, and Mona Livholts. *Discourse and Narrative Methods*. Sage, 2015.

Te Punga Somerville, Alice et al. "Indigenous Conversations About Biography." *Biography: An Interdisciplinary Quarterly*, vol. 39, no. 3, 2016.

Thomas, William I., and Florian Znaniecki. *The Polish Peasant in Europe and America*. Dover Publications, 1958 [1918].

Thomson, Rachel, and Julie McLeod. *Researching Social Change*. Sage, 2009.

# Forms

# 1 Writing Memoir

*Claire Lynch*

## Between

I started writing memoir in the spaces in between. I wrote the first version sitting on a wipe-clean hospital chair, wedged between two incubators. When our baby twins were in hospital, I kept a notebook in my pocket to keep track of the doctors' updates on saturation rates and blood volume. At night, when the babies slept and we didn't, I started to write about our new family. Later, when we were all home, I wrote scraps of memoir between mushing carrots and wiping tiny chins. Sometimes I wrote whole pages during the miraculous hours when two babies napped at the same time. As the babies grew, so did the memoir, and I found space to write between the things I know as a theorist and the things I'm learning as a writer.

It's a good time to be a theorist of memoir. G. Thomas Couser has gone so far as to argue that we live in "an age—if not *the* age—of memoir" (3). It is also a good time to be a reader with bookstores and publishers catering to what Julie Rak calls the "memoir boom", noting the "thousands of people [. . .] buying, borrowing, downloading, and reading memoirs" (3). Does it follow that it is also a good time to write memoir? The question of timing is a crucial one for memoir writers. Those who write "within" an experience are often criticised for a lack of reflection; those who write with the benefit of hindsight are accused of forgetting or fictionalising. Writing memoir is a risky business. Writing about one's own life is, of course, potentially exposing, but at least the revelations are self-inflicted. Writing about the lives of others presents a quite different ethical dilemma. Do memoir writers have a responsibility to the lives and life stories that intersect with their own? When Couser asserts that memoir has the power to "*do* things fiction cannot" (176), he refers to the genre's potential to connect readers via real-life experiences and memoir's capacity to challenge and inspire. But memoir has other side-effects, too, lawsuits for libel, say, divorces, or media scandals. In the case of family memoirs, parents risk betraying their children's privacy; children lay bare their parents' flaws. Families are rife with the private stories memoirists thrive on—the question is, do they have the right to make them public?

## Ethics

In some sense, all methodologies are a response to the practical question: what *can* be done and, the ethical question, what *should* be done. Paul John Eakin points out that:

> When we tell or write about our own lives, our stories establish our identities both as content—I am the person who did these things— and as act—I am someone with a story to tell.
>
> (5)

Memoir emerges here as an affirmation, a claim that the life, and the story, have value. One might well argue that there is something inherently immodest in this but it is hardly unethical. Except, that is, that the disproportionate power of the "I" in memoir forces the author into ethical challenges at every turn. On the one hand, as Rachel Robertson observes, is the temptation to make oneself "more attractive and better behaved than I feel I really am" (305). On the other, is the protection offered by self-deprecation, the defensive tactic of making jokes at one's own expense in order to show just how unbiased the memoir is. In their essay on "The Ethics of Laughter" in memoir, Kylie Cardell and Victoria Kuttainen ask: "What kind of ethical position is available to the life writer who also wants to make his audience laugh?" (106). There is a scene in my memoir about being the only woman in the "Dads' Group" at an antenatal class. It is the section I always choose to read aloud because I know it is funny, not least because it involves linking arms with a group of strangers and pretending to be a dilating cervix. I'm glad it makes people laugh, I want them to, but I also know that the memory behind that scene is not funny. I was destabilized, excluded, undermined by the way the teacher treated me in that class but I chose not to say that. I chose to make a joke from it. Cardell and Kuttainen understand that:

> Whether the response is one of laughter or shame, the humorous life narrative makes overt recognitions of the performative, exhibition-istic, and immodest nature of self-representation. Both comedy and autobiography depend on the creation of intimacy for success.
>
> (112)

I don't think of my representation of the antenatal class as dishonest or unethical, but I do recognise that it is "performative". If anything, the choice to dissemble pain through humour might be a more revealing statement about my personality. In any case, it is my story to tell, my right, we might even say, to represent myself as I see fit. The real question is, do I have the same rights when it comes to representing other people?

## Do No Harm

For Jeffrey Rosen, the answer is quite clear, when he argues that "there are few acts more aggressive than describing someone else" (206). If this is true, it is an aggression all memoirists are guilty of. By its very nature, memoir is a multiple, not singular, narrative, positioning the author against a specific backdrop, reflecting on the lived experiences that are atypical, or representative, of a particular time and place. A life story simply cannot be told without, in some way, telling the life stories of the friends, relatives, lovers, enemies, neighbours, colleagues, and so on, who give that story meaning. Since this is such an inevitable by-product of the genre, it is, I think, revealing that the language used to describe it is always so transgressive. While Rosen thinks of writing about other people as necessarily "aggressive", Robertson believes that "to represent others is to steal their story" (307). She goes on:

> When you write autobiographically about yourself and others, you are giving yourself some form of authority in relation to "the truth" of your tale. Others, including readers, may question that authority, may resist the exercise of power.
>
> (Robertson 311)

This authorial "authority" grows out of the very practice of writing, the precisely chosen language, the arranging and editing of sentences, even the (conscious or unconscious) censorship of certain aspects of the narrative. If I choose to flatter or humiliate myself in my memoir, that is my business; in either case, the image I portray demonstrates "the exercise of power", to use Robertson's terms. By contrast, those I write about are powerless. If I am callous in my descriptions, real people's feelings might be hurt. If I disguise, change names, or merge multiple people to protect them, I could face charges of not writing memoir at all. One might well argue that the principal ethical challenge of writing memoir is the fact that the people I am trying to recreate on the page are also the people living in my house.

The most obvious solution to this is to redistribute power by offering a right of reply, or even the right to veto, to those written about in the memoir. Of course, this idea is unworkable in many cases. Very often a memoir emerges from a context of a challenging or even abusive relationship. Giving such a person the right to veto their portrayal in a memoir would be to return to the harmful power dynamics the memoir seeks to dissolve. Equally, in cases where the person is portrayed favourably and has an ongoing relationship with the author, their input may not always be to the literary benefit of the text. For all the trouble it might cause, the author needs to hold tight to his or her "authority". In my own case, I felt that I should, at least, allow my partner to read drafts before I sent them to a wider audience because it was, in a palpable sense, her story too. As she read, I would quiz her, "have I gone too far there? Is that how you remember it too?" I wanted reassurance that I had captured a recognisable version of the experiences we had shared. Contra Rosen and Robertson, I didn't think it necessary to "steal" her story at the expense of mine, but I did need to find a way to manage the ethical balancing act of telling our story on my terms. As she read the drafts, she described not so much a feeling of reading about herself but rather of reading about a character that stood in for her, a parallel self, acting out her story. The same mode of distancing allows me to control the narrative and, I hope, protect the real people who exist outside the text. After all, "these characters are both people in my own life and creations of my fingers on the computer keyboard" (Robertson 305).

All that said, the right to reply is only of use to those with the capacity to reply. One of the major topics of my memoir is my children. I am writing about them when they are too young to read and (mercifully) too young to offer me a detailed critique of their representation. Certainly, I don't want them to be embarrassed by what I have written, but I also understand that children are embarrassed by their parents whether or not they write a book about them. I am careful not to compromise their privacy or make fun of them, but I cannot predict which aspects of my writing might seem too revealing when, or if, they read it as adults. This is not an idle concern; as Zachary Snider warns, "writing about family in fiction, memoir, or nonfiction can indeed affect real-life relationships" (104). In recent years, Karl Ove Knausgaard's *A Death in the Family: My Struggle Book 1* (2012) has become shorthand for a type of memoir that alienates and outrages those represented within it. It is also a huge success by many of the measures we might typically apply, including popularity with readers, critical acclaim, and translation. Yet, as Michael Sala puts it,

> what is perhaps most "real" in Knausgaard's writing is not the painful details that his extended family might wish to contest or suppress in this book—but the force, the violence, that underpins their particular arrangement in the text, the anxiety and doubt about the self that in a sense is unresolvable and self-inflicted and unquantifiable, a product of the mind.
>
> (168–169)

It is not, in other words, *what* Knausgaard writes about others that makes the text so contentious but *how* he relates their lives to his own in an "unresolvable" cycle of revelation. One metric of a memoir's success must surely be the impact on the author's own life. Knausgaard often expresses regret in interviews, acknowledging that the work has damaged relationships, caused harm. His wife and friends have given interviews contradicting the author's account. Snider is right to warn that

> ethically, writing about one's family is one of the biggest risks that a writer, especially a memoirist, can take, one that determines whether or not his family will ever speak to him again.
>
> (101)

Am I walking into the same trap? Like so many, my memoir takes into account my adult life as a parent and, to some extent, my child-hood memories of being parented. These relationships are so central to many people's lives yet, John Barbour argues, critical works rarely explore "how the writer's relationships to her parents and to her chil-dren influence each other, especially as these relationships are the focus of moral scrutiny" (74). My memoir exists because becoming a parent permanently shifted my sense of how I exist in relation to others, or as Snider captures so neatly: "Having a child of my own has made me con-sider someone else's future even more so than my own—as both a parent *and* as a writer" (104).

## Writing

Learning how to write memoir (as opposed to writing *about* memoir) has taught me how much I did not know about it. When I sit at my desk to write I hear the siren call of search engines and library catalogues; I want to work my way through bibliographies and indexes. I am happy there, but I can't find what I need. Couser advises memoir writers to employ "methodological transparency":

> disclosing to readers just what a narrative is based on—personal memory, consultation with other parties, documents, diaries, tape recordings, e-mail, and so on. Readers deserve to know just what they are reading so that they can respond accordingly. There's no harm in reminding readers that memoir is, after all, by its very nature, a fallible, subjective and often deliberately artful representa-tion of the past.
>
> (65)

Readers probably do "deserve" this, but searching one's own soul turns out to be much harder than searching a database. For comfort I try to construct a sort of archive, gathering up documents and images that might jog my memory. I look at pictures of the babies in hospital, all tubes and wires, to remind me of how frail they were; but it is hard to recreate the worry I felt when, three years later, I can hear them in the garden hap-pily trying to knock apples down from a tree. My diary from that time is sporadic and completely devoid of any helpful material for a memoir. Perhaps I was too emotionally overwhelmed to write in it; perhaps I was just too busy. The scribbles in my diary and the photos taken on my mobile phone are documentary evidence, but they are not reflection. As Couser points out, memoir demands a shaping of memories, images, and texts into something that has meaning for others. Although I write, in part, for them, I am conscious that my daughters may see things differently; in time, their memories and diaries may contradict my story. Still, I carry on writing. It will be years before they can read it, perhaps years more before they can tell me what they think. Worst still, they might yet grow up to produce their own "deliberately artful representation" of me. It will, no doubt, serve me right.

## Works Cited

Barbour, John D. "Judging and Not Judging Parents." *Ethics of Life Writing*, edited by Paul John Eakin. Ithaca, NY: Cornell UP, 2004, pp. 73–100. Print.

Cardell, Kylie, and Victoria Kuttainen. "The Ethics of Laughter: David Sedaris and Humour Memoir." *Mosaic: A Journal for the Interdisciplinary Study of Literature*, vol. 45, no. 3, 2012, pp. 99–114. *Project Muse*. Web. 10 June 2018.

Couser, G. Thomas. *Memoir: An Introduction*. New York: Oxford UP, 2012. Print.

Eakin, Paul John. *Ethics of Life Writing*. Ithaca, NY: Cornell UP, 2004. Print.

Rak, Julie. *Boom! Manufacturing Memoir for the Popular Market*. Ontario: Wilfrid Laurier P, 2013. Print.

Robertson, Rachel. "Carving, Forging, Stealing." *Life Writing*, vol. 7, no. 3, 2010, pp. 305–315. *Taylor & Francis*. Web. 20 Apr. 2013.

Rosen, Jeffrey. *The Unwanted Gaze: The Destruction of Privacy in America*. New York: Vintage, 2001. Print.

Sala, Michael. "Knausgaard's *My Struggle*: The Interplay of Authority, Structure, and Style in Autobiographical Writing." *Life Writing*, vol. 15, no. 2, 2016, pp. 157–170. *Taylor & Francis*. Web. 2 Feb. 2017.

Snider, Zachary. "Mom and Dad Will Hate Me: The Ethics of Writing About Family in Memoir-Fiction." *New Writing*, vol. 14, no. 1, 2017, pp. 98–105. *Research Gate*. Web. 10 June 2018.

# 2 Archival Methods in Auto/Biographical Research

*Maria Tamboukou*

This chapter draws on my research in the Archives and Manuscript Division of the New York Public Library (NYPL). This involved me working with auto/biographical documents of women trade unionists in the garment industry in the first half of the twentieth century, and more particularly with the papers of Rose Pesotta (1896–1965) and Fannia Cohn (1885–1962), two of the very few women vice-presidents in the history of a predominantly women's union, the International Ladies Garment Workers Union (ILGWU). Among the many themes that have arisen from my research and informed a range of conference papers, methodology workshops, journal articles, and books, in this chapter I explore auto/biographical paths within the archive, something that informs all my work on this project. The chapter unfolds in three moves: imaging, living, and writing the archive.

## Imagining the Archive

The questions we carry with us into an archive are important because they will have shaped the preparatory work we have done for the research, which is both theoretical and practical. It is the time before the researcher arrives at the archive that I want to consider here, by raising a seemingly simple question: when does archival work begin? Looking back at my journeys in a number of archives in the UK, France, and the USA, where I have conducted research over the past twenty years, one of the patterns I can discern is that of multiple beginnings. Following a research question and immersing ourselves in the relevant literature is of course a recurrent mode of tracking and identifying archival sources, but it is only one of many. Sometimes beginnings emerge while we already work in an archive and we encounter a line of writing, a document, a person, or a source that we want to trace further. But even when such new beginnings emerge in the middle of a process, they still demand planning and preparation to be realised as concrete archival projects.

Archival research is a process that is conceived as part of a wider research project but develops its own life, puts forward its own demands, and requires specific responses to the questions and problems it raises. The latter are both intellectual and material and always interrelated as such. The material conditions of possibility for archival research always include intricate space/time arrangements, both local and global. Take for example my NYPL project on the papers of women trade unionists. This started through my reading of autobiographical documents of seamstresses in the first half of the twentieth century; Rose Pesotta emerged as an intriguing figure in this body of literature, and this is how I decided to follow her in the archive. The only way I could have access to her papers was physically to visit the New York Public Library; but in order to secure funding, I had to make sure that her papers were not available in any digitised or other form that would be accessible in different and possibly cheaper ways.

But once in the archive, new beginnings emerge, around people, documents, and sources that had not been thought about when designing the research. In my case with Pesotta's papers, two new projects erupted from the archive: 1) the importance of women workers' education, a theme that made me return to the NYPL the following year to work with Fannia Cohn's papers; and 2) Pesotta's epistolary friendship with Emma Goldman through her involvement in the anarchist labour movement, something that sent me to Emma Goldman's papers at Berkeley the following year as well (Tamboukou, "Good Night and Good-Bye").

## Living the Archive: Space/Time/Matter Rhythms

No matter how well we have prepared, once we find ourselves in an archive, we have to adapt to new conditions and contexts, synchronise ourselves with its space/time rhythms, and in this way become organically entangled in it. It should be remembered here that archives and libraries are powerful power/knowledge institutions and like other organisations impose strict time/space restrictions and regulations. Over the years I have worked in archives, I have understood that allowing myself time to get to know these rules and adapt to different archive systems, as well as to the diverse rules and regulations prevailing, is as important as finding, reading, or transcribing documents. In this light, "start slowly" would be my suggestion for researchers visiting an archive for the first time. But as the research proceeds, we also have to take into consideration that speediness and slowness should be considered in their interrelation, for archival research is a question of rhythm, and it is the depth of the understandings that result that we are primarily interested in.

What is also important to bear in mind is that researchers need not upset the archivists they will need to work with. The archive is their workplace, while we researchers will only temporarily reside there. In this light, a researcher cannot just storm an archive and do things instantly from the beginning, no matter how experienced, well published, or famous they are.

It is also worth remembering that a researcher's relationship with archivists may continue well after leaving the archive in question. They are the people we may need to contact for additional or missing information, or if more photocopies are needed, for instance. It is these archivists who will also facilitate permission to reproduce and other copyright processes when the stage of publishing research outputs is reached. Archivists are thus importantly involved in the whole research process, and acknowledging their contribution should be part of archival research ethics more widely.

In raising these concerns, my point is that the materiality and sociality of the archive is crucial for the entire research process and that as researchers we should not separate the physical, social, and intellectual dimensions of the archival research we carry out. But what does it mean to become organically involved in an archive? I address this question by drawing on Henri Lefebvre's ideas about the "rhythmanalysis" of different spaces.

"What we live are rhythms, rhythms experienced subjectively", Lefebvre wrote in his major work, *The Production of Space* (206). But it was only at the end of his academic life, when perhaps he had more time to indulge his love for music (being a pianist as well as an intellectual and activist) that he wrote a small book on *Rhythmanalysis*.

In following Lefebvre's method of rhythmanalysis, I have thus considered space/time rhythms as constitutive of archival practices and therefore of the knowledges that can derive from archival research. An archive is a dynamic space traversed and indeed constituted by multiple rhythms and is thus open to new ideas and encounters. Moreover, an archive is not restricted within buildings or other architectural arrangements, majestic though some of them might be. Conceived as an entanglement of space/time rhythms, the archive extends into the world, both in terms of its immediate locality as well as with reference to its global position in colonial histories, as influentially discussed by Ann Stoler (*Along the Archival Grain*).

During the summer of my research in the NYPL, I followed the rhythms of New York, a city that was the hub of the US garment industry in the first half of the twentieth century. Living in the "fashion district" of middle Manhattan and walking up and down streets still full of garment workshops was thus a spatial experience that was entangled in the daily rhythms of my archival understanding. Indeed, spatial and temporal serendipities had an unexpected impact on my research. When I went to New York in summer 2011, I chose my accommodation in the "fashion district": it was within walking distance from the NYPL and it felt comfortable, as I had not lived in New York before. It was quite accidentally that my visit in 2011 coincided with the centenary commemoration of the *Triangle Fire*, one of the most tragic events in the history of the garment industry in the US, when 146 young immigrant women garment workers died while trying to escape the burning building wherein they were locked (see Stein). Reading women's immediate impressions of this event in their letters was thus a moving experience framed within different temporalities: "I suppose you are still waiting for the letter of which I spoke to you in my card of last week yet. I could not write, I could not do anything for the last two or three weeks, the Triangle tragedy had a terrible affect upon me", Pauline Newman (1887–1986) wrote to her friend Rose Schneiderman (1882–1972) on 12 April 1911, just a month after the disaster (Rose Schneiderman Papers). For Cohn, the Triangle Fire was not just a shock but also a turning point in her life, as she wrote in an autobiographical letter to a friend much later in her life (see Tamboukou, "The Autobiographical You" 271).

Reading these letters a hundred years later in the heart of a city that staged a series of mnemonic practices to remember these events, and also reflecting upon women's current position in the world of work, had a significant impact upon my own affective understanding in the archive. Dipesh Chakrabarty has argued that a relation of contemporaneity allows historical time to unfold and disrupts "the empty, secular and homogeneous time of history" (113). In this light, leaping into Triangle Fire times and places became a condition of possibility for a genealogical understanding of the hardships of women garment workers' lives. I read Pauline Newman's letters in the archives of the Tamiment Library, which is literally around the corner from the Triangle Fire Building, after having visited the exhibition that the students of New York University had co-curated as part of the commemoration events. This opened up a third space of understanding where "time present and time past collapsed" (Dinshaw 121). Indeed, by reading letters written in different times—just after the event, as well as forty years later—by women who had witnessed it, and who had also worked to make it part of the history of political struggles around women's labour, made me feel like a body immersed in multiple and heterogeneous times.

Thus, during my research at the NYPL archives, my actuality as a researcher was becoming a blurring sensation of past and present images, spaces, and times. This co-existence of different spacialities, temporalities, and urban rhythms influenced my understanding, as well as my theoretical and methodological orientations within the archive. Attention to "rhythmanalysis" places the researcher in the middle of his/her sense-data, thus challenging the distinction between subjects and objects of research, the world as it is and the world as we perceive it. As I have written elsewhere, archival research can be considered in parallel with the epistemological restrictions and limitations of any scientific experiment conducted within a laboratory, including acknowledging that the way an archival project is set up will affect its outcomes and findings (Tamboukou, *Archival Research*). It is while living/thinking in between other spaces and different temporalities and in the realm of the sociological imagination that ideas have emerged, themes have been followed, ideas have been coined, and also "narrative personae"—that is, archival people, both real (as they did live) and imaginary (in terms of my internal conversations with them)—have come to life.

## Writing the Archive: The Narrative Fabric of Archival Research

As researchers, we become entangled in a web of archival stories, irrespective of whether we do narrative analysis or not with the documents we find in archives. In considering stories in the archive, we are of course mindful of Steedman's provocative warning that "archives contain practically nothing, just disconnected fragments of documents and lists, collected for purposes forgotten or not to be known" (18). Archival research is indeed a process of finding fragments and working with discontinuities. It is here, however, that narrativity becomes a way of assembling disparate and sometimes disconnected pieces and fragments into a design that has a meaning.

What I want to highlight in this section is the difficulty of grappling with "the return from the archive". There are many issues to consider about "the return". There is the question of how to manage the welter of archival data that the researcher comes back with. There is the problem of how to reconnect with the world left behind while in the archive, while retaining the memories, affective bonds, and imaginary travels that were experienced while in the archives. And, also, there is the small detail of writing, of creating the publications that were promised to funders but are also important to the academic self you hopefully still inhabit. This is where the importance of narrative sensibility emerges: stories are traces of human existence and human actions, Hannah Arendt has famously suggested. Without stories, there is no history; it is through stories that we are entangled in the web of human relations (*The Human Condition*). Drawing on the Arendtian take on narratives, I suggest that it is through narrativisation that we create meaning in archival research.

## By Way of Conclusion

What I have tried to show throughout this chapter, is that space, time, and matter are crucial not only in our understanding of how an archive becomes but also in how the researcher and the archive create an assemblage that fuses divisions and separations between the subjects and objects of the research and further problematises a range of dualisms, such as mind/body, texts/readers, reason/experience, memory/

imagination, reality/representation—in short, the world as it is and the world as we perceive it.

In drawing on my experience of working at the New York Public Library with the papers of women trade unionists in the garment industry, I have shown the more general applications of this approach. Also, throughout the chapter I have emphasised that archival research is always a situated process with emerging questions, problems, and issues, and these need to be addressed and dealt with in an ongoing way. This multi-modality of engaging with and raising questions about the archive in itself creates an archive of methodological approaches that can be drawn upon, by always bending "previous rules" and charting new paths.

What I therefore hope readers will gain from this chapter is an understanding of archival research as an entanglement of intellectual and material practices with multiple points of emergence, some unforeseen destinations, as well as a wide variation of flows and rhythms (see Moore et al., *The Archive Project*). In this light, being-in-the-archive is both a journey and an adventure that needs a map and a compass, but it will certainly also open up its own paths. I hope that some of the analytical trails and methodological moves suggested in this chapter will be helpful in orienting researchers in their archival journeys to come.

## Archival Sources

Fannia M. Cohn papers. Manuscripts and Archives Division. The New York Public Library. Astor, Lenox, and Tilden Foundations (NYPL/FCP/MSS588).

Rose Pesotta papers. Manuscripts and Archives Division. The New York Public Library. Astor, Lenox, and Tilden Foundations (NYPL/RPP/MSS2390).

Rose Schneiderman papers. The Tamiment Library and Robert F. Wagner Labor Archives Collection (RSP/TAM/18).

## Works Cited

Arendt, Hannah. *The Human Condition*. Chicago: U of Chicago P, 1998 [1958]. Print.

Chakrabarty, Dipesh. *Provincializing Europe: Postcolonial Thought and Historical Difference*. Princeton, NJ: Princeton UP, 2000. Print.

Dinshaw, Carolyn. "Temporalities." *Twenty-First Century Approaches: Medieval*, edited by Paul Strohm. Oxford: Oxford UP, 2007, pp. 107–123. Print.

Lefebvre, Henri. *The Production of Space*. Translated by Donald Nicholson-Smith. Oxford: Blackwell, 1991 [1974]. Print.

———. *Rhythmanalysis: Space, Time and Everyday Life*. Translated by Stuart Elden and Gerald Moore. London: Continuum, 2004. Print.

Moore, Niamh et al. *The Archive Project: Archival Research in the Social Sciences*. London: Routledge, 2016. Print.

Steedman, Carolyn. *Dust*. Manchester: Manchester UP, 2001. Print.

Stein, Leon. *The Triangle Fire*. Ithaca, NY: Cornell UP, 1962. Print.

Stoler, Ann Laura. *Along the Archival Grain: Epistemic Anxieties and Colonial Common Sense*. Princeton, NJ: Princeton UP, 2009. Print.

Tamboukou, Maria. "Archival Research: Unravelling Space/Time/Matter Entanglements and Fragments." *Qualitative Research*, vol. 14, no. 5, 2014, pp. 617–633.

————. "The Autobiographical You: Letters in the Gendered Politics of the Labour Movement." *Journal of Gender Studies*, vol. 25, no. 3, 2016, pp. 269–282.

————. "Good Night and Good-Bye: Temporal and Spatial Rhythms in Piecing Together Emma Goldman's Auto/Biographical Fragments." *BSA Auto/Biography Yearbook*, vol. VI, 2013, pp. 17–31. Durham, NC: BSA Auto/Biography Group. Print.

# 3    Zines

*Anna Poletti*

When I started my doctoral studies on life writing in Australian zines in 2002, I had not really thought about methodologies before. Having studied philosophy and literary studies, I was well versed in theoretical approaches and aesthetics. I knew that either (or both) could produce methodological differences among scholars because a psychoanalytic reading of a text asks different questions, and finds different evidence, than one informed by the preoccupations of (say) feminist or postcolonial theory. But, as the debates in literary studies about close reading over recent years have demonstrated, all I really knew was that my methodology was textual analysis.[1] My job, as I saw it then and still tend to see it now, is that of a critic: to undertake a specific kind of reading and interpretation that puts texts into conversation with each other; to contextualise them (i.e., draw out and explore the works' connection to the political, social, historical, technological, aesthetic, and economic conditions of their production, circulation, and reception); and to speculate on what I think the conversations between texts and their contexts tell us about what life writing is and what its uses can be. In 2002, I knew I had to read widely enough across a variety of disciplines—history, media and cultural studies, material culture studies, social theory, and of course my home discipline of literary studies—in order to be able to do this. In that sense, I thought my other methodology was simply *reading*.

Because zines had not been the subject of systematic scholarly research in Australia when I undertook my research, my first job was to access the primary texts. Over the course of three years, I amassed an archive of around 2500 zines and engaged in various (analogue) methods of organising them and the notes reading all these zines generated. While zines were an unusual text type to study in the context of literary studies at that time, these methods of undertaking research were not unusual: all humanities scholars have to gain access to the their texts, analyse them and organise their findings.[2] However, in order to get access to zines, I had to participate in a subculture structured by rules entirely different to those of institutionalised forms of cultural production and circulation.[3] Indeed, it was the non-institutional status of zines—the fact that, at that time, they were not systematically collected by libraries, sold widely, or housed in archives—that made them an attractive object for studying contemporary life writing. This non-institutionalised—essentially punk—approach to literary production and circulation was an unexplored and exciting space where life writing was being written and read, and was shaping the way people thought about life.

As I explore in *Intimate Ephemera*, one of the things that made me want to study zines was the unique way they enact and mediate the relationship between author and reader. As a cultural practice, this can be understood in terms of zines' close relationship with and adaptation of the founding principles of punk, which disregards standards of competence and merit as requirements for artistic production in favour of a democratic model of making art. It celebrates the aesthetics of amateurism in direct rejection of the aesthetics and ideologies of institutional culture and forms. However, practically speaking, studying this cultural practice demanded that I adopt an entirely unexpected method. Sure, I could buy zines from zine makers, zine distributors, and the few stores that sold them. But in order to access the mode of circulation and reception that is central to zines, I would have to make a zine to trade. It was clear that many zine makers preferred trading zines to selling them and, in the early months of starting my research, I was quickly becoming aware of the demand of reciprocity that drives zine culture, an impulse noted in earlier writing on zines by Kate Eichhorn ("Sites") and Jennifer Sinor. It was clear to me, and indeed many zine makers said this to me directly, that if I wanted to study zines I had to make them; not only because people often preferred trade as a means of sharing and acquiring zines, but because the researcher (or at least the kind of researcher I was trying to become) cannot stand outside the context they research. (My reading of Donna Haraway and feminist theories of situated knowledges had taught me that much.[4])

Thus, over the course of my doctoral studies I made a zine called *Trade Entrance*,[5] which documented the experience of doing a PhD on life writing in zines. There were seven issues of *Trade Entrance*, the last issue culminating with the experience of receiving my examiner reports and passing my degree. In what follows, I reflect on the process of making *Trade Entrance* as a methodology for undertaking research on zines, but also more broadly on zine making as a methodology for documenting, reflecting on, and communicating about the research process and its aims. I will tease out how zine making produces a structured space for research practice. This space enables and materialises a practice of thinking differently that has surprising benefits for the more formalised elements of research, such as engaging scholarly debate and producing scholarly writing.

## The Zine as a Form of Communication

Produced, circulated, and read within a subcultural context influenced by punk, zines are—as a textual object—handmade publications, most often produced on a photocopier.[6] While adhering to a distinct and coherent set of material characteristics, zines can be about whatever their maker wants them to be. Many zines approach their subject matter—whether it be lived experience, popular culture, local history, cooking, parenting, or politics—through the lens of the personal. However, you will also regularly encounter a form of writing closer to cultural criticism in zines (particularly fanzines).

In 2002, when I first started writing to zine makers to ask them if I could buy their zines—or their entire back catalogue—they would often express surprise that I was "allowed" to study zines at university. For this reason, *Trade Entrance* often narrated the process of doctoral research with the aim of communicating about cultural research to a non-scholarly audience. Specifically, it sought to present my personal experience of designing and undertaking a large research project to the community who produced the texts I was reading.[7] It felt very important at the time that I was talking to zine makers on the terms they set (in zine form, in a personal voice) rather than expecting them to be interested in scholarly modes of communication.

Talking to the community about the research I was doing was a direct response to the call for participation that underscores zines as a do-it-yourself (diy) mode of cultural production (Duncombe; Poletti 59–103), but methodologically, making *Trade Entrance* was a means for me to periodically reflect on and describe the progress of my work to someone other than my thesis supervisors. Writing *Trade Entrance* allowed me to imagine an audience of people actually interested in my research and ideas—an important and rare thing, given the sense of isolation that can characterise doctoral research. Writing for an implied reader who is interested in my work, but is not a scholarly reader who must be convinced of its value or unique contribution to knowledge, was an enormously beneficial process for me in terms of honing my ways of writing about my ideas, and for testing out ways of thinking in what felt like a more welcoming environment. Vitally, it gave me a sense of connection through communicating about an experience as it unfolded.

Because zine culture is a space that celebrates idiosyncratic interests and personal writing, the benefits of writing about scholarly interests in the zine community can be experienced by researchers *not* working on zines. While my zine was of particular interest to some zine makers and zine readers, zine culture—because of its proximity to fan cultures—is home to readers who are willing to read way beyond their own personal interests, as evidenced by the popularity of zines on topics considered niche within mass models of publishing (Duncombe). What matters, stylistically, is that the zine gives the reader access to the topic through the idiosyncratic lens of the zine maker. This is what zine readers love, no matter how obscure the topic.

## The Zine as Research Journal

This sense of writing about the unfolding research, in retrospect, makes *Trade Entrance* a kind of research journal. I have since used the methodology of journaling when visiting archives and have found it invaluable as a way to record and document the generative, at times overwhelming, experience of being in the archive. Learning the rigours of scholarly writing is a vital part of the doctoral process, but I also see now that having this other kind of personal writing where the "I" of the researcher has a place created a parallel writing space that ultimately benefitted the more formal writing that was the thesis. The zine provides the experience of communicating about one's research, while also creating a structured space in which one has permission to write and think *differently*.

## The Zine as an Opportunity to Think Visually

Aesthetically, culturally, and politically, zines are a parasitic media form,[8] making use of obsolescent and current media. A key element of this is the appropriation and reuse of images in the form of collage, a staple of the zine aesthetic. Making *Trade Entrance* required me to think about what kinds of images, visual textures, and fonts might serve my goal of reflecting on and communicating about the research process. In my years as an undergraduate, I had never considered the aesthetic qualities of my work or thought visually about ideas (beyond the construction of Venn Diagrams in first year philosophy). Because zines are written, laid out, copied, and assembled by their makers, the entire process of textual production becomes a creative practice of thinking about the topic of the zine. Producing *Trade Entrance* sent me into library sales, opportunity shops (thrift stores), and second-hand bookstores in search of visual material. For this reason, making a zine occasioned thinking about the representation and communication of ideas entirely differently and progressed the process of generating and evaluating ideas. Crucially, because collage is not a form of visual communication that serves singular perspectives, I could think analogously about the process of scholarly writing—of being in dialogue with the ideas of other scholars and the idea of scholarship as a conversation—free from the tentativeness that attends an actual attempt to participate in that conversation. Collage is a technique of material destruction of source texts. This violence of cutting and reformatting blurs the boundary between self and other (original text and source), allowing for an exploration of the transformative and pleasurable potential of destruction and remaking (Halberstam

136). As I negotiated the fraught intellectual questions of incorporating the voices of zine makers and other scholars into my scholarly writing, making collages became a process of taking up and embracing a greedier, more explicitly appropriative form of engagement with texts. Having no formal training in visual art, it was also an opportunity to experience the distinct pleasures of amateur cultural production: my collages weren't very good, which was part of the point. They did, however, create a mimetic process by which the question of the role of vision in my scholarship could be explored.

## The Zine as a Materialisation of Situated Knowledges

In theorising the importance of situated knowledges as a methodology for feminist research, Haraway sought to recuperate vision as an embodied and located practice central to knowledge production. Only a methodology of embodied objectivity, Haraway argues, can anchor the epistemological claims of feminist research while enacting the feminist rejection of the fallacy of objectivity that produces universalising knowledge and its subjugatory effects. Making a zine while studying zines allowed me to situate myself within the textual culture that I was studying on the terms set by that culture. The contribution to my knowledge about zines that came from making and trading one is impossible to quantify. Yet making a zine and trading a zine was not an engagement with methodologies associated with qualitative methods of social science such as participant observation. Practically speaking, I was not trained in those methods, nor was my research supervised in such a way that those methods were explicitly incorporated into the aims or findings of the research. The research practice and intellectual style of my supervisor, Ivor Indyk, was in retrospect, very influential here. As a literary scholar, editor, and publisher, Indyk's work is inherently of and within the literary field, rather than standing outside it with the view to analysing its products. As an editor of the (now defunct) literary journal *Heat*, and before that *Southerly*, and the founder of Giramondo Publishing, Indyk's research practice is grounded by *doing* literature as much as interpreting it. In this sense, he was the perfect supervisor for a project that sought to make the argument that thinking about zines as literature—rather than as sociological documents—was worthwhile.

## The Zine as a Methodology

Zines are a highly self-reflexive textual form. Zine makers often narrate how making zines about lived experience, their interests, political opinions, or as a means of validating non-scholarly research is a generative process, rather than a representational one. It is for this reason that I think of *Trade Entrance* as a core part of the methodology of the work I undertook on zines, and have outlined here the benefits of making zines for the research process more generally. As a structured textual form that can be easily connected to a global network of readers, the zine offers the researcher an important alternative place for testing ideas and ways of framing, trying out positions and approaches, and engaging in remediating scholarly work into different formats—such as collage. True to the spirit of diy, I have used this chapter as process of self-authorisation, placing *Trade Entrance*, and zines, into a methodological frame without institutional permission. Albeit belatedly.[9]

## Postscript: The Afterlives of Methodologies

Janice Radway has proposed studying the "afterlives" of zines produced in the riot grrrl movement as a means of understanding how the zine makers "developed a commitment to extending the reach and effects of zines into the future" (144). Along with recent work by Kate Eichhorn (*The Archival Turn*), Jessie Lymn, and the network of zine librarians, Radway partly wants to consider how institutional engagements with zines—such as scholarship, institutional collections and so on—relate to the world-building and world-changing potential of zine making and reading. Making *Trade Entrance* was a vital part of the research process, and as with many elements of methodology, its material trace is less important than the process of making it in terms of its contribution to the research.[10]

Yet, as many zine makers know, the increased institutional interest in zines—which my own PhD and scholarly monograph contribute to—has created the somewhat uncomfortable situation that zines that were made to process and document a particular moment in time, and enable a specific aim (whether it be research, self-reflection, community building, or something else), are now housed in university and government libraries that, in principle, will hold them indefinitely. Trapped in the amber of institutional collecting, the small, partially anonymous, ephemeral zine made to facilitate a very specific form of sociality in a specific time and place is now available for future readers to interrogate. The material trace of the methodology that informed the writing of *Intimate Ephemera* is now available in the State Library Victoria (SLV) in Melbourne, as copies of the zine were included in collections donated by zine makers whom I had traded zines with. When I donated my zine collection to the SLV before relocating to the Netherlands in 2016, I left in the complete set of *Trade Entrance*, despite my discomfort that some future scholar— keen to debunk central claims of the argument in *Intimate Ephemera*— could comb the writings of my younger self as she learned the process of research for proof of her ineptitude and wrong steps in her thinking.

Yet as a document of the development of my situated knowledge about zines, *Trade Entrance* is an important counternarrative to the scholarly argument presented in *Intimate Ephemera*. For this reason, the sense of exposure I feel about its continued availability is worth enduring.

## Notes

1. See Best and Marcus; Culler; Love; Weed.
2. See Philippe Lejeune's *On Diary* for an important and encouraging description of how literary scholars can undertake research on texts that are not published in the traditional, institutional sense.
3. I was already involved in artist-run initiatives dedicated to writing and performance, and had encountered zines through my involvement as Manager of the National Young Writers' Festival (NYWF) held in Newcastle, Australia, in 2000. Those early days of the NYWF were a mix of DIY approaches to cultural production, and an attempt to create a space for younger writers as a way to enact the generational critique of Australia's cultural landscape developed by Mark Davis in *Gangland*. NYWF has now, along with the Emerging Writers' Festival in Melbourne and other initiatives, largely succeeded in advancing recognition of young writers in the Australian literary field.
4. While a vital part of the research process, and acknowledged in the thesis in the spirit of what Philippe Lejeune refers to as the "honesty" that requires us to contextualise our research (29), a thorough discussion of my zine making practice was not included in the thesis or in the book that resulted from it. I am grateful to Kate Douglas and Ashley Barnwell for the invitation to reflect more fully on this methodology twelve years later.
5. The title of the zine reflected the fact that undertaking a PhD brought with it a sense of personal discomfort and being out of place. As a woman from a working-class background seeking entrance to the academy, I often experienced a kind of class dysphoria when in conversation with my professors, teaching staff, and fellow students. I am from a family of tradespeople. See Carolyn Steedman's *Landscape for a Good Woman* for an explication of working-class autobiography. Unlike Steedman's retrospective autobiographical narrative in that book, *Trade Entrance* was a writing of class dysphoria from within it, rather than an analysis of it. *Trade Entrance* also signalled my interest in trading the zine (rather than selling it), and in it being my first zine (my entrance into zine culture).
6. Zines can also be produced using letterpress, risograph, and other analogue print technologies. See for example the monthly letterpress zine *Ker-bloom!* by Art Noose, produced in the United States, and the zines made by members of The Rizzeria collective in Sydney, Australia (www.rizzeria.com/).
7. A methodological note about my research on zines at this time: zines had been studied in cultural and media studies such as Henry Jenkins' canonical discussion of fandom in *Textual Poachers: Television Fans and Participatory Culture* (1992), and Stephen Duncombe's defining *Notes from the Underground: Zines and the Politics of Alternative Culture* (1997). However, they had not been comprehensively discussed as literary or aesthetic works. My (perhaps naïve) intention with my doctoral research was to read zines as literature, and in making this choice I set myself the task of trying to learn how to read them (Poletti 3). For this reason, I did not utilise interviews with zine makers as a method. Kirsty Leishman's earlier work, based on interview material, had already documented zine makers' perspectives on their work and community.
8. Marc van Elburg, founder of the Zinedepo in Arnhem, the Netherlands, is writing a series of zines explicating this idea.
9. There is a significant body of scholarship on the pedagogical uses of zines in teaching literacy and social justice in a range of educational contexts; see Congdon and Blandy; Desyllas and Sinclair; Jacobi; Rallin and Barnard.
10. The print run of each issue *Trade Entrance* was around thirty copies. I would trade them, sell them at zine fairs, and send them to friends.

# Works Cited

Best, Stephen, and Sharon Marcus. "Surface Reading: An Introduction." *Representations*, vol. 108, 2009, pp. 1–21.

Culler, Jonathan. "The Closeness of Close Reading." *ADE*, vol. 149, 2010, pp. 20–25.

Congdon, Kristin G., and Doug Blandy. "Zinesters in the Classroom: Using Zines to Teach About Postmodernism and the Communication of Ideas." *Art Education*, vol. 56, no. 3, 2003, pp. 44–55.

Davis, Mark. *Gangland: Cultural Elites and the New Generationalism*. 2nd ed. Allen and Unwin, 1999.

Desyllas, Moshoula Capous, and Allison Sinclair. "Zine-Making as a Pedagogical Tool for Transformative Learning in Social Work Education." *Social Work Education*, vol. 33, no. 3, 2014, pp. 296–316.

Duncombe, Stephen. *Notes From Underground: Zines and the Politics of Alternative Culture*. Verso, 1997.

Eichhorn, Kate. *The Archival Turn in Feminism: Outrage in Order*. Temple UP, 2013.

———. "Sites Unseen: Ethnographic Research in a Textual Community." *Qualitative Studies in Education*, vol. 14, no. 1, 2001, pp. 565–578.

Halberstam, Jack. *The Queer Art of Failure*. Duke UP, 2011.

Haraway, Donna J. "Situated Knowledges: The Science Question in Feminism and the Privilege of Partial Perspective." *Simians, Cyborgs and Women: The Reinvention of Nature*. Free Association Books, 1991, pp. 183–201.

Jacobi, Tobi. "The Zine Project: Innovation or Oxymoron?" *The English Journal*, vol. 96, no. 4, 2007, pp. 43–49.

Jenkins, Henry. *Textual Poachers: Television Fans and Participatory Culture*. Routledge, 1992.

Leishman, Kirsty. "Becoming Zine: The Place of Zines in Australia's Cultural Life." MPhil dissertation, U of Queensland, 2004.

Lejeune, Philippe. *On Diary*. Edited by Jeremy D. Popkin and Julie Rak. Translated by Katherine Durnin. U of Hawai'i P, 2009.

Love, Heather. "Close But Not Deep: Literary Ethics and the Descriptive Turn." *New Literary History*, vol. 41, no. 2, 2010, pp. 371–391.

Lymn, Jessie. "The Zine Anthology as Archive: Archival Genres and Practices." *Archives and Manuscripts*, vol. 41, no. 1, 2013, pp. 44–57.

Poletti, Anna. *Intimate Ephemera: Reading Young Lives in Australian Zine Culture*. Melbourne UP, 2008.

Radway, Janice. "Zines, Half-Lives, and Afterlives: On the Temporalities of Social and Political Change." *PMLA*, vol. 126, no. 1, Jan. 2011, pp. 140–150.

Rallin, Aneil, and Ian Barnard. "The Politics of Persuasion Versus the Construction of Alternative Communities: Zines in the Writing Classroom." *Reflections*, vol. 7, no. 3, 2008, pp. 46–57.

Sinor, Jennifer. "Another Form of Crying: Zines: Girls Zines as Life Writing." *Prose Studies*, vol. 26, nos. 1–2, Apr.–Aug. 2003, pp. 240–264.

Steedman, Carolyn. *Landscape for a Good Woman*. Virago, 1986.

Weed, Elizabeth. "The Way We Read Now." *History of the Present*, vol. 2, no. 1, 2012, pp. 95–106.

# 4  Objects and Things

*Gillian Whitlock*

The idea that the recent turn to posthumanism and new materialisms, and their "new ways of thinking about living matter" (Coole and Frost 24) in the humanities, offers opportunities for research in life narrative seems tenuous. After all, biography is traditionally firmly anchored in key tenets of western humanism. An elementary principle of conventional understandings of "biography" in western traditions is a central assumption that the "bio" is a human subject, conventionally the lives of individual men, narrated from birth to death (Hoberman). In this schema, a seemingly natural order of things separates persons, objects, and things: persons are individuated and singular; objects are commodities. However, "thinking about living matter" in its various manifestations as "posthumanism" (Wolfe), or the "nonhuman turn" (Grusin), or "new materialisms" (Coole and Frost) questions these boundaries, and in life narrative now there is a turn to thresholds where these distinctions are transactional, and creaturely things come to vibrant life.

In *Evocative Objects*, an edited collection of autobiographical essays, Sherry Turkle defines objects as "things we think with" and companions in life experience:

> We find it familiar to consider objects as useful or aesthetic, as necessities or vain indulgences. We are on less familiar ground when we consider objects as companions to our emotional lives or as provocations to thought. The notion of evocative objects brings together these two less familiar ideas, underscoring the inseparability of thought and feeling in our relationship to things. We think with the objects we love; we love the objects we think with.
>
> (5)

In questioning what makes an object evocative, Turkle evokes the notion of the "testimony of object narratives", and how everyday objects in particular can become part of our inner lives. So, for example, Edmund De Waal's family memoir *The Hare With Amber Eyes* focuses on the transactions of a collection of netsuke, small Japanese carvings, across centuries. These are objects that emit an "existential hum": things that "retain the pulse of their making". Here a collective familial memoir is told through these powerful objects that pass through many hands to become repositories of a generational history. In tracking the transactions that mobilise this collection, De Waal traces a family history and, it follows, the catastrophic history of European Jews last century. Turkle concludes by gesturing to the changing frontier between humans and objects: we will need to tell ourselves different stories, she suggests, as we begin to live with objects that challenge the boundaries between the born and created, and between humans and everything else (326).

In "The Cultural Biography of Things", Igor Kopytoff points out that the conceptual polarity of individualised persons and commoditised things is recent and, culturally speaking, exceptional. He turns to slavery to demonstrate how persons become objects, commoditised as property. Kopytoff's biographical approach to enslavement as a process suggests that processes of commoditisation and singularisation, of persons to things, can be ongoing. It follows from this that the commoditisation of other things may be seen similarly, and in doing the biography of a thing we can ask questions that usually shape the trajectory of life narratives of persons.

> Where does the thing come from and who made it? What has been its career so far? . . . What are the recognised "ages" or periods in the thing's "life" . . . what happens to it when it reaches the ends of its usefulness?
>
> (66)

Researchers in auto/biography studies have been working on this frontier for some time now, exploring what the turn to new materialisms brings to thinking about life narratives—in work on new technologies, for example (Rak and Poletti; Zuern and McNeill). Here there is a decisive break with Romantic notions of selfhood and authorship, and the humanism and individualism of the European Enlightenment. These are different stories that emerge as the boundaries between self and other are radically reconfigured. We are, argues Cary Wolfe, "not that 'auto-' of autobiography studies that humanism 'gives to itself' " (119). Just as Kopytoff's essay was germinal in dismantling the boundary between persons and things, so Jane Bennett's *Vibrant Matter* (2010) has led the way in opening new ways of thinking about that "auto" that inhabits life narrative. For Bennett, objects are not evocative and companionable attachments to individual human subjects; nor are they obedient, passive repositories of family history. Rather, "vibrant" matter challenges the parsing of life into dull matter (objects, things) and vibrant life (us, beings). A dispersed agency intervenes: things have the capacity to act as forces with trajectories, propensities, and tendencies of their own, as "actants". The category "object" does not neatly divide the animate from the inanimate, the material from the immaterial, or the human from the non-human (Candlin and Guins 2).

Jane Bennett asks us to imagine a testimony of things, a startling prospect given the production and dissemination of testimony is embedded in humanism, in claims for recognition that appeal to human rights and humanitarianism (Wilson and Brown 4–9); testimony itself has been compared to "human remains", a speaking for the dead, and integral to campaigns for social justice (Franklin and Lyons viii). The non-human turn often concerns scholars engaged social justice projects (feminism, postcolonialism, and critical race studies, for example) that work to protect vulnerable subjects from dehumanisation and objectification, and classification as a non-human object or thing that is commodified, incarcerated, and dispensable (Grusin xviii). In *How We Become Posthuman*, N. Katherine Hayles anticipates these concerns, taking up Kopytoff's point that the status of the human has always been a privilege of the few, that conceptions of the "human" are historical, and cultural. Thinking in terms of new materialisms does not mean the end of humanity, Hayles suggests. It offers resources for rethinking the liberal humanist view of the self specifically, and questioning conceptions of the human organised in terms of hierarchies of speciesism and anthropocentrism. These are ideas "that may have applied, at best, to that fraction of humanity that had the wealth, power and leisure to conceptualise themselves as autonomous beings exercising their will through individual agency and choice" (286). "The human" is entangled variously in nature, culture, and technology; the state or condition of the human "being" is made, remade, unmade in proximity to a "widened field of alterity: animate and inanimate, natural and artificial, living and dead, organic and mechanistic" (Fuss 3).

Both the possibilities and risks of engaging with the testimony of things are acute in the research field of refugee studies, where for ethical and political reasons human subjects remain essential to rights discourse. Refugees and asylum seekers occupy the conceptual borderlands where demarcations of humans, animals, and things are fragile and easily eroded. They are, as Zygmunt Bauman points out in *Wasted Lives*, frequently consigned to the abject. Erasing the humanity of asylum seekers and denying their rights is a standard protocol in the management of border control, as unwelcome strangers threaten the body of the nation, and are "ejected beyond the scope of the possible, the tolerable, the thinkable" (Kristeva cited in Ahmed 86). Now, given the recent historical surge in mass migration and a resurgence of discourses that dehumanise asylum seekers and refugees, it is more than ever necessary to explore how life narrative, which has been so essential to the social history of the sovereign self, can engage with the limits of the human, such as Bennett's concept of the testimony of things, in its repertoire of research methodologies. Kelly Oliver points out that bearing witness to the ways that one is rendered a thing or an object is paradoxical in that things and objects cannot testify. "While the act of witnessing itself is a testimony to one's subjectivity, the narrative of oppression tells the story of one's objectification and silence. How can we speak the silence of objectification?" (98).

Several recent projects on refugees and asylum seekers, and a startling autobiographical novel by a refugee, engage with this question now.

## Remains

In his "The Land of Open Graves: Living and Dying on the Migrant Trail" Jason De Léon "documents" the lives of undocumented migrants crossing the Sonoran Desert in Arizona, moving from Mexico to the USA. An installation based on De Léon's book, "States of Exception", presents a display of relics: the debris that remains in the wake of these migrants—backpacks, shoes, water bottles, Bibles (Barnes et al.). On occasion, they find human remains in the desert. Reviewers have questioned whether this is "art" (Cotter), and whether the aestheticisation of emptiness and ruins is an adequate response to the ethical questions raised by the representation of human subjects seeking asylum in Europe (Lisle np). This scepticism about the politics of displaying waste matter to record the presence of asylum seekers recurs in response to Ai Wei Wei's installation of debris, the life vests abandoned on the beaches of Lesbos, at the Konzerthaus in Berlin in the summer of 2015. In this case, ethical concerns about displays of debris were heightened by Ai Wei Wei's earlier controversial appropriation of the image of the drowned child, Alan Kurdi (Neuendorf). Although these two projects are geographically remote, they are conceptually similar in an orientation to a testimony of things. These installations turn from social activism oriented to "human rights and narrated lives" (Schaffer and Smith), which "gives face" and a name to humanise and individualise the dispossessed (Edkins x), to an activism that demands we bear witness to the testimony of things—waste matter, including the corpse.

Grief and loss inhabit asylum seeker archives, and asylum seekers are themselves haunted by the spectral presence of the corpse. As I have argued elsewhere, the real and potential deaths of asylum seekers in transit has been invoked to justify inhumane policies of mandatory indefinite detention and border control by Australian governments in the recent past, a faux humanitarianism that justifies violations of human rights (Whitlock, "A Testimony of Things"). The association of humanitarianism and the presence of the dead as silent witnesses is generic—Thomas Laqueur traces the formulation of "human" in "human rights" back to the late eighteenth century, and he points out that "human" and "life" as well as "death" and "the dead" took on new meanings in this period. Bringing the dead into public recognition incorporated them into what Laqueur refers to as "a remade world of the living", where the dead exerted an ethical claim (38); the dead came to insist on being seen as never before in campaigns to ameliorate the suffering of those without social power—women and children, slaves, Indigenous peoples, prisoners, and animals. In Laqueur's view, the distinction between the human and the animal, human beings and things, is never secured.

Refugees and asylum seekers return now, in times of mass migration, as bodies that mark the boundaries between citizen and alien; the familiar and the strange; the human and the animal and the thing. As Hannah Arendt points out in her writing on the surge of refugees in Europe following the Holocaust, humans bear rights by law, not by being human in any essential way, and asylum seekers are positioned in the borderlands at the limits of the human. It is no surprise that installations of debris that marks the passages of these people and the insistence of the corpse on being seen (with that spectacular instance of the image of the dead child that Ai Wei appropriates) return, not only in campaigns on behalf of asylum seekers but also in their own testimonies from the borders where they insist on their status as grievable life: "I am not a 'death meat' of Australia", proclaims "Nima", an Iranian refugee "lying on a bed like a corpse" on Nauru, where over 900 refugees and asylum seekers—men, women, and children—remain subjected to processing (Hekmat 1).

"How should I read these?" Helen Hoy asks, responding to the demands that Indigenous literature makes on its readers, and on the limits of research methodologies grounded in western ontologies and epistemologies. Similarly, the Australian Indigenous critic Jeanine Leane questions how settlers engage with Indigenous Country and its "nourishing terrain" where the boundaries between the animate and inanimate, the living and the dead, the organic and the mechanistic establish an order of things outside western humanism. Recently, Behrouz Boochani's autobiographical novel *No Friend but the Mountains*, which draws on Kurdish and Pacific Indigenous knowledges, makes similar demands of its readers. Boochani is a Kurdish Iranian refugee who also remains in limbo on Manus Island in Papua New Guinea following the closure of the Australian Regional Processing Centre there. His narrative is inspired by philosophical knowledges and Indigenous non-anthropocentric traditions: a trans-species understanding that draws on Kurdish folklore and resistance, Persian literature, sacred narrative traditions, local histories and nature symbols, and ritual and ceremony, including Manusian thought and culture. It is a unique creation of the camp. The refugees held in Manus Prison have "modified their perception and interpretation of life . . . transfigured into different beings", argues Boochani (363), and in this extraordinary example of "Australian–Persian literature" (370) this carceral creativity and interpretation of life animates plants and animals, objects and landscapes, myth and legend, as well as the punitive power complex of the "Kyriarchal System" of the prison. Here a trope that records a profound disturbance in the order of things in the Australian Pacific camps returns: "A prisoner is reduced to a useless piece of meat to be destroyed" (303). Boochani is convinced, writes his principal translator Omid Tofighian, that had the refugees not established a relationship of respect with the environment and animals, the force of the prison would have killed them: "nature works with the prisoners to combat the system" (xxiv).

*No Friend but the Mountains* deliberately turns aside from "the refugee industry" and appeals for empathic humanitarian witness, and it is, as the writer Richard Flanagan suggests in paratexts, "a strange and terrible book" that is a difficult read for Australians, as beneficiaries whose citizenship is secured by this offshore detention regime (ix). The production of this text transforms conventional understandings of "translation" as the genesis of this refugee voice emerges across different domains, media, and languages. Omid Tofighian's paratext, the "Translator's Tale", explains this process. This novel was "thumbed" by Boochani into his smartphone in Farsi, and then transferred via WhatsApp and converted to PDFs, so a network of consultants, confidants, and translators engage in simultaneous planning, writing, and translating. Authorship is transformed into a collaborative and philosophical activity here, and, although the text becomes hard copy and finally moves from screens to paper, Boochani's Twitter handle is recorded on the cover, a reminder of the multiple digital domains where he appears as a narrating "I". The affordances of technologies and "digital life" in the production of identities online (Rak and Poletti 5) are essential to the agentic assemblages that authorise refugees now. And yet, there are enduring traditions: unsurprisingly (given the ubiquitous and uncanny presence of the dead in these borderlands), Tofighian's "Tale" records that this work of translation was a continuation of a work of mourning, inaugurated by the eulogies for his father. His first meeting with Behrouz on Manus is on the day that the body of refugee Hamed Shamshiripour is found in suspicious circumstances, and Tofighian's "Tale" records the names of those who have died in offshore detention on Manus, Nauru, and Christmas Islands. Boochani's decolonial novel ends with a lamentation on the death of Reza Barati at the Manus Island Regional Processing Centre in 2014.

Life narrative has always been caught up with the limits of the human, in "posting" lives (Whitlock, "Posthuman Lives"). What it means to be human is a question that is embedded in auto/biography in western modernity. Thinking on objects and things alerts us to testimonial narrative as a threshold, caught up in the constant and relational making of the human and the non-human, entangled in nature, culture, and technology. Now, research methodologies that turn to objects and things alert us to the essential place of auto/biography in the history of human being, and its presence at borderscapes where the making of the human and recognition of "grievable life" (Butler) remain works in progress.

## Works Cited

Ahmed, Sara. *The Cultural Politics of Emotion*. Routledge, 2004.

Barnes, Richard et al. "State of Exception." An Exhibition of the Undocumented Migration Project, 2013. https://issuu.com/humin/docs/state_of_exception. Accessed 21 Sept. 2018.

Bauman, Zygmunt. *Wasted Lives: Modernity and Its Outcasts*. Polity, 2014.

Bennett, Jane. *Vibrant Matter: a Political Ecology of Things*. Durham: Duke UP, 2010.

Boochani, Behrouz. *No Friend But the Mountains*. Picador, 2018.

Butler, Judith. *Frames of War: When Is Life Grievable?* Verso, 2009.

Candlin, Fiona, and Raiford Guins. *The Object Reader*. Routledge, 2009.

Cotter, Holland. "For Migrants Head North, the Things They Carried to the End." *New York Times*, 3 Mar. 2017. http://undocumentedmigrationproject. com/media/state-of-exception-opens-in-new-york-city-thursday-february 2nd-2017/. Accessed 21 Sept. 2018.

De Léon, Jason. *The Land of Open Graves: Living and Dying on the Migrant Trail*. U of California P, 2015.

De Waal, Edmund. *The Hare With Amber Eyes: A Hidden Inheritance*. Chatto & Windus, 2011.

Edkins, Jenny. *Face Politics*. Routledge, 2015.

Fuss, Diana, editor. *Human, All Too Human*. Routledge, 1996.

Grusin, Richard, editor. *The Nonhuman Turn*. U of Minnesota P, 2015.

Hayles, N. Katherine. *How We Became Posthuman*. U of Chicago P, 1999.

Hekmat, Abdul Karim. "I am Not a 'Death Meat' of Australia." *The Saturday Paper*, 15–21 Sept. 2018, pp. 1–4.

Hoberman, Ruth. "Biography: General Survey." *Encyclopedia of Life Writing: Autobiographical and Biographical Forms*, edited by Margaretta Jolly.

Hoy, Helen. *How Should I Read These?* U of Toronto P, 2001.

Kopytoff, Igor. "The Cultural Biography of Things: Commoditization as Process." *The Social Life of Things: Commodities in Cultural Perspective*, edited by Arjun Appadurai. Cambridge UP, 1986, pp. 64–91.

Laqueur, Thomas "Mourning, Pity, and the Work of Narrative in the Making of 'Humanity,'" in *Humanitarianism and Suffering: The Mobilization of Empathy*, ed. Richard Ashby Wilson and Richard D. Brown. Cambridge: Cambridge University Press, 2009. 38–39.

Leane, Jeanine. "Tracking Our Country in Settler Literature." *JASAL*, vol. 14, no. 3.

Lisle, Debbie. "Emptiness, Ethics and Disgruntlement." Unpublished paper, "Visuality and Creativity in Global Politics", The U of Queensland, 1 Nov. 2018.

Neuendorf, Henri. "Ai Weiwei Commemorates Drowned Refugees With Public Installation During Berlin Film Festival." *artnet news*, 15 Feb. 2016. https:// news.artnet.com/art-world/ai-weiwei-life-jackets-installation-berlin-427247. Accessed 21 Sept. 2018.

Oliver, Kelly. *Witnessing. Beyond Recognition*. U of Minnesota P, 2001.

Rak, Julie, and Anna Poletti, editors. *Identity Technologies: Constructing the Self Online*. U of Wisconsin P, 2014.

Schaffer, Kay, and Sidonie Smith. *Human Rights and Narrated Lives*. Palgrave Macmillan, 2004.

Turkle, Sherry. *Evocative Objects: Things We Think With*. The MIT P, 2007.

Whitlock, Gillian. "Posthuman Lives." *Biography*, vol. 35, no. 1, Winter 2012, pp. v–vxi.

———. "A Testimony of Things." *Challenging the Humanities*, edited by Tony Bennett. Australian Academy of the Humanities/Australian Scholarly, 2013, pp. 17–32.

Wolfe, Cary. "What is Posthumanism?" Minneapolis: U of Minnesota Press, 2009.

# 5 Social, Media, Life Writing

## Online Lives at Scale, Up Close, and In Context

*Aimée Morrison*

Self-representation in social media *performs work* in the world that is autobiographical, interpersonal, and, increasingly, institutional and public. Fundamentally, social media is predicated on the production, dissemination, reception, and response to and of various sorts of texts by and about the self. For example, consider: a series of real-time, informal status updates on Facebook that accumulate into a sort of history over time; an ultrasound photo captioned and shared via Snapchat as a pregnancy announcement; the publication of details of new jobs, new degrees, and big moves on Twitter; the careful crafting of a visual identity through staged photos of the self on Instagram linked into broader communities of practice through hashtags. Digital self-representations in social media constitute a form of life writing in the most capacious sense. Auto/biography as a field of study thus offers rich theoretical insights upon which to found interpretation and analysis of life writing on social media. Arguably, the literary practice of auto/biography studies can be considered a *key field* upon which to make sense of social media.

At the same time, social media life writing is profoundly, fundamentally mediated and networked in ways that exceed or challenge auto/biography's existing methodologies and frameworks. Social media is comprised, obviously, of individual utterances produced by individual people, each with their own authorship agenda, style, goals, and audiences. But the texts these authors produce are also substantially determined by sharing platform, authoring hardware, and quality of network access. Social media texts can take the form of viral YouTube videos, heavily filtered images, repurposed memes, textual captions or narratives, posts of all kinds networked among themselves with hashtags. They can be aural, textual, pictorial, photographic, or, more usually, some combination. Each of these multimedia fragments can act as components of life stories, as representatives of a group of similar texts comprising genres, as gambits in private or public conversations, or as aesthetic or cultural objects—or some combination of some or all of these. Further, social media life writing texts can be deliberately optimised to better spread via the sorting algorithms of different platforms such that a certain type of autobiographical production might be determined to be more legible and appropriate to one platform over another—that is, social media life writers are attuned to how the platform foregrounds or supresses certain kinds of speech, increasing or decreasing its reach in ways that can be purposefully engaged. Social media life writing texts may be, on the other hand, optimised for privacy or circumscribed sharing within bounded audiences—constructing intimate publics with limited searchability, for example. Together, all these characteristics of social media life writing push us to consider authorship as attuned to technical, social, and generic exigencies as much as to simply literary or creative ones. Social media life writing texts, that is, are complex and multimodal sets of objects, practices, and meanings that require interdisciplinary competencies to understand, analyse, and interpret. Additionally, of course, the massive scope, scale, and variety of such texts further requires new methods for text selection: how to choose which of the millions of Instagram accounts to focus on, for example, and how to justify such a choice as wise or even useful?

Methodological innovation is required; in this piece, I elaborate the particular methods (and their interdisciplinary theoretical underpinnings) that I have developed over ten years of researching and publishing in social media life writing. I propose a method for grouping social media life writing practices into distinct rhetorical genres, for establishing criteria by which to choose exemplary or representative texts for close reading (or perhaps distance reading as well), and for analysing and understanding the rules for producing successful texts or utterances in those genres.

## Inter/Disciplinary Contexts

Digital self-representation in online social media is autobiographical, purposive, multimodal, and social. The relevant literature thus draws first and foremost from the literary study of auto/biography, from rhetorical genre theory, and from new media studies/digital humanities. Auto/biography studies is based in close reading of life writing texts and attends to particular narrative strategies and other literary techniques. Crucially, the constructed personae represented in life writing texts are examined in light of (primarily) poststructuralist, feminist, and raced theories of the construction of the human subject (see Smith and Watson, *Reading Autobiography*, for a general overview). Auto/biography scholars themselves have been calling for the development of "more advanced visual and cultural literacies" (Whitlock and Poletti vi) when confronting these new kinds of texts. Indeed, auto/biography scholars have undertaken some of the most nuanced readings of online autobiographical acts, and I would acknowledge in particular the important research published in a 2003 special issue of *Biography* entitled "Online Lives" (Zuern)—and then revisited in a second special edition on the same topic in 2015 (McNeill and Zuern). The recent *Identity Technologies: Constructing the Self Online* (Poletti and Rak) is the first edited collection to push this mode of enquiry forward in a more formal and systematic way. In auto/biography studies, rightly, the primary mode of analysis remains close reading, supported by an attention to the material conditions of production and the broader cultural contexts in which such texts are produced, are published, and gain an audience.

Rhetorical genre theory (Miller) proposes that communicative acts can be categorised on the basis of the social goal they aim to accomplish. My work on "personal mommy blogging", for example, defined that genre by its exigence of building communities of new mothers grappling with role conflict as they transitioned into their new maternal status in relative social isolation (Morrison, "Autobiography", "Suffused", "Compositional"). Rhetorical genre theory has come to be applied more widely to social media research, as in the recent collection *Genres on the Internet* (Giltrow and Stein). Online ethnography is also rapidly developing a scholarship around these methods (Markham and Baym; Horst and Miller; Hine; see instances in Gajjala et al. 2007, 2008). Rhetorical genre theory is supported by literary strategies of close reading and surface reading (Best and Marcus), and ethnographic methods of thin description (Love): the first attends to the interpretation of the actual words or images used by online social subjects, and the second places these utterances in a broader context of (textual and multimodal) speech acts, in order to fully describe a community of practice. Rhetorical genre theory proposes a type of structural analysis that seeks to understand, first, the *why* of a communicative practice, and then to catalogue and consider the *how* of communication, developing insight into what constitutes the discursive field of successful or sensible utterances. As with literary genre, rhetorical genre considers formal and thematic linkages between texts (broadly construed) but adds a particular focus on the pragmatics of communication, keeping at the forefront of analysis the question of the unmet needs genres emerge to address.

In new media studies, scholars theorise the interaction of technology, culture, human subjects, intention, and reception. New media studies also has a strong foundation in poststructuralist and postmodern theories, as well as an underpinning in the materialities of the underlying digital technologies. Important work on social media practices has been produced (e.g., boyd; Jenkins et al.; Noble and Tynes; Thumim; van Dijck) in media studies and in sociology, although much of this work cannot account for individual texts or practices as auto/biography would, focusing instead on the issues at scale, in quantitative and qualitative studies. In its insistence on accounting for affordances and constraints of hardware and software platforms, such work also grounds analysis of the mutually determining relationships between platform, user, and genre (e.g., Evans et al.; Ellison and Vitak; Morrison, "What's").

These fields ground the methodology as a general case. Necessarily, as we will see, each research foray into different social media practices will discover and outline different rhetorical genres, each with different participant communities, practices, and purposes, and so all research will draw on relevant work in other fields: in my own work, for example, this has included research into motherhood as a social role and identity category, feminist media studies, critical race studies, queer theory, and disability studies.

## Methodology

In short, interdisciplinary fields and methods are drawn together to understand the full action of social media life writing in the world. I propose, therefore, a mixed methods process employing some combination of the following depending on the particular case: close reading and surface reading methodologies drawn from literary fields; grounded theory study design drawn from sociology (Bryant and Charmaz; Charmaz); thin and thick description drawn from anthropology and ethnography; and the delineation and interpretation of the software and hardware affordances drawn from new media studies (Kirschenbaum; Noble; Norman).

In practice, research proceeds along the following pathway: Explore and Engage; Categorise; Select; and Interpret. Stages are iterative and necessarily overlap, as data collection and organisation are informed by interpretive or analytical work, which in turn is moderated by secondary research as well as increased exposure to the primary materials.

- *Stage 1—Explore and Engage*: The first step involves wide exploration and reading among linked texts (images on Instagram tagged "#effyourbeautystandards", and those that link to them, for example) in order to get a sense of the scale and scope of a set of practices: who does it, how, and why? This reading practice is embedded, context-driven, and interpretive; it traverses a field of texts rhizomatically, across webs of connection, in order discern emergent patterns from a diffuse set of instances. It is attentive to platform. This step draws from grounded theory: a deep and exploratory reading of communities of practice and the authoring subjects within them, to determine the contours of appropriate and context-sensitive research questions to guide all further enquiry. Exploration crosses from primary texts, to discussion of practices by the community of users itself in blog posts delineating proper practices or deviations from them, to mainstream media treatments, to scholarly literature on similar practices by similar subject or addressing similar aims. The goal here is to read a lot, to read very broadly, to read generously, in order to develop an emerging sense of discursive field at issue and the rhetorical exigence seeking assuagement.

- *Stage 2—Categorise*: From this emergent sense of the contours of a given set of practices or a community, second, follows a thin description of the practice: a main outcome of the research is precisely in this work of meticulously describing what constitutes membership in the community, the goals of communication, and the boundaries of shared practices, as well as themes and content. This thin description gives a full contextual reading of the purpose of the communications and how they perform meaningful work in a given community. Such descriptions then trace the outlines of a specific rhetorical genre, delineating *who* comprises the community of practice, *what* goals they aim to accomplish through these communications, and *how* these goals are advanced through specific and describable compositional practices. This process proceeds iteratively alongside Stage 1.

- *Stage 3—Select:* In the third stage of research, both exemplary (unusually skilled or somehow noteworthy to the broader community of practice) instances of the determined genre and representative (typical of the larger class) ones are chosen to serve as target texts for analysis and interpretation. This work employs literary strategies of discernment and discrimination, modes of scholarly judgement that animate any choice of primary text in print or otherwise. Rhetorical genres at scale ("fat fashion selfies", or "the Kiki challenge") must be described at the more general level of purpose, strategy, and community as I suggest above. But literary analysis is difficult to perform on a huge and fragmented corpus of texts such as might be collected using big data methodologies like keyword search scraping, or random sampling of texts from the internet meeting certain parameters. As this work is also grounded in auto/biography, it is necessary to select (and to justify the selection of) a far smaller number of instances in order to address more particular, ground-level manifestations or instances of the genre in daily practice: how to account for auto/biography, that is, in the singular. This stage begins during the refinement process of Stage 2 and consists of sifting through sufficient unique instances to surface and document exemplary and representative texts for interpretation and analysis. A note, also, on ethics: understandably queasy about subjecting everyday life writers to the full critical academic treatment (see Felski), scholars often focus on the most highly public or visible examples online, as quasi-public figures. However, this risks misrepresenting the full variety of online practices, crucially disguising the fact that the overwhelming bulk of online self-representation is as vital as it is obscure. In my own work, this qualm is obviated by simply asking writers for permission to quote from their work, and giving them enough of the context in which it will appear that they can make an informed judgement. Most say yes, and those who do not have their wishes respected. In this way, I feel I have been better able to show the great skill and creativity by authoring subjects who would never otherwise come to critical attention (see Morrison, "Laughing", for examples of such collaboration). More elaboration of this ethical dimension, of engaging truly everyday life writers, is required to produce viable critical practices.

- *Stage 4—Interpret:* Fourth, these exemplary and representative instances are subjected to literary-inflected close reading practices that interpret the means by which each instance performs the work central to the genre described in Stage 2, and which characteristics mark it as an exemplary or representative instance. A study of fat fashion selfies, for example, would distinguish fat activist or fat liberationist practice from more amorphous "body positivity" selfies online; make the case for "Fat Fashion Selfie" as a distinct rhetorical genre (or subgenre) with shared formal and communicative features; surface examples of such selfies that are very normal and ordinary, and others that are particularly noteworthy; and explain how each fits into the genre by attention to specific and individual characteristics of each photo: software platform, pose, lighting, or filter, hashtag use, caption, deployment of clothing and accessories, number of likes or reblogs, follower networks, and more. This stage most closely approximates the production of standard academic articles and conference papers and draws on modes of literary close reading informed by auto/biography studies' poststructuralist understandings of the means by which both selves and narratives are constituted, as well as design studies and new media studies' insistence on the interplay between platform, technology, and production.

Everyday subjects perform autobiographical acts online as a condition of social media participation. Such autobiographical acts can be understood to constitute micro-acts of life writing that accrete over time into forms of memoir, or into cross-sectional purposive political speech through hashtags, for example, or which articulate new forms of social identity and social belonging through the development of rhetorical genres attentive to unmet expressive needs. The overwhelming number of texts and writers is matched only by the development and proliferation of new genres of speech, writing, and action. To understand these autobiographical acts requires, thus, attention to context, community, platform affordance, and scale, even as we wish to keep our attention focused as well on individual texts or utterances. The above methodology proposes to allow for any number of such avenues to be pursued.

## Works Cited

Best, Stephen, and Sharon Marcus. "Surface Reading: An Introduction." *Representations*, vol. 108, no. 1, Nov. 2009, pp. 1–21.

boyd, danah. *It's Complicated: The Social Lives of Networked Teens*. Yale UP, 2014.

Bryant, Antony, and Kathy Charmaz, editors. *The SAGE Handbook of Grounded Theory*. Paperback ed., Reprinted. Sage Publication, 2011.

Charmaz, Kathy. *Constructing Grounded Theory*. London: SAGE. 2014.

Dijck, José van. *Mediated Memories in the Digital Age*. Stanford UP, 2007.

Ellison, Nicole B., and Jessica Vitak. "Social Network Site Affordances and Their Relationship to Social Capital Processes." *The Handbook of the Psychology of Communication Technology*, edited by S. Shyam Sundar. John Wiley & Sons, Ltd, 2015, pp. 203–227.

Evans, Sandra K. et al. "Explicating Affordances: A Conceptual Framework for Understanding Affordances in Communication Research: Explicating Affordances." *Journal of Computer-Mediated Communication*, vol. 22, no. 1, Jan. 2017, pp. 35–52.

Felski, Rita. *The Limits of Critique*. The U of Chicago P, 2015.

Gajjala, Radhika et al. "Epistemologies of Doing: E-Merging Selves Online." *Feminist Media Studies*, vol. 7, no. 2, 2007, pp. 209–213.

———. "Racing and Queering the Interface: Producing Global/Local Cyberselves." *Qualitative Inquiry*, vol. 14, no. 7, 2008, pp. 1110–1133.

Giltrow, Janet, and Dieter Stein, editors. *Genres in the Internet: Issues in the Theory of Genre*. Vol. 188. John Benjamins Publishing Company, 2009.

Hine, Christine. *Ethnography for the Internet: Embedded, Embodied and Everyday*. Bloomsbury Academic, An imprint of Bloomsbury Publishing Plc, 2015.

Horst, Heather A., and Daniel Miller, editors. *Digital Anthropology*. English ed. Berg, 2012.

Jenkins, Henry et al. *Participatory Culture in a Networked Era: A Conversation on Youth, Learning, Commerce, and Politics*. Polity P, 2015.

Kirschenbaum, Matthew G. *Mechanisms: New Media and the Forensic Imagination*. MIT P, 2008.

Love, H. "Close Reading and Thin Description." *Public Culture*, vol. 25, no. 3 71, Oct. 2013, pp. 401–434.

Markham, Annette N., and Nancy K. Baym, editors. *Internet Inquiry: Conversations About Method*. Sage Publications, 2009.

McNeill, Laurie, and John David Zuern. "Online Lives 2.0: Introduction." *Biography*, vol. 38, no. 2, 2015, pp. v–xlvi.

Miller, Carolyn R. "Genre as Social Action." *Quarterly Journal of Speech*, vol. 70, no. 2, May 1984, pp. 151–167.

Morrison, Aimée. "Autobiography in Real Time: A Genre Analysis of Personal Mommy Blogging." *Cyberpsychology: Journal of Psychosocial Research on Cyberspace*, vol. 4, no. 2, 2010. www.cyberpsychology.eu/view.php?cisloclanku=2010120801&article=5.

———. "Compositional Strategies of Conflict Management in Personal Mommy Blogs." *Feminist Media Studies*, vol. 14, no. 2, Mar. 2014, pp. 286–300.

———. "Laughing at Injustice: #DistractinglySexy and #StayMadAbby as Counternarratives." *Digital Dilemmas*, edited by Diana C. Parry et al. Springer International Publishing, 2019, pp. 23–52.

———. "'Suffused by Feeling and Affect': The Intimate Public of Personal Mommy Blogging." *Biography*, vol. 34, no. 1, 2011, pp. 37–55.

———. "'What's on Your Mind?': The Coaxing Affordances of Facebook's Status Update." *Identity Technologies: Producing Online Selves*, edited by Anna Poletti and Julie Rak. U Wisconsin P, 2013, pp. 112–131.

Noble, Safiya Umoja. *Algorithms of Oppression: How Search Engines Reinforce Racism*. New York UP, 2018.

Norman, Donald A. "Affordance, Conventions, and Design." *Interactions*, June 1999, pp. 38–42.

Poletti, Anna, and Julie Rak, editors. *Identity Technologies: Constructing the Self Online*. The U of Wisconsin P, 2014.

Smith, Sidonie, and Julia Watson. *Reading Autobiography: A Guide for Interpreting Life Narratives*. 2nd ed. U of Minnesota P, 2010.

Thumim, Nancy. *Self-Representation and Digital Culture*. Palgrave Macmillan, 2012.

Whitlock, Gillian, and Anna Poletti. "Self-Regarding Art." *Biography*, vol. 31, no. 1, Winter 2008, pp. v–xxiii.

Zuern, John. "Online Lives: Introduction." *Biography*, vol. 26, no. 1, 2003, pp. v–xxv.

# 6   Studying Visual Autobiographies in the Post-Digital Era

*Sarah Brophy*

From webcomics to Ted Talks, and to selfie travelogues and iPhone documentaries, digitisation is profoundly reshaping both the aesthetic composition and the circulation of visual auto/biography. We are living and conducting scholarly work in the age of what Wendy Hui-Kyong Chun calls "habitual new media", a turn of phrase that invites us to wonder, critically, about the untold, ordinary extent of digital culture's reach into every corner of life. Yet, as Gillian Rose acknowledges in her essential reference text *Visual Methodologies*, the pervasiveness of digital technologies in the realm of visual culture is not yet matched by "digital methods for analyzing visual images", and, in particular, we do not have "a selection of off-the-shelf software tools for analysing digital visual materials using digital methods" (292–293). In the absence of digital tools that can be readily and effectively adopted by the non-programmer, how can scholars go about critically engaging with the phenomena of large-scale, multi-platform, or otherwise digitally mediated visual auto/biographies?

Some pilot projects do, of course, exist. The *Selfiecity* project, with its ambitious use of facial recognition software as well as of Amazon-sourced Mechanical Turk workers to tag and analyse a dataset of over 600000 user-generated digital portraits based on a week-long 2013 sample, imagines the media artefacts it has collected as data ripe for computational analysis. As Elizabeth Losh has pointed out, *Selfiecity*'s largely "positivistic" approach "ignores how people are embedded in complex rhetorical situations", while relying on a problematic form of outsourced labour and hinging its sorting and analysis on biased normative markers, such as a static, binary notion of gender (1649, 1653). Meanwhile, corporate and state entities are working to figure out how to analyse selfies and to put them to work in a range of cultural, economic, and political domains. Launched in December 2017, Google's popular "Art Selfie" app directly solicits users' role in content production by inviting you to take a temporary selfie, which it then matches with images in the database drawn from a reported 1500 participating cultural institutions. Thirty million selfies were uploaded in the first few days: selfie-makers become the digital workers on a massive scale, and the product is the refinement of tools for biometric data analysis (Lange; Mahdawi).[1] Consider, too, the use of self-ies in electoral and activist campaigns, across a wide political spectrum, to foster resistance, as Kathleen Rodgers and Willow Scobie have argued with reference to pro-sovereignty Inuit self-representational practices, or to produce a hegemonic effects, as Anirban Baishya has argued of PM Narendra Modi and the Hindu nationalist BJP's mobilisation of voter selfies in the 2014 Indian General Election. These selfie-related examples suggest that accessing and analysing the "serial, cumulative practices" (Walker Rettberg 36) of social media users across varying scales of pro-duction and dissemination is a key methodological and ethical problem.

What is more, visual testaments which seem predominantly narrative at first glance are also now thoroughly "automediated", in the sense pro-posed by Julie Rak, for "the product (media about a maker)" has become more and more entangled with "the process of mediating the self, or auto" (161). Take, for example, Jennifer Brea's 2017 film *Unrest*, which gives a detailed feature-length account of the writer-director's experience living with myalgic encephalomyelitis (ME), a condition also often also described as chronic fatigue syndrome (CFS). Most immediately recogni-sable as belonging the genre of "personal documentary", *Unrest* is now streaming on Netflix after having significant success on the documentary film festival circuit at sites including Sundance and Hot Docs. Signifi-cantly, *Unrest* is accompanied by a major digital apparatus, consisting of a website, Brea's personal Twitter and Instagram accounts, an intricate press kit, several different trailers on YouTube and Vimeo, Unrest VR ("interactive non-fiction experience"), a Ted Talk by Brea, and an activ-ist campaign associated with the hashtags #TimeForUnrest and #MEAc-tion. Clearly, we need a robust visual methodology for the digital era, one capable of addressing the full range of visual and cultural modes of production today across seemingly disparate media.

With layered processes and sites of mediation in mind, I propose that the "paradox" (292) noted by Rose when she points to the surge of digi-tal–visual culture and the lack of digital methods is not so much to be lamented in the hopes of a better day for the computational. For what emerges here in the probably uncloseable gap[2] is the continuing relevance of approaches grounded in auto/biography studies, visual culture stud-ies, and feminist media studies. Even if there were—indeed, when there are—more low-barrier digital tools for scholars of differing technological skill levels to analyse re/mediated visual content, we would still need to commit to a self-reflexive set of practices. Digital transformations there-fore require that auto/biography scholars experiment with new ways of conceptualising and approaching digital/visual interfaces while reflect-ing all the while on questions of ethical praxis. Inventiveness and criti-cal reflexivity have been demanded by my work on a particular form of convergence: the relationship between artists' projects and their social media presence, particularly the solicitation of user participation in art installations and performance works, ranging from Kara Walker's "A Subtlety" and Bree Newsome's tearing down of the Confederate flag at the South Carolina statehouse (Brophy, "#FreeBree" and "Stickiness"), to Yayoi Kusama's "Infinity Mirrors". While I currently have the benefit of research assistants and digital librarian staff to support webscraping from Twitter, allowing me to produce datasets amenable to tagging and computer-assisted analysis as well as visualisations using Voyant, and while I have also had a chance to play with Documenting the Now's protocol,[3] more vernacular and/or "manual" methods have remained indispensable in order to contend, critically and ethically, with the impact of digital environments, aesthetics, and archiving on the study of visual auto/biography and the considerations of power and ethics intrinsic to it.

## Encountering Visual Auto/Biography in Digital Environments

It is, first of all, indispensable that we describe the architecture of the online spaces that generate and hold the digitally mediated visual artefacts and communities that concern us. We need to understand where and how we are located and constituted as viewers of digital media. As Aimée Morrison explains in her analysis of the rhetorical implications of Facebook's architecture, affordances are the structures of a particular environment makes possible/impossible for users (117–119). Critically analysing the affordances of particular platforms by describing our encounters with them, also known as a "walkaround", is especially generative when deployed comparatively, as Stefanie Duguay does in her comparison of the relative conservativism of Instagram by contrast with the unruly possibilities of the now-defunct Vine for celebrities navigating public queerness. Simultaneously, then, it has proven essential to my research to track and archive what Sidonie Smith and Julia Watson identify as the proliferating "paratexts" that are a signal feature of autobiography in the digital era (85–87). Self-documentation and self-promotion on social media have become de rigueur for artists and museums alike, and publicity can furthermore hinge on controversy, which generates its own archive of debates and para-curatorial interventions by visitors, critics, and other members of the public. In my current work on Kusama's "Infinity Mirrors" exhibition, for instance, the analysis would be incomplete without an analysis of the promotional materials, which now increasingly merge with the vernacular rhetorics of social media platforms as in this example of the Art Gallery of Ontario's use of an anonymised selfie in one of the artist's mirrored chambers in its outreach strategy (Figure 6.1). Here, the kaleidoscopically refracted image of the viewer's hands taking the selfie is paired with a quote from Kusama, in effect folding together the artist's subjectivity with that of the visitor (and the PR staff) and collapsing existential and promotional agendas.

# Instagram

**1,255 likes**

**agotoronto** "I fluctuate between feelings of reality and unreality. I am neither a Christian nor a Buddhist. Nor do I possess great self-control. I find myself stranded in a strangely mechanized and standardized, homogenous environment." #infiniteKUSAMA
Reminder that this is the LAST weekend to

*Figure 6.1* Instagram post by @agotoronto tagged #infinitekusama. Author screenshot. Saturday, 26 May 2018.

69%
match

**Interior 178 (Meg)**

Jude Rae

Canberra Museum and Gallery
Google Arts & Culture

*Figure 6.2* Google "Art Selfie" app result. Author screenshot. Tuesday, 23 January 2018.

In walking around platforms and navigating paratexts, the researching subject inevitably (if ambivalently) puts herself in the picture along the way: generating a few art selfies of my own (Figure 6.2) was necessary in order to explore the inter/face of the Google app, to grasp the way its algorithm prioritises matching skin colour and hair colour/style, above all, and imparts a feeling of dissatisfaction that makes one inclined to produce "just one more".

## Making Digital–Visual Archives

The aggregate but also ephemeral and emergent nature of digital media entails that visual autobiography scholars must ongoingly re/constitute their own archives for any given project. In my research practice and in my graduate research seminar on "Selfie/Culture", I find that there is ongoing value in assembling and sharing a virtual commonplace book, using an existing web clipping, compositional, and/or archiving tool, such as Evernote, Tumblr, Pinterest, OneNote, or Instagram. In the course assignment, the explicit aim of the commonplace book is not only to consider the immediate utility of one or more quotidian digital tools, but also to make a linkage to an autobiographical notetaking tradition and in the process to become more critically attuned to their design affordances and, in an autoethnographic way, to reflect on the relationship between one's own platform presence(s) and research practice, including what Morrison has, in a lecture for the DHSI, elucidated as the quotidian "fan" and remix practices of attending to and making meaning that are so often the lively heart of digital media studies research (qtd in Losh 1650). While the paratextual penumbra often prove transitory, with links rendered inactive when one goes back to look at them again weeks, months, or years later, screenshots and recording tools such as Webrecorder.io can yield relatively stable archives, or one can also decide that the most practical and ethical option is to reflect on the dynamics leading to the original source's disappearance.

## The Politics of Digital–Visual Aesthetics

As we locate ourselves in digital environments and assemble digital–visual archives, rigorous attention needs to be paid, too, to the questions of what we are looking at and how we are looking. Gillian Rose astutely critiques the longstanding ties of a compositional approach to an entrenched elitist idea of connoisseurship or the "good eye" that would concentrate on works of genius so as to celebrate their aesthetic richness (82–84). However, I want to underscore that close consideration of the "content, form, and experiencing" of media artefacts (60) remains necessary in order to perceive the affective and the political dimensions of visual culture, including, not least, both digital photography's role in practices of "survivorship" (Murray 512) and the "mixed feelings" of vernacular or family photography (Brown and Phu). While critical visual methodologies tend to prioritise the vocabularies of semiotics, discourse analysis, and audiencing/circulation in order to emphasise social and political meaning (Rose 82–84), as Brown and Phu contend in their critical and curatorial work on queer and diasporic photographic archives, "for marginalized subjects, family photographs are technologies of the otherwise, both documenting and instantiating a multisensory rhetoric that counters repressive social constructs" (156).[4] Attention to sensuous dimensions (composition, texture, synesthetic effects) is thus inextricable from the critical work of imagining "alternative digitalities", as Anna Munster emphasises in her discussion of embodiment in new media (172). But, given the accretive nature of new media and especially where they meet social media, quotidian

tools that can offer insights into larger scales of critical and political significance should not be overlooked either. In particular, a Google reverse
image search (especially perhaps when performed with a cleared browser
cache) can help to gauge the scale of an image's distribution, usual and
unusual remediations, and what an image is competing with in the digital mediascape. When I was researching the radical impact of Bree Newsome's flagpole climb, for instance, Google helped me to see and interpret
the significance of the fan memes and gifs against the backdrop of a not
only banal but normative and omnipresent white supremacist iconography
associated with the Confederate flag (Brophy, "#FreeBree"). At the same
time, and equally important, closely and thickly describing the sensory
qualities of visual/digital images in our scholarship is a fundamental issue
of disability access, in tune with calls by self-identified "non-visual learn-
ers" such as artist, curator, and activist Carmen Papalia for a push beyond
ocularcentrism in our research methods and exhibition designs.

## Power, Agency, and Ethical Praxis

I offer the above account of some of the directions that I have explored in
my research and graduate teaching with some hesitation, for such an ite-
mised account of methods and tools can only be provisional. Fortunately,
longstanding and new work in the traditions of visual culture studies
and auto/biography studies offer enduring resources to help us discern
and exercise our responsibilities in the new field of born-digital, web-
extended, and remediated autovisuality that I have been mapping. In his
essay revisiting Marxist art critic John Berger's critical model for the era
of the selfie, Ben Davis has pointed out that much of the visual content
uploaded on photo-sharing platforms speaks the language of what Berger
identified as oil painting's and advertising's shared investment in glam-
our: of possession and of envy, the wistfully aggressive daydreams of
capitalism, in which we can be for a moment among the successful striv-
ers, or, in eighteenth-century terms, the landed gentry. Berger's model is
just as illuminating on a methodological level, as Davis suggests, for the
mass reproduction of images in print media give rise to everyday collage
practices that make new meanings and resonances out of

> letters, snapshots, reproductions of paintings, newspaper cuttings,
> original drawings, postcards. On each board all the images belong to
> the same language and all are more or less equal within it, because
> they have been chosen in a highly personal way to match and express
> the experience of the room's inhabitant.
>
> (30)

Ultimately, as Berger summarises, "we only see what we look at" (8). The
activities of the researcher, like those of the ordinary, socially situated

viewer (which we should not forget that we also are), bring materials into the perceptual field, making them available for multiple forms of engagement, along the lines of what Morrison describes as fan practices and what Katie Warfield understands, in Karen Barad's new materialist terms, as the "agential cuts" we enact as we explore our technologically mediated world as producers, consumers, and critics (2).

Grappling responsibly with matters of agency, authorship, owner-ship, and data privacy and security is one of the most pressing issues my graduate students and I face as we go about activities including social media webscraping, gathering, and compiling media clippings, engaging in critical analysis of image sets, and referencing digitally mediated visual self-inscriptions in our essays. It is to intersectional feminist media stud-ies that auto/biography scholars working with visual materials can turn for a substantial body of work on digital research ethics to guide our work on autobiographical forms such as selfies, digital documentaries, and remediation more generally. Moya Bailey, in her work on the health care and community work effected by black trans women through online self-presentation, community-building, and advocacy, proposes that

> the creation of media by minoritarian subjects about themselves and for themselves can be a liberatory act. These acts of image redefini-tion actually engender different outcomes for marginalized groups, and the processes by which they are created to build networks of resilience that far outlive the relevant content. Black women and queer and trans folks reconstruct representations through *digital alchemy*.

> (para 31; italics in original)

Resonating with Bailey's concern to align research projects with social justice aims through practices of "connection, creation, and transfor-mation" (para 34), Dorothy Kim's discussion of "the ethics of digital bodies" issues a powerful call to understand that "gender, race, ability, sexuality are just as marked on digital Twitter avatars as they are in real physical interactions". Current scholarship at the meeting point between critical disability studies, visual media scholarship, and digital practices shows a range of possibilities for ethical engagement. For instance, the feminist and disability oriented research of Carla Rice and her Project Re: Vision research team, which involves video production by partici-pants, hosts this material in a password protected site, whereas Tamar Tembeck, who did not collaborate with Karolyn Gehrig (the originator of the critical disability project #hospitalglam), recognised the artist's status as emerging and sought her permission to reproduce screen caps. Thus, while some scholarship on visual autobiography in the era of social media pursues an ethical path forward by prioritising direct collabora-tion with subject-participants (as exemplified by the research programs of Rice et al., Bailey, and Brown and Phu), not all will be or need to be collaborative in this precise way. Insights into digitally mediated visual autobiographies can come, too, from close sensory and compositional engagement with carefully selected smaller samples (as in the work of Murray, DasGupta, Tembeck, and Warfield).

In the context of the Selfie/Culture research seminar mentioned earlier, I encourage students to focus on public-facing projects/accounts and to consider, further, that public settings may not always confer an assumption of publicity (Highfield and Leaver), especially if a social media account is not highly followed. Especially as projects move towards public dissemination in venues such as online magazines, book chapters, and journal articles, but ideally from the outset, it is vital to seek permission to reproduce working artists' visual images, even if those images have a parallel "public" life on social media, and to consider how precisely to crop and situate them in order to draw out their online framing and circulation in a responsible and accurate way. I also maintain that the best practice for major programs of research is to apply for a full institutional ethics review, in order to clarify best practices in digital culture research, including the importance of abiding by Terms of Service and moments when there is a case for describing (rather than visually reproducing), anonymising, or indeed redacting a reference to a media artefact or commentary (Tiidenberg and Baym 3–4).

It is the task of the visual auto/biography scholar in the age of digital reproduction to recognise the distinctively collaged, multi-platform, accretive dimensions of visual self-portraiture and self-narration today. It is also our individual and shared responsibility to devise research practices that bring digital visualities into critical view as problems of power, agency, and ethical praxis in a ongoingly reconfigured visual–digital field.

## Acknowledgements

Thank you to my colleague Andrea Zeffiro and to research assistants Adan Jerreat-Poole and Paige Maylott for ongoing conversations about best practices. The research program that I am reflecting in this chapter, entitled "Selfie culture, feminist/crip/mad autobiographical art, and social justice imaginaries", is supported by an Insight Grant from the Social Sciences and Humanities Research Council of Canada.

## Notes

1. Google is not alone in its exploration of facial recognition. As Christy Lange notes, similar biometric software has also been rolled out as an interactive feature of Facebook's photo functions and by Apple with the advent of its iPhone X.
2. I say uncloseable in part because changes to data security and privacy in the wake of the Cambridge Analytica scandal and investigations into data

breaches mean that it is becoming more rather than less difficult to engage in webscraping of platforms containing a mix of private and public accounts. Note the near-shutdown of public API access for Instagram and parent company Facebook in April 2018.
3. *Documenting the Now* hosts a robust community of practice for social media archiving. See www.docnow.io/.
4. While Rose raises the possibility that phenomenological or sensory approaches to working with visual sources may be just as depoliticising as the fine art/art historical use of this approach has tended to be (81), I would underscore that the politically transformative importance of tactile or otherwise haptic engagements with visual media artefacts and archives has been championed and developed by scholars in Black Atlantic/diaspora studies (Campt; Sharpe), cultural anthropology (Taussig), new media (Munster), and comparative feminist visual studies (Brophy and Hladki; Tamboukou).

## Works Cited

Bailey, Moya. "#transform(ing)DH Writing and Research: An Autoethnography of Digital Humanities and Feminist Ethics." *Digital Humanities Quarterly*, vol. 9, no. 2, 2015. www.digitalhumanities.org/dhq/vol/9/2/000209/000209.html.

Baishya, Anirban K. "#NaMo: The Political Work of the Selfie in the 2014 Indian General Elections." *International Journal of Communication*, no. 9, 2015, pp. 1686–1700. http://ijoc.org/index.php/ijoc/article/view/3133.

Berger, John. *Ways of Seeing*. British Broadcasting Corporation and Penguin, 1973.

Brophy, Sarah. "#FreeBree: Witnessing Black Artivism Online." *No More Potlucks*, 1 Jan. 2018. http://nomorepotlucks.org/site/freebree-witnessing-black-artivism-online-sarah-brophy/.

———. "The Stickiness of Instagram: Digital Labour and Post-Slavery Memory in Kara Walker's 'A Subtlety.'" *Cultural Critique*, forthcoming.

Brophy, Sarah, and Janice Hladki. "Visual Autobiography in the Frame: Critical Embodiment and Cultural Pedagogy." *Embodied Politics in Visual Autobiography*. U of Toronto P, 2014, pp. 3–28.

Brown, Elspeth H., and Thy Phu. "The Cultural Politics of Aspiration: Family Photography's Mixed Feelings." *Journal of Visual Culture*, vol. 17, no. 2, pp. 152–165. https://doi.org/10.1177%2F1470412918782352.

Campt, Tina. *Listening to Images*. Duke UP, 2017.

Chun, Wendy Hui-Kyong. *Updating to Remain the Same: Habitual New Media*. MIT P, 2016.

DasGupta, Sayantani. "Quickening Paternity: Cyberspace, Surveillance, and the Performance of Male Pregnancy." *Embodied Politics in Visual Autobiography*, edited by Sarah Brophy and Janice Hladki. U of Toronto P, 2014, pp. 31–47.

Davis, Ben. "Ways of Seeing Instagram." *Artnet News*, 24 June 2014. https://news.artnet.com/exhibitions/ways-of-seeing-instagram-37635.

Duguay, Stefanie. "Lesbian, Gay, Bisexual, Trans, and Queer Visibility Through Selfies: Comparing Platform Mediators Across Ruby Rose's Instagram and Vine Presence." *Social Media and Society*, Apr.–June 2016, pp. 1–12. http://journals.sagepub.com/doi/abs/10.1177/2056305116641975.

Highfield, Tim, and Tama Leaver. "A Methodology for Mapping Instagram Hashtags." *First Monday: Peer Reviewed Journal on the Internet*, vol. 20, nos. 1–5, Jan. 2015. http://firstmonday.org/article/view/5563/4195.

Kim, Dorothy. "Social Media and Academic Surveillance: The Ethics of Digital Bodies." *Model View Culture: Technology, Culture, and Diversity*, 7 Oct. 2014. https://modelviewculture.com/pieces/social-media-and-academic-surveillance-the-ethics-of-digital-bodies.

Lange, Christy. "Surveillance, Bias and Control in the Age of Facial Recognition Software." *Frieze*, 4 June 2018. https://frieze.com/article/surveillance-bias-and-control-age-facial-recognition-software.

Losh, Elizabeth. "Feminism Reads Big Data: 'Social Physics', Atomism, and Self-iecity." *International Journal of Communication*, 2015, no. 9, pp. 1647–1659. http://ijoc.org/index.php/ijoc/article/view/3152.

Mahdawi, Arwa. "Finding Your Museum Doppelganger Is Fun—But the Science Behind It Is Scary." *The Guardian*, 16 Jan. 2018. www.theguardian.com/commentisfree/2018/jan/16/find-your-art-doppelganger-facial-recognition-technology-frightening.

Morrison, Aimée. "Facebook and Coaxed Affordances." *Identity Technologies: Representing the Self Online*, edited by Anna Poletti and Julie Rak. U of Wisconsin P, pp. 112–131.

Munster, Anna. *Materializing New Media: Embodiment in Information Aesthetics*. Dartmouth CP, 2006.

Murray, Derek Conrad. "Notes to Self: The Visual Culture of 'Selfies' in the Age of Social Media." *Communicating Identity/Consuming Difference*, special issue of *Consumption, Markets, and Culture*, edited by Jonathan Schroeder, vol. 18, no. 6, 2015, pp. 490–516. https://doi.org/10.1080/10253866.2015.1052967.

Papalia, Carmen. "An Accessibility Manifesto for the Arts." *Canadian Art*, 2 Jan. 2018. https://canadianart.ca/essays/access-revived/.

Rak, Julie. "Life Writing vs. Automedia: The Sims 3 Game as a Life Lab." *Online Lives 2.0*, special issue of *Biography*, edited by Laurie McNeill and John David Zuern, vol. 38, no. 2, Spring 2015, pp. 155–180. https://doi.org/10.1353/bio.2015.0015.

Rice, Carla et al. "Pedagogical Possibilities for Unruly Bodies." *Gender and Education*, vol. 1, no. 2, 22 Nov. 2016. https://doi.org/10.1080/09540253.2016.1247947. Accessed 20 Aug. 2017.

Rodgers, Kathleen, and Willow Scobie. "Sealfies, Seals, and Celebs: Expressions of Inuit Resilience in the Twitter Era." *Interface: A Journal for and about Social Movements*, vol. 7, no. 1, May 2015, pp. 70–97. www.interfacejournal.net/wordpress/wp-content/uploads/2015/06/Issue-7-1-Rodgers-and-Scobie.pdf.

Rose, Gillian. *Visual Methodologies: An Introduction to Researching With Visual Materials*. 4th ed. Sage, 2016.

Sharpe, Christina. *In the Wake: On Blackness and Being*. Duke UP, 2016.

Smith, Sidonie, and Julia Watson. "Virtually Me: A Toolbox About Online Self-Presentation." *Identity Technologies: Representing the Self Online*, edited by Anna Poletti and Julie Rak. U Wisconsin P, 2014, pp. 70–98.

Tamboukou, Maria. "Painting the Body: Feminist Musings on Visual Autographies." *Embodiment*, special issue of *a/b: Auto/Biography Studies*, edited by

Sarah Brophy, vol. 33, no. 2, 2018, pp. 327–345. https://doi.org/10.1080/089 89575.2018.1445584.

Taussig, Michael. *I Swear I Saw This: Drawings in Fieldwork Notebooks*. U of Chicago P, 2011.

Tembeck, Tamar. "Selfies of Ill Health: Online Autopathographic Photography and the Dramaturgy of the Everyday." *Social Media and Society*, Jan.–Mar. 2016, pp. 1–11. http://journals.sagepub.com/doi/abs/10.1177/2056305116641343.

Tiidenberg, Katrin, and Nancy Baym. "Learn It, Buy It, Work It: Intensive Pregnancy on Instagram." *Social Media and Society*, Jan.–Mar. 2017, pp. 1–13. https://doi.org/10.1177%2F2056305116685108.

*Unrest*. Directed by Jennifer Brea, Shella Films/Little by Little Films, 2017.

Walker Rettberg, Jill. *Seeing Ourselves Through technology: How We Use Selfies, Blogs, and Wearable Devices to See and Shape Ourselves*. Palgrave, 2014. https://link.springer.com/book/10.1057%2F9781137476661.

Warfield, Katie. "Making the Cut: An Agential Realist Examination of Selfies and Touch." *Selfies: Mediated Inter-Faces*, special issue of *Social Media and Society*, edited by Katie Warfield et al., Apr.–June 2016, pp. 1–10. http://journals.sagepub.com/doi/abs/10.1177/2056305116641706.

# 7  Biography

*W. Craig Howes*

I will begin with a linguistic commonplace: some languages—German, for example—have words that distinguish between *knowing* something and *knowing how to do* something, while others—English, for instance—do not. In the case of biography, the difference lies between *knowing* a great deal about the genre's common forms, history, and canonical texts, and *knowing how* to select a subject, conduct the requisite research, and then organise, draft, revise, and publish a new instance of the genre. These forms of knowledge need not be mutually exclusive. Many noted biographers have also been critics and theorists of biography—Leon Edel, Nigel Hamilton, Richard Holmes, Hermione Lee, Ira Nadel, and Carl Rollyson come to mind.

I have written elsewhere about how some scholars draw sharp, even combative lines between biography and life writing, at least partially because of differing assumptions about what it means to write, or write about, a life ("What Are We Turning From?"). Here I want to explore what the editors of this volume have referred to as "the value of different methodological approaches to the study of life narratives", and especially the value of "interdisciplinary" and "new methods and perspectives". (As I am a co-editor of *Biography*, which declared itself *An Interdisciplinary Quarterly* from its inception in 1978, this only makes sense.)

My own method will be derivative and highly indebted. I want to suggest that recent published conversations about Indigenous biography, conducted by Indigenous scholars, offer "something different and perhaps even transformative to the larger field of biographical studies" (241).

\*

The most common methods for examining biography tend to be reasonable and old. Course syllabi or published overviews can be organised chronologically, starting with Genesis, the Christian gospels, or Sima Qian, then moving on to Plutarch, Aubrey, Dr Johnson, Carlyle, Strachey, and Woolf, concluding perhaps with some prominent contemporary biographer. Or the approach can be anatomical, with such

genres as hagiography, the brief life, the two fat volumes about the
great man, and the psychoanalytic study examined in turn. Traditional
biography courses, including my own, tend to offer a mixture of both.[1]

What, then, could an "interdisciplinary" or "new" method be? My
own speculations have been strongly shaped by my experience as a co-
editor of the academic journal *Biography*, and in particular, by our Summer 2016 Special Issue on "Indigenous Conversations about Biography".
For certain special issues, we invite guest editors to send out a call for
papers, to select some participants from the abstracts received, and to
invite other participants as especially desirable for the planned issue. We
then bring everyone together for a four-day working seminar in Honolulu; the guest editors organise and supervise the discussion.

For this issue, our guest editors were Alice Te Punga Somerville
(Māori), Daniel Heath Justice (Cherokee Nation), and Noelani Arista
(kanaka maoli), and from the very beginning, they adopted, customised,
or rejected parts of our common practice in accordance with what they
felt would actually be useful and productive. Because they wanted to create "a conversation about Indigenous lives, the ways we understand them,
the way we represent them, and the responsibilities that come from doing
this work in a good way", they resolved to bring "a trans-Indigenous,
multidiscipline, multivocal community into expansive dialogue about
what it means to think about Indigenous lives and what it means to *do*
Indigenous biography" (239).

Knowing and knowing how—at first glance, there seemed to be nothing new here. As it turned out, though, much about the approach was
novel. As the editors explain in the issue's introduction, "Conversations"
was the key term. They wanted above all to explore the questions "we get
to ask once people who identify and are recognized by others as Indigenous get in a room and say, 'Okay, what shall we talk about?'" So,
given the issue's theme, the seminar would be driven by "what interests *us* about Indigenous lives" (240). Because the editors believed that
"gone are the days when it was interesting to engage in long taxonomi-
cal discussions about what we are talking about when we talk about
'Indigenous'" (239), they chose to focus "on Indigenous people as the
biographers rather than the biographees", since such biographies were
"too often studied for how they engage colonial subjects rather than for
the ways they center their own contexts and concerns both within and
beyond settler colonialism" (240–241).

How the seminar participants got into the room was the first departure from *Biography*'s standard operating procedure. The editors did
not want to issue an open call for papers. Instead of assembling a large
list of potential participants, then honing it down to a select few, the
editors invited a cluster of people whom they wanted in that initial
shared space, with the numbers and participation increasing as the process unfolded.

As with our previous symposia, the participants circulated drafts of their individual projects before arriving in Honolulu. But during the on-site discussions, the editors emphasised the development of a shared and cumulative understanding, as *knowing* and *knowing how to do* biography fluctuated in relation to individual location, Indigenous community, and need. Before everyone arrived in Honolulu, the editors sent out a list of possible conversation topics in the form of questions. Those who have studied life writing for a while may recognise the importance of the questions reproduced below, but the theme granted them an added bite and urgency.

> What use do Indigenous scholars in a range of disciplines have for life writing?
> How do Indigenous biographers engage the relationship between individual and collective lives?
> How do non-human and ancestral lives figure in Indigenous biographical work?
> What are the ethical considerations for Indigenous biographers, whether the subject is from their own community or another?
> What kinds of subjects, methods, accountabilities, and archives do Indigenous people who work with biography make visible?
> How is the biographical conceived through different genres of chant, dance, and performance in and out of Indigenous language?
> How might Indigenous scholars problematize the concept of "biography," or "life writing," across multiple oral literary genres and contexts?
>
> (242)

Given the range and critical edge of these questions, we can at least consider whether biography has any real substance or relevance to the proposed conversation at all.[2] But here was my second major methodological lesson. However much you might problematise a term, it can still have real and material effects. For this reason, the editors retained "biography" as an organising concept "because that term is well-known in Indigenous circles and one way to start a conversation is to use terminology that feels familiar" (243). Familiar, but not necessarily congenial or ultimately necessary. Given the longstanding and widespread mistreatment of Indigenous biographical subjects, all participants "took seriously the potential impacts, both positive and negative, of representing Indigenous lives", and "for some, what this means is questioning the entire enterprise of biography itself" (244).[3]

My third methodological lesson arose from how the editors created a scholarly discussion that both respected the specificity of participants' contributions while fostering legitimate and useful comparisons. For the seminar, the editors paired up the participants. One pragmatic result was that while each person was summarising then discussing their work, the partner took notes, so that the presenter could concentrate fully on the responses. Later, the partners went over each other's notes, discussing the relevance and value of each question and comment to their projects. Each writer thus interacted with the other participants, the editors, and their partner—three distinct yet related interlocutors all fully invested in producing the eventual special issue.

Following the seminar, the preparation of the issue followed fairly standard editorial operating procedures. The contributors had deadlines. To varying degrees, they produced their work in tandem with their partners. They then received detailed feedback from the special issue editors, who determined when the essay was ready for copyediting. The *Biography* staff prepared copyedited versions for review and approval, and then page proofs, while at the same time securing the necessary permissions for images or other copyrighted material.

But the commitment to sustained conversation led to another methodological innovation. When the articles were ready, the editors solicited two written reactions to each one from "writers whose Indigenous and disciplinary roots are different from the author of the essay to which they respond". In addition, these writers "were invited to write in any form or style they chose" (245). As a result, the number of participants in the conversation increased from eleven—the three co-editors and the eight seminar attendees—to twenty-seven. These responses also increased the number of genres in the collection: "Some are traditional essays; some are poems; some are conversations; some are letters; some combine elements of all of these and others". And one final note—many of the essays were themselves dialogues. Elle-Máijá Apiniskim Tailfeathers' "Conversation" with Helen Haig-Brown and Lisa Jackson, two other Indigenous filmmakers, explores "the process and motivations of and responses to their (auto)biographical films" (236). And in Jordan Wilson's account of "Listening to Musqueam Lived Experiences", he suggests how "group storytelling can inform other forms of representation such as biography and ethnography" (238).

According to the editors, the "one thread" woven through the collection is "an insistence on Indigenous biographies as more than past-tense histories of study, but rather, as meaningful and ongoing living relationships in the world" (246). In keeping with the ever-extending nature of the conversation, however, they also tried to "offer something different and perhaps even transformative to the larger field of biographical studies" (241). That they succeeded in attracting the attention of still larger fields was confirmed by the Council of Editors of Learned Journals, which bestowed its award for Best Special Issue for 2016–2017 upon the collection. The judges praised in particular the "innovative and effective" editorial decisions, which resulted not only in "a fascinating, original list of guiding questions and a variety of different forms, including traditional essays, poetry, letters, responses, and more", but an "especially clear, self-reflective, and engaging" Introduction as well. "An altogether impressive achievement", in short, on the part of our guest editors (Award Citation).

What, then, can biography scholars and practitioners learn, as opposed to appropriate, from such an interrogation of standard methods? Weaving my own way back through this chapter, I would start by asking how we can make biography, as a discipline and a practice, something more than "past-tense histories of study". Though biographers at times gesture in their introductions or afterwords toward claims that their lives enact "meaningful and ongoing living relationships in the world", the familiar template is a beginning, middle, and end synopsis of someone's completed life, created through encounters with other sources and accounts more closely resembling extractions than conversations. Put more starkly, it is hard to imagine most biographers starting their process by asking the individuals, communities, or previous biographers related to or heavily invested in the subject's life "What kind of biography do *you* want?" Analogies to critiques of the common practice of ethnography, and of the impact of research on many Indigenous and minority communities, should be obvious, and biographers could at least entertain the possibility of asking such questions.

A second methodological consideration would be the possibility of collaboration, or even "co-labor-action", in Alicia Partnoy's sense.[4] The familiar biography involves a single author writing the life of a single subject. Boswell's Samuel Johnson. Edel's Henry James. Ellmann's James Joyce. Lee's Virginia Woolf. Isaacson's Leonardo. Could it be possible to think of biography as a collective venture, arising out of expansive but rigorous conversations between many researchers, relatives, friends, and enemies, living and dead? At stake here are some deeply embedded notions of authorship and art—and some equally established conventions of intellectual property and publishing. At the very least, however, the questions raised by the "Conversations" editors suggest that entertaining such a possibility could have some interesting results.

A third benefit could result from theorists and practitioners imitating Indigenous scholars in problematising "the concept of biography, or 'life writing,' across multiple oral literary genres and contexts". The method here would be to extend the range of "subjects, methods, accountabilities, and archives" employed or consulted when doing biography. Some life writing scholars have been heavily engaged in such efforts; this is in fact what some biography scholars consider to be the problem with life writing.[5] But one hundred years after the appearance of *Eminent Victorians*, Lytton Strachey's reference to the "fat volumes, with which it is our custom to commemorate the dead" still resonates, and so does his suggestive, though needlessly violent, call for the "explorer of the past" to "attack his subject in unexpected places", "fall upon the flank, or the rear", or "shoot a sudden, revealing searchlight into obscure recesses, hitherto undivined" (9–10).

As the editors of "Indigenous Conversations about Biography" note, we are all "familiar" with what biographies tend to be. But surely the impulse to represent another person's life, or to evaluate the success of such a representation, can withstand and even benefit from the most searching and extensive discussion of supposedly self-evident methodological truths. Or as Alice Te Punga Somerville and Daniel Heath Justice suggest to all of us, "we can unpack, repack, and throw out terms once we're at the table, but there is still life in this old term 'biography' yet" (243).

## Notes

1. For a variety of approaches to teaching biography, see Fuchs and Howes *passim.*, and McNeill and Douglas *passim.*
2. In fact, people have suggested that changes in the content of *Biography* over the years represent an abandonment of what its title promises. See Binne De Haan, "The Eclipse of Biography in Life Writing".
3. These discussions of "biography" often paralleled Linda Tuhiwai Smith's landmark work on "research" in *Decolonizing Methodologies*.
4. See both "Disclaimer Intraducible: My Life / Is Based / on a Real Story" and "Concealing God: How Argentine Women Political Prisoners Performed a Collective Identity".
5. See De Haan and Renders, "Biography in Academia" and "Biography Is Not a Selfie".

## Works Cited

Award Citation for Best Special Issue 2017. "Indigenous Conversations about Biography," *Biography: An Interdisciplinary Quarterly*. Award Ceremony, Council of Editors of Learned Journals Annual Meeting. Modern Language Association Convention, January 5, 2018, New York City, NY.

De Haan, Binne. "The Eclipse of Biography in Life Writing." *Theoretical Discussions of Biography: Approaches From History, Microhistory, and Life Writing*, edited by Hans Renders and Binne De Haan. Brill, 2014, pp. 177–194.

Fuchs, Miriam, and Craig Howes, editors. *Teaching Life Writing Texts, Options for Teaching*. Modern Language Association, 2007.

Howes, Craig. "What Are We Turning From? Research and Ideology in Biography and Life Writing." *The Biographical Turn: Lives in History*, edited by Hans Renders et al. Routledge, 2017, pp. 165–175.

McNeill, Laurie, and Kate Douglas, editors. "Teaching Lives: Contemporary Pedagogies of Life Narrative." *a/b: Auto/Biography Studies*, vol. 32, no. 1, 2017.

Renders, Hans. "Biography in Academia and the Critical Frontier in Life Writing: Where Biography Shifts Into Life Writing." *Theoretical Discussions of Biography: Approaches From History, Microhistory, and Life Writing*, edited by Hans Renders and Binne De Haan. Brill, 2014, pp. 169–176.

————. "Biography Is Not a Selfie: Authorisation as the Creeping Transition From Autobiography to Biography." *The Biographical Turn: Lives in History*, edited by Hans Renders et al. Routledge, 2017, pp. 159–164.

Smith, Linda Tuhiwai. *Decolonizing Methodologies: Research and Indigenous Peoples*. 2nd ed. Zed Books, 2012.

Somerville, Alice Te Punga et al. "Indigenous Conversations About Biography." Special Issue of *Biography: An Interdisciplinary Quarterly*, vol. 39, no. 3, 2016.

Strachey, Lytton. *Eminent Victorians*. Penguin, 1986 [1918].

# 8 Research Methods for Studying Graphic Biography

*Candida Rifkind*

Graphic biographies have not received as much attention as the more critically acclaimed landmarks of auto/biography (Art Spiegelman's *Maus*; Marjane Satrapi's *Persepolis*; Alison Bechdel's *Fun Home*) and graphic journalism (Joe Sacco's *Palestine*; Sarah Glidden's *Rolling Blackouts*). Auto/biography comics studies has produced important critical volumes by Michael Chaney, Hillary Chute, Elizabeth El-Rafaie, and Charles Hatfield, among others, that provide examples of how to combine narrative and formal analysis and pay attention to story as well as style within the broader historical, geopolitical, and socio-economic contexts in which artists produce what Whitlock terms "autographics". Andrew J. Kunka synthesises this body of scholarship in his handbook, *Autobiographical Comics*, and emphasises that the key question for research on these texts arise from life writing theory more generally: who is the "I" of the auto/biographical comic and how do the multiple selves of artist, narrator, focaliser, and character make themselves present on the page? Given the prominence of individual and collective trauma in auto/biographical comics scholarship, this central question leads to related concerns around practices of testimonial and witness, representations of memory and history, and depictions of the self as emerging artist. Certainly, some of the key themes that Kunka and others see recurring in auto/biographical comics are also common in alternative graphic biography: childhood and coming-of-age, personal and historical trauma, the quotidian and the banal, illness, ageing, and dis/ability, gender and sexuality, and race and ethnicity. However, there is relatively little research on graphic biography as a distinct genre that poses its own specific set of aesthetic and philosophical questions.

The first step in researching graphic biography is developing a definition of the field itself. I define graphic biography as comic books (standalone or multi-volume compilations) by one or more persons, about the life experiences of a different real person or people. As capacious as this category may be, since it allows for collaborative graphic biographies by multiple artists, or collective graphic biographies of multiple subjects, such as members of a family, its key organising principle is that the primary subject is not the artist herself, even if she draws or writes herself in to the comics sequences at some points. Whereas graphic memoirs and auto/biographies attract questions about how the cartoonist objectifies herself into a caricature on the page, how she recalls and narrates her past experiences from the present, and how she understands her individual life narrative to be part of familial, communal, national, or global narratives, graphic biography raises a different set of aesthetic, philosophical, and political questions. For this reason, defining the field itself is the first step in formulating my research methodology, even though every boundary I draw is both porous and provisional.

The forms and styles of graphic biographies vary widely, from sketchy black-and-white ink and pencil to pale watercolour washes to vibrant colour, and from illustration to caricature, realism to expressionism and surrealism. As well, many graphic biographies reproduce archival elements, such as photographs and letters, even as they play with the very idea of verifiable proofs and documentary evidence. In this way, they are often part of the archival turn that Jared Gardner has observed in recent American comics. By focusing on graphic biography as a contemporary form of popular culture and knowledge production, I draw on comics studies, life writing studies, biography theory, film studies, and celebrity studies to ask a series of interrelated questions:

- How can comics construct and deconstruct the "biographical illusion" of a knowable, linear, coherent life? How do artists negotiate pre-existing mythologies of their subjects, and to what extents are they explicit about lacunae and inventions in the life narrative?
- How can comics engage readers affectively through visual style to offer both a feel for the person and what they felt? How do artists reproduce, remediate, or reject the visual culture of their subjects, from paintings to photographs to biopics?
- How can comics' primary techniques, cartooning and caricature, express the complex interiorities and socio-political realities of real lives?

These questions help to focus the study of how alternative graphic biographies often challenge some or all of the conventional criteria of a good biography: veracity (documentary rather than creative storytelling); sequence (birth to death narrative arc); comprehensiveness (no events excluded or minimised); and verifiability (can be proven through historical documents or sources) (Greene 739–41).

As much as there is stylistic and narrative diversity in the field of alternative graphic biography, the field remains overshadowed by mainstream and educational graphic biographies that depict the trials and achievements of positive role models for young readers in conventional cartooning styles. The first methodological decision I had to make was how to

frame my interest—not in these formulaic, didactic series for young readers, which far outnumber and outsell alternative graphic biographies, but
rather in those works that are experimental, avant-garde, and occasion-
ally disorienting and confusing versions of well-known lives. Reading
Leigh Gilmore's *The Limits of Autobiography: Trauma and Testimony*
introduced me to the notion of "limit cases" that exceed the conventions
of a genre, yet engage with some of its central premises and parameters—
in her case autobiography and in my case graphic biography. Rather than
attempting to survey the entire field of cultural production, from educational to alternative graphic biographies, Gilmore's method of studying
"limit cases" helped me to direct my own research to the outliers in the
field, those that fit with Bart Beaty's theory, developed in relation to contemporary French *bandes-desinnée*, of alternative comics as a form of
"unpopular culture", comic books that are generally closer to the visual
arts than superhero or supermarket comics.

   As a literary critic working across the fields of biography studies and
comics studies, I have turned to the formal methodologies of semiotics
and narratology to consider how comics have unique tools and techniques to externally focalise a life narrative. For instance, cartoonists
can play with temporality (multiple moments on the same page), irony
and disjuncture (words and images do not match), visual style (realistic, painterly, minimal, surreal, abstract, retro, parody, pastiche), visual
code switching (from comics to photographs, newspaper clippings, letters, diaries, diagrams, and other signifiers of the "real"), and perspective (focalising what the character sees, remembers, dreams, or imagines).
This might serve as a formal checklist to work through when analysing a
specific sequence in a graphic biography, but there is a larger core set of
topics that shape my research methodology as a textual scholar informed
by literary studies, media and cultural studies, film theory, affect theory,
and feminist theory.

## Genre

My training as a literary critic will always compel me to ask about a
work's generic affiliations: what narrative and visual genres does each
work join, resist, echo, subvert, or pastiche? As helpful as the rich criticism on prose biography has been to researching graphic biography, I am
increasingly convinced that film studies focused on the biopic are more
relevant to developing a poetics of graphic biography. First, both film
and comics biographies are often based on one or more prose biographies
and/or autobiographies that they filter, amalgamate, or cite. Sometimes
this debt to a prose biography appears before the text, as with Paulo
Parisi's acknowledgement that his graphic biography, *Coltrane*, is drawn
largely from Lewis Porter's prose biography. Another formal similarity
is that both biopics and graphic biographies must compress lengthy life

narratives and amalgamate secondary characters due to the constraints of form. This often leads to both selectivity and summary, using key moments in a life to stand in for longer periods. Also, film and comics share the ability to juxtapose moments through either editing or sequencing. In some cases, this complies with the popular psychological reading of adult behaviour as determined by childhood trauma. This is certainly how Peter Bagge represents Margaret Sanger's motivation to dedicate her life to the struggle for reproductive rights in *Woman Rebel*. Using a loopy, classic Warner Brothers-style of caricature, Bagge shows key moments in the early life of Sanger—controversial birth control educator, founder of Planned Parenthood, and possible eugenicist. Early on, he draws a young Margaret, recently qualified as a nurse, frustrated that she is legally prohibited from educating impoverished women about birth control. Combined with her childhood memories of her Catholic mother's multiple painful pregnancies, these moments come to justify Sanger's lifelong dedication to the cause for reproductive rights. So, we also need to understand that graphic biography shares with the biopic the formal urgency to dramatise scenes of the life in sequences that invite closure from the reader (filling in the gaps), and that this can produce cause-and-effect readings of life events. The question for the researcher then becomes: what generic affiliations does the work have with prose and cinematic biographies, and how does comics' form mediate the expectations of these genres? These questions about genre direct methodological approaches towards literary, cinematic, and cultural histories of specific forms and fictional as well as life writing precedents for the graphic biography's visual and verbal narrative.

## Paratexts

It has become a convention for graphic biographies to include paratextual materials before or after the comics narrative. Chester Brown's *Louis Riel* tells the life story of this controversial leader of the Métis people—a Canadian Indigenous group of people of mixed European and First Nations ancestry whose distinct identity was formed by the 1800s. Riel was hanged for treason and remains a contested figure in Canadian history and politics. Brown's innovation of supplementing his comics biography with a foreword, thirty-nine pages of endnotes, and a bibliography has been adopted by numerous subsequent graphic biographers. These paratexts at once authorise the cartoonist's historical representation, declares her position on controversial questions about the life, and acknowledges moments of invention for narrative purposes. Such paratextual material in prose sometimes takes up more space than the comics life story. In *Who Is Ana Mendieta?*, Christine Redfern and Caro Caron's graphic biography of this Cuban-American feminist performance artist takes up nineteen pages, while a hand-drawn replication of newspaper clippings and two essays take up another twenty-three pages. All of this non-comics material in alternative graphic biographies serves a legitimating function that both foregrounds the text's authority and reminds us that biography is a genre of competing discourses and truth claims. In many alternative graphic biographies, the paratextual material invites in the uninformed reader and separates out the didactic work of explication and documentation from the comics representation of the life story. It also authenticates the comic book and positions the cartoonist as responsible researcher and artistic auteur, rather than, in Beaty's words, "a cultural hack slaving away to turn out mass-mediated product" ("Autobiography" 229–230).

## Style and Affect

Alternative graphic biographers sometimes reproduce older visual styles or reference a specific artistic movement to convey a sense of the historical moment as well as the pastness of their subject's life. In *Isadora*, Sabrina Jones' Art Nouveau lines and pictorial flourishes reflect the Edwardian bohemian aesthetic the avant-garde dancer Isadora Duncan embodied. Frank Young and David Lasky's collective biography, *The Carter Family*, tells the story of this "founding family" of American country music through adapting the styles of 1920s and 1930s newspaper comics, from single panel gags to daily strips to Sunday supplements. In *The Boxer*—the story of young Hertzko Haft, a Polish Jew who survived Auschwitz—Reinhard Kleist's stark expressionism to depict a Holocaust narrative echoes 1920s and 1930s German Expressionism. Kleist uses dark shadows and blurry images at peak moments to ask readers to fill in the details. Cartoonists can exploit comics' traditions of fantasy and surrealism, and echo comics history itself, inviting the research question: how does the cartoonist use visual style to both locate their subject in time and place and invite readers to imagine what it felt like to live their experiences?

## Remediation

Graphic biographers must create a pictorial icon of an other, a real person whose image often already circulates in visual discourse through photographs, films, portraits, and so on. From these, the cartoonist draws a caricature, based on simplification and exaggeration, to transform the physical reality of the person's face and body through a signature style. Somewhat surprisingly, relatively few graphic biographies include photographs of their subjects—one exception is the publicity shot at the end of the comics narrative of Harry Haft in Kleist's *The Boxer*, which is also the cover of the prose biography by Haft's son. Instead, there is a pattern of cartoonists using photographs or film and television footage of their subjects as uncredited visual source materials. Throughout *King*, Ho Che Anderson uses analogue and digital technologies to alter some of the most iconic photos of his subject, Martin Luther King, Jr., and to layer archival images of African American oppression behind the man himself to illustrate his political and psychological motivations. Another visual field available to cartoonists is the body captured in motion by film and TV cameras, especially when the subjects were professional athletes, performers, or politicians in the age of broadcasting. In Wilfred Santiago's *Bull on Parade: The Michael Jordan Story*, the representation of this famous figure's kinetic body on the basketball court draws on televised games in ways that thematise his public image as all we can ever know of the real man. When it comes to subjects who were themselves artists, graphic biographers may choose to remediate their subjects' works within the diegesis of the panels, as Barbara Stok does in *Vincent*, about Van Gogh's final years. Cartoonists thus often reference directly or remediate obliquely the existing visual culture of the subject, which might bring competing visual discourses, such as painting and comics, into tension or conflict (Groensteen). So, when graphic biographies work with photographs, paintings, film, or television materials by or about their subjects, researchers need to investigate the narrative and aesthetic work these intermedial representations perform in the text.

## Biomythology

Researching graphic biographies thus requires studying the larger visual and verbal cultural mythology of the subject. Cultural mythologies have long been the stuff of mainstream comics that draw their characters as supernatural beings, heroes, and demons, often in disguise to the mere mortals around them. It is not surprising, then, that alternative graphic biographies often represent their subjects as different from prevailing norms, as the subjects of specific destinies or callings—a generic convention Dennis Bingham also sees in biopics—whose impact on the world is only evident after their deaths. To write a book chapter on Ho Che Anderson's *King*, I explored the existing biomythology of Martin Luther King, Jr., across popular culture and learned from African American studies about the role he played in the post-Civil Rights era. For an article on Lauren Redniss' *Radioactive*, I studied the history of Marie Curie life narratives, from popular culture to her role in the history of science, and situated this illustrated version of the subject within almost a century of gendered representations of Curie as the female scientist par excellence. My research methodology includes studying both primary and secondary sources that construct and challenge the subject's cultural mythology. Ultimately, researching graphic biography comes back to the overlapping discourses of contemporary biography theory and comics theory, and to approaching the works as visual–verbal multimodal life narratives in which form and content operate dialectically to at once construct and deconstruct the very idea of knowing and showing the life of an other person and a celebrated persona.

## Works Cited

Bagge, Peter. *Woman Rebel: The Margaret Sanger Story*. Montreal: Drawn & Quarterly, 2013. Print.

Beaty, Bart. "Autobiography as Authenticity." *A Comics Studies Reader*, edited by Jeet Heer and Kent Worcester. Jackson, MS: UP of Mississippi, 2009, pp. 226–235. Print.

———. *Unpopular Culture: Transforming the European Comic Book in the 1990s*. Toronto: U of Toronto P, 2007. Print.

Bechdel, Alison. *Fun Home: A Family Tragicomic*. Belmont, CA: Wadsworth, 2007. Print.

Bingham, Dennis. *Whose Lives Are They Anyway? The Biopic as Contemporary Film Genre*. New Brunswick, NJ: Rutgers UP, 2010. Print.

Bourdieu, Pierre. "The Biographical Illusion." *Identity: A Reader*, edited by Paul Du Gay et al. London: SAGE, 2000, pp. 297–303. Print.

Brown, Chester. *Louis Riel: A Comic-Strip Biography*. Montreal: Drawn & Quarterly, 2003, rev. 2013. Print.

Chaney, Michael, ed. *Graphic Subjects: Critical Essays on Autobiography and Graphic Novels*. Madison, WI: U of Wisconsin P, 2011. Print.

Chute, Hillary. *Disaster Drawn: Visual Witness, Comics, and Documentary Form*. Harvard UP, 2016. Print.

———. *Graphic Women: Life Narrative & Contemporary Comics*. Gender and Culture ser. New York: Columbia UP, 2010. Print.

El-Rafaie, Elizabeth. *Autobiographical Comics: Life Writing in Pictures*. UP of Mississippi, 2012. Print.

Gardner, Jared. *Projections: Comics and the History of 21st Century Storytelling*. Stanford UP, 2012. Print.

Gilmore, Leigh. *The Limits of Autobiography: Trauma and Testimony*. Ithaca, NY: Cornell UP, 2001. Print.

Glidden, Sarah. *Rolling Blackouts*. Montreal: Drawn & Quarterly, 2016. Print.

Greene, Mott T. "Writing Scientific Biography." *Journal of the History of Biology*, vol. 40, no. 4, 2007, pp. 727–759. JSTOR. Web. 24 June 2018.

Groensteen, Thierry. "Biographies of Famous Painters in Comics: What Becomes of the Paintings?" *ImageTexT*, vol. 9, no. 2, 2017. Web.

Hatfield, Charles. *Alternative Comics: An Emerging Literature*. Jackson, MS: UP of Mississippi, 2005. Print.

Jones, Sabrina. *Isadora Duncan: A Graphic Biography*. New York: Hill & Wang, 2008. Print.

Kleist, Reinhard. *The Boxer: The True Story of Holocaust Survivor Harry Haft*. New York: SelfMadeHero, 2014. Print.

Kunka, Andrew J. *Autobiographical Comics*. Bloomsbury Comics Studies. New York: Bloomsbury, 2017. Print.

Parisi, Paolo. *Coltrane*. London: Jonathan Cape, 2012. Print.

Redfern, Christine, and Caro Caron. *Who Is Ana Mendieta?* New York: Feminist P, 2011. Print.

Sacco, Joe. *Palestine Collection*. Seattle: Fantagraphics, 2001. Print.

Santiago, Wilfrid. *Michael Jordan: Bull on Parade*. Seattle: Fantagraphics, 2014. Print.

Satrapi, Marjane. *The Complete Persepolis*. New York: Pantheon Books, 2007. Print.

Spiegelman, Art. *The Complete Maus: A Survivor's Tale*. New York: Pantheon Books, 1997. Print.

Young, David M., and David Lasky. *The Carter Family: Don't Forget This Song*. New York: Abrams, 2012. Print.

# 9    Working With Family Histories

*Ashley Barnwell*

In the past few decades, family history research has become enormously popular as a life writing practice. Around the world people create family trees, weaving together family names and dates with local and national history to anchor their kin in narrative time. As material culture, family histories are most often composed as genealogical charts, memoirs, albums, and intertextual collages of words and image. Increasingly, they are taking digital form on web 2.0 platforms such as Ancestry.com, and "genie-blogs", where people post tales of ancestors and share the trials and triumphs of the research process. Semi-autobiographical fictions such as Alice Munro's *The View from Castlerock* (2006), Kate Grenville's *The Secret River* (2005), and Michael Ondaatje's *Running in the Family* (1982), to name just three of many examples, draw from family history research. Family history has also been an important genre in recent life writing scholarship, with giants of the field such as Nancy K. Miller (2011), Marianne Hirsch and Leo Spitzer (2011), and Alison Light (2014) penning autobiographical books about tracing ancestors and returning to homelands. Family histories are often sparked by the impulse to know who you are, where you come from, who you belong to, and to be able to give an account of these things. It is also a distinctively relational form of life writing. In these texts, our lives are woven into an intricate web of kinships and connections that, once recovered and rekindled, can unsettle the story of the self as much as they anchor it (Watson; Barnwell; Rak).

An array of guides on how to collect and compose family histories are available online and in print (Kempthorne; Cass; Annal). They instruct researchers on where to begin: ask older relatives what they remember about ancestors, heirlooms, and photographs; check census records and pore over old newspapers; mine both private and public archives for fragments, clues, and details. These books of advice, as well as online genealogy forums, can help you resolve mysteries and break down "brick walls", when misspelt names or conflicting dates halt progress. What I address here goes beyond these more practical aspects of how to search for family history. I will consider methodological questions about family history as a life writing practice: what kinds of stories can we tell with and about family history? What narrative choices are required in selecting which events or ancestors to omit or include? And what ethical considerations arise when we tell shared stories that may present different sensitivities for various family members or communities of readers? First I outline three narrative approaches to writing family history as an "inspiration kit", and then I turn to ethical questions we might consider when writing about family lives.

## What Kinds of Stories Can We Tell With and About Family History?

When I have presented my own studies of family historians' life writing and literature, it has been common to hear other scholars wryly describe what they see to be the too indulgent or sentimental aspects of people's auto/biographical accounts of their family's past. Family histories do risk falling into both of these categories (which in itself reveals something interesting about the kinds of affects writing and reading about family can summon), but they also have the power to tell stories that are rich and multi-layered in their exploration of everyday, domestic life as it changes over time. For both those writing family histories and those analysing them, it is important to think about how stories about one family are also—in diverse ways—stories about families more broadly.

Family histories represent specific family lives but also ask questions about the ethics and politics of how families are represented in public life and within and across different cultural contexts. Both Tanya Evans and Julie Rak argue that family histories have a "radical" potential (Evans 50; Rak 481) to challenge and revise social scripts. Alison Light argues that to recognise this potential, "family detectives in search of lost ancestors need to be democrats; their forebears are far more likely to be dustman than noblemen, labourers than landowners" (xxii). Family memoirs that detail the shared impacts of illegitimacy, adoption, divorce, mental illness, and other stigmatised experiences can extend our social understanding about familial relationships and challenge cookie-cutter images of family life. Because family histories are relational, they can also decentre the traditional Enlightenment subject of classical auto/biography and reveal the wider social networks that shape individual lives. As Marianne Hirsch and Nancy K. Miller note, "legacies of the past, transmitted powerfully from parent to child within the family, are always already inflected by broader public and generational stories, images, artifacts, and understandings that together shape identity and identification" (4).

Family histories can take on many plots and narrative structures, and often include meditations on the process of collating and telling a narrative. For this reason, stories of ancestors can be read as life writing texts and as texts about life writing. Popular genealogy-themed television programs like *Who Do You Think You Are?* (Lynch) display the intertextual nature of family histories, as documents that weave narratives in and through photographs, objects, places, letters, diaries, archives, and so on. They require the life writer's competence working across several different forms, and therefore the author of a family history will likely find themselves visiting several of the chapters in this book. One of the main methodological approaches to family history is elicitation: the use of material cultures to conjure the stories and memories of the family. More than just evidence, Hirsch argues that such materials operate as "points of memory" that "enable us to reflect [. . .] on how memory and transmission work both to reveal and to conceal certain [. . .] recollections" (xix). Here I outline three narratives for framing family histories that combine intertextuality and elicitation: object stories; travel stories; and photo stories.

### Object Stories

Several successful family histories have been structured around a family heirloom or collection of inherited objects. For example, in his award-winning *The Hare with Amber Eyes* (2010), Edmund De Waal uses objects as a narrative device for tracing the plight of the family across generations. De Waal tracks his family's history from 1871 to 2009 via the passing down of a collection of small Japanese sculptures. Every phase in the life of the object accompanies a phase in the life of the family, and the heirlooms signify the continuity of familial bonds. Miller similarly presents inherited objects as the inspiration for her own genealogical hunt—*What They Saved: Pieces of a Jewish Past* (2011). After her father passes, Miller discovers a drawer of family memorabilia in his Danish credenza, including photographs, letters, locks of hair in an old soap box, and a map and deed to a plot of land in Israel. Miller writes, "these strange things provided clues, almost an invitation, to follow where they lead" (4). The contents of the drawer direct her toward distant relatives, unknown lives/sides of her parents, and faraway homelands. Miller explains that the objects become the key narrative mechanism for illuminating her family narrative: "I've conjured stories from my objects about the people to whom they once belonged. They've become evidence, telling details of a family history that was until now lost to me" (5). In both of these texts, objects lend the family history a narrative focus and momentum. But Light reminds writers that inheritance is a mark of wealth and such stories are only available to certain families. When she came to write *Common People* (2014), her working-class family had not bequeathed jewels or porcelain, hand-written letters and diaries, or studio portraits from which to conjure tales. Light asks: What story can be told about the absence of these things? "Was their lack of belongings a sign of deprivation or of mobility?" (xxvi).

## Travel Stories

Tracking the family's mobility via travelling to ancestral homelands is also a popular narrative structure for family histories and can be a powerful way to explore loss and disconnection. By linking story and place, these texts often deal with experiences of migration, diaspora, or dispossession. In *Rites of Return* (2011), Hirsch and Miller explain that with the rise of family history, the "desire for return to origins and sites of communal suffering has progressively intensified" (3). Return to places is especially important in family histories that deal with violent and traumatic pasts, including Transatlantic slavery, the Holocaust, or frontier violence in settler colonial states.

Family histories based on travel are often intertextual and contain reprints of maps and archival and family photographs of places. As Hirsch outlines in *Ghosts of Home: The Afterlife of Czernowitz in Jewish Memory* (2011), written with Leo Spitzer, narratives of return often de-centre family stories, locating them firmly in a wider ecology of local and national histories. She describes the book as "a family and communal memoir spanning three generations that explores the afterlife, in history and memory, of the city of Czernowitz" (xiii). Hirsch is interested in the city because it is the land of her ancestors, but she anchors her desire to know this place via a portrait of the city itself, rather than just her own family's paths through it. With Czernowitz as the axis, Hirsch builds a family history that intersects with public history in concrete and embodied ways. As a critical consideration around narratives of ancestral return, Miller and Hirsch caution that writers should be wary about how they can reify nation-based identities and static conceptions of who belongs where (8).

## Photograph Stories

Salman Rushdie's auto/biographical essay *Imaginary Homelands* (1991) melds travel and photograph narratives to structure a diasporic family history. An old family photograph underpins Rushdie's account of a trip back to Mumbai. Used as the comparative basis for the story, the differences between the black-and-white photograph of his father's house and the real place—vivid with colour and transformed by the passage of time—reveal how Rushdie's memory and subjectivity reconstruct the past. The photograph, used at the very beginning of the essay, ignites a deeper discussion about nostalgia and the relation between diaspora and homeland. In *Family Secrets: Acts of Memory and Imagination* (1995), Annette Kuhn marks out the methodological value of family photographs—as channels for elicitation—by calling them "memory texts". She devises a framework for reading "memory texts" via "memory work", where researchers are guided to consider the content, context, production, and currency of family images. Kuhn argues that by working with photographs, writers develop a "critical consciousness [. . .] that reso-nates across individual and collective" (9) and build a rich sociohistori-cal context for autobiography. In overtly political works of fiction that are based on family history materials, engagement with the source and intended purpose of family photographs can be a central narrative drive. For example, in Kim Scott's novel *Benang* (1999), the protagonist Har-ley Scat, a young Australian Aboriginal man, keeps a photograph that features family members but was produced to demonstrate a theory of eugenics and justify assimilationist policies in colonial Australia. The photograph, in its complex multivalence for Harley, registers the tension between family identities and the national governance of those identities, a key focus in *Benang*. Whether used in the process of research or as a narrative device within the life writing itself, the photograph can be a powerful means to elicit and mediate memories.

## Ethical Issues

The writer of a family history may begin with a burning question about their own identity, or desire to solve a mystery about their ancestors. In this sense, they can be very personal stories. But in the process of knit-ting together family lines and perhaps revealing family secrets, the lives of more than just the author are put on display. As autobiographies but very often also biographies of a collective, family histories and memoirs pose complex ethical questions about representation and privacy. Often the sensitivities around events can vary within a family: what may be a curious and intriguing story to one branch of the family may be an unspeakable grief to another branch, depending on their proximity to a family tragedy, for example, and their experience of its repercussions. The collective ownership of family stories makes their telling sensitive. Australian life writing is rich with examples of collaborative family sto-rytelling that authors could consult to explore the ethics and politics of narrating shared lives. Texts such as Kim Scott and Hazel Brown's *Kay-ang & Me* (2005) and Rita and Jackie Huggins' *Auntie Rita* (1994) can-didly explore the methodological questions that accompany the telling of intergenerational family stories and offer inspiration for how narratives can be authored collectively—again intertextual, combining both written and oral accounts.

As Leigh Gilmore has written, contemporary memoir has been influ-enced by a confessional, tell-all culture (16). The idea that a work of life writing must expose every finding is limiting. As with all social research, authors might consider the impacts that their representations of fam-ily life have upon their families, but also on readerships who may be affected by public texts representing family in specific ways. Such discus-sions arose among Indigenous academics in Australia after the publica-tion of Sally Morgan's *My Place* (1989), a family memoir that opened up important national conversations about the Stolen Generations, but was in some cases problematically taken as *the* definitive representation of this life experience (Brewster 15). Ethical concerns about the representation of specific family members can be extended to the representation of families more broadly, particularly if the story is likely to operate as social commentary. To address the dually personal and shared nature of family stories, the writer of a family history could seek to balance interrogating norms about family life with being careful not to unnecessarily fracture living relationships. As Jeanine Leane explains, when writing about her family history she carefully chose what information to share, to refer to in oblique or impressionistic ways, or to leave out entirely (Leane, Chapter 16, this collection). If sensitivities are present, it is possible to tell a family history that uses creative and narrative techniques that can both explore and protect family knowledge, while also posing candid questions about how we read and represent families through and across time. The methodological and ethical questions about how to tell life stories that cross inter- and intra-generational lives outlined in this chapter could inform both the writing *of* family histories and critical writings *about* family histories.

## Works Cited

Annal, David. *Easy Family History: The Beginner's Guide to Starting Your Research*. Bloomsbury, 2013.

Barnwell, Ashley. "The Genealogy Craze: Authoring an Authentic Identity Through Family History Research." *Life Writing*, vol. 10, 2013, pp. 261–275.

Brewster, Anne. *Reading Aboriginal Women's Autobiography*. Sydney UP, 1996.

Cass, Deborah. *Writing Your Family History: A Practical Guide*. Crowood, 2012.

Evans, Tanya. "Secrets and Lies: The Radical Potential of Family History." *History Workshop Journal*, vol. 71, 2011, pp. 49–73.

Gilmore, Leigh. *The Limits of Autobiography: Trauma and Testimony*. Cornell UP, 2001.

Grenville, Kate. *The Secret River*. Text Publishing, 2005.

Hirsch, Marianne, and Nancy K. Miller. *Rites of Return: Diaspora Poetics and the Politics of Memory*. Columbia UP, 2011.

Hirsch, Marianne, and Leo Spitzer. *Ghosts of Home: The Afterlife of Czernowitz in Jewish Memory*. California UP, 2011.

Huggins, Rita, and Jackie Huggins. *Auntie Rita*. Aboriginal Studies P, 1994.

Kempthorne, Charley. *For All Time: A Complete Guide to Writing Your Family History*. Boynton/Cook Publishers, 1996.

Light, Alison. *Common People*. Penguin Books, 2014.

Lynch, Claire. 2011. "Who Do You Think You Are? Intimate Pasts Made Public." *Biography*, vol. 34, no. 1, 2011, pp. 108–118.

Miller, Nancy K. *What They Saved: Pieces of a Jewish Past*. University of Nebraska Press, 2011.

Morgan, Sally. *My Place*. Fremantle P, 1989.

Munro, Alice. *The View From Castle Rock: Stories*. Chatto & Windus, 2006.

Ondaatje, Michael. *Running in the Family*. Picador, 1982.

Rak, Julie. "Radical Connections: Genealogy, Small Lives, Big Data." *a/b: Auto/ Biography Studies*, vol. 32, no. 3, 2017, pp. 479–497.

Rushdie, Salman. *Imaginary Homelands: Essays and Criticism*. Granta Books, 1991.

Scott, Kim. *Benang*. Perth: Fremantle P, 1999.

Scott, Kim, and Hazel Brown. *Kayang & Me*. Fremantle P, 2005.

Watson, Julia. "Ordering the Family: Genealogy as Autobiographical Pedigree." *Getting a Life: Everyday Uses of Autobiography*, edited by Sidonie Smith and Julia Watson. Minnesota UP, 1996, pp. 297–323.

# 10 Tracing Emotional Bonds in Family Letters

## A Pursuit of an Epistolary Melody

*Leena Kurvet-Käosaar*

"I believe that our letters are like music, like 'Lieder ohne Worte' between us if we care about each other. What matters, is the melody—that is, how we feel". These lines were written by my maternal grandmother Helga Sitska (b. 1911) to her sister Aino Pargas (b. 1922) sometime in the mid-fifties, shortly after the sisters had re-established contact after Aino left Estonia during the great escape to the West in the fall of 1944.[1] A conceptualisation of sorts of the sisters' adaptation of the epistolary medium, this brief extract captures an important aspect—the affective value—of their correspondence spanning over thirty-three years in over 500 letters and dozens of postcards and anniversary cards. For me, the process of cataloguing, reading, and interpreting the correspondence—the most extensive textual record of my family of all times—has been a complex journey where personal concerns of re-building a relationship with two important foremothers and acquiring new insights into my family history have intertwined with a scholarly interest in the correspondence.

As a mode of communication no longer actively pursued today even in its more current formats, such as emailing, letter writing is a demanding autobiographical practice to engage with, whether in the format of a scholarly inquiry or as an exploration fuelled by personal and family history related concerns. On the one hand, working with letters requires the systematisation of the epistolary corpus in terms of its duration, frequency, and characteristic textual and communicative features as well as situating it within relevant socio-cultural contexts. On the other, tracing the dynamics of communication of a correspondence requires an engagement with the epistolary exchanges as a (life)writing practice consisting of different materially embedded processes and activities. In my chapter, I attempt to balance the analysis of the textual features of the correspondence with a focus on writing strategies that support the creation and maintenance of emotional bonds with a discussion of referential aspects of the letters, in particular with regard to censorship issues. I will conclude with exploring the question of the possibilities and limits of accessing the correspondence as a (lifelong) life writing practice as an experiential and experimental way of engaging with the correspondence from a personal and familial perspective.

Belonging to the category of "everyday letter writing" (Barton and Hall 2–3; see also Jolly and Stanley 93), the correspondence can be viewed as a creative and resourceful exploration of the possibilities of the epistolary medium by ordinary individuals, shaped by complex socio-political circumstances that almost completely cancelled out all other means of contact and communication between the correspondents. Not exceptional in essence, the correspondence is an example of building and maintaining kinship ties, friendships, and also professional contacts across the Iron Curtain in the Baltics. A number of such correspondences between figures of cultural importance can be found in various archives, for example in the Archives of Cultural History of the Estonian Literary Museum. Preserved correspondences between ordinary individuals across the Iron Curtain, in particular those available for research, are extremely rare. As such, the correspondence offers valuable insights into the transnational communication dynamics of the Cold War period, making visible both the possibilities and limits of epistolary exchange across the Iron Curtain on the level of ordinary individuals. An extensive and elaborate example of migrant correspondence, the letters contain numerous thematic foci and writing strategies considered characteristic of such correspondences in general, and in particular with regard to recent interest in (migrant) letters as "a lens onto the intimate, emotional and rational mappings of minds" (Cancian and Wegge 352) where attempts at "stitching together the ripped mesh of transnational kinship ties" (Khanenko-Friesen 8) play an important role.[2]

"How has it happened that our lives have taken so diverging routes?" Aino writes on 17 September 1957, hoping one day to be reunited with her sister, as they "belong together even though [they] are now separated by such vast distances". As one strategy for reconstructing and maintaining sisterly bonds, variations of verbal confirmation of closeness form a distinct affective thread in the letters, foregrounding kinship ties and affinities of character, sharing similar worldview, or simply expressing deep love and longing for each other. Sharing memories is an equally important strategy that serves to strengthen the intimate bond between the sisters.[3] In a letter from March 1957, Helga views the existence of memories, the fact that the sisters have "wandered along many paths side by side in [their] childhood", as a source of blessing and happiness, proposing to "make the most of them" for reuniting the sisters. The common figurative reference to life course as a path to be followed here functions as a reminder of the importance of shared life experience within the sisters' life course, attempting to create a sense of security, continuity, and consolation under radically different circumstances. These lines also show that different strategies of restoring and maintaining an intimate bond were applied in the correspondence in a self-conscious and reflective manner. Other strategies of intimacy involve, for example, imagining sharing the same physical space that include descriptions of studying each other's photographic images (sometimes even with a magnifying glass), pretending to have a real face-to-face conversation and descriptions of imaginary (sightseeing) trips meant to familiarise each other with their respective surroundings.

Different strategies for constructing and maintaining close intimate relationships and for the creation of transnational family ties in the correspondence illustrates well David Gerber's claim that "immigrant letters are not principally about documenting the world, but instead about reconfiguring a personal relationship rendered vulnerable by long-distance, long-term separation" (143). Nevertheless, exchanging updates of recent developments in their lives and familiarising each other with the details of everyday life constitute an important and extensive share of the correspondence. Yet I would argue that the informational value of these updates depends to a considerable extent on the manner in which they are mediated. Most importantly, both sisters make a considerable epistolary effort to create a common ground and a sense of familiarity with each other's daily lives.

A focus on the possibilities of tracing relationship dynamics and affective modalities in the letters foregrounds "the textual and rhetorical dimensions" of letters (Stanley 223), the "epistolary performance" or "personae" adopted (Jolly and Stanley 93; see also Cockin 152; Maybin 152), and recurring tropes and cultural references as well as narrative structuring. Yet, as Liz Stanley emphasises, "letter writing is always located *in* actual things . . . that have a material, social, temporal and spatial reality", and it is the dynamics between the referentiality of letters and textual mediation that should guide any analytic approach to letters (212). In the current case, the correspondence was to an important extent shaped by tense socio-political circumstances, limiting the range of topics that could be discussed in the letters, determining the frequency and duration of the epistolary exchange, and even shaping its dominating affective modalities.

Regarding information on the daily life of my family in Soviet Estonia in particular, an awareness of censorship and risks to the well-being of corresponding parties considerably influenced what could be said in the letters, and how. Although I have discovered no actual traces of the operation of the Soviet censorship system in the correspondence (such as, for example, missing pages, crossed-out sections, or markings on the envelopes), instances of the use of various measures of precaution can be found in the letters. Responding to Aino's inquiry about a mutual friend, Helga writes that she "lives somewhere far away, somewhere in the Soviet Union" (2 February 1958), with her response trying to communicate to Aino in code the fact that her friend had been sent to the Gulag. In addition, Helga's letters contain several examples of a writing strategy aimed at "thwart[ing] the censors" referred to as "subterfuge" (Hannah 1339), most commonly regarding basic everyday life matters, such as catering for the family's financial needs, employment possibilities, and managing household responsibilities. In contrast to Aino's detailed overviews of her life in Harlow in the UK and later in the US, Helga is noticeably laconic and evasive with regard to most aspects of her family's everyday life, also carefully avoiding any discussions of her disposition toward the Soviet regime that she quietly resisted throughout her life. It is only from casual remarks concerning trivial matters, often containing gaps or discrepancies, that a careful reader could get an idea of her life's realities (e.g., difficulties in finding proper professional employment due to political reasons, struggling to make both ends meet) behind the Iron Curtain. If Aino was able to decipher these subtle messages, she never reflected on that in her letters and never brought up possibly politically risky topics. From the perspective of the political circumstances, an emphasis on emotional bonds and discussion of more abstract matters less obviously connected to the realities of everyday life also emerge as relatively safe foci that could be pursued without major risks of compromising the continuation of communication.

As the sisters' relationship was almost entirely confined to the epistolary, their lives, lived in vastly different socio-political and material contexts on two different continents, were not only represented in their correspondence but in a way also "lived" within the limits and possibilities of the medium (see Stanley 210). As Philippe Lejeune has argued, similarly to diary-keeping, correspondence is also a practice, "a way of living before it is a way of writing" (Lejeune 153), a set of activities that is anchored in the correspondents' everyday life contexts yet also constitutes a distinctive spatio-temporal intersubjective experiential sphere. In the sisters' correspondence, reflections on the process of letter writing—of composing the letters in their heads for weeks: of carefully choosing a writing time uninterrupted by household chores or work responsibilities: of creating a special mood by listening to music: of placing a photo of the other on the desk in front of them while writing; of apologising for hastily written letters or delays in their response—form a common thematic thread, functioning as a confirmation of the importance of the (epistolary) relationship.[4] Of equal importance is the process of engaging with each other's letters, reading and rereading, sharing the letters with other family members but also cherishing the letters as material objects "possess[ing] physical authority rooted in closeness to the writer's body [. . .] a form of bodily trace that underwrites, and sometimes dominates, its text" (Jolly 208).

Working with the correspondence of my grandmother and great aunt has been an insightful and inspiring journey, an occasion for reflecting upon (my) family history and a possibility of familiarising myself with the practice and theoretical and critical considerations of letter writing. The sisters' letters highlight the capacity of ordinary individuals who become writers not by choice but by necessity to adopt to their medium skilfully and with considerable resourcefulness. Organising the letters chronologically, charting key events in the sisters' lives as represented in the correspondence, tracing different textual strategies and epistolary personae developed, and both reconstructing the more immediate referential contexts of the correspondence and exploring the ways in which the correspondence was shaped by larger historical and socio-political factors has enabled me to estimate the letters as a valuable source for research of migrant correspondences. The easy accessibility of a nearly complete corpus of both sides of the correspondence, my relative familiarity with the lives and immediate experiential contexts of the correspondents, and the fluent and elaborate writing style of the letters of both sisters have certainly been considerable contributing factors in the process. Similar to other life writing scholars working on their family archives, I also cannot deny the comforting effect of subjecting the life writings of my family members to "scholarly analysis through contrasts and comparisons and the arrangement of examples in orderly patterns" (Popkin 183). Being able to situate the life experience of my grandmother and great aunt within the larger framework of migrant correspondences and sharing many of its general concerns, characteristic textual features, and writing strategies has enabled me to view it within the scope of common human experience in terms of patterns of mobility in the twentieth century. The knowledge I have gained through these critical frameworks and socio-cultural contexts have also to a great extent facilitated the initial process of emotionally coming to terms with an extensive and often overwhelming source of my family history.

Yet I also realise that the critical distance such an approach has provided me, though doubtless appropriate for a scholarly investigation, has also kept me from facing the more complex task of finding a way to personally engage with the dynamics of the correspondence that, despite its familial contexts, constitutes a deeply private epistolary world, a gradually unfolding lifelong dialogical life narrative. Viewing letter writing as an integral part of life experience, G. Thomas Couser argues that (family) letters should not be regarded as "an epiphenomenon thrown off by the 'real life' of which they are the tantalizing written remains" but rather as "the actual stuff of life itself—preserved moments" (890). The extensive corpus of the sisters' letters offers multiple detailed insights into different aspects of constructing and maintaining an intimate epistolary relationship. Yet the correspondence is nevertheless nearly impossible to grasp. It is a lifelong life writing practice rooted in the sisters' everyday lives but that also entails the creation of a separate experiential space inhabited throughout their adult lives.

For a secondary reader of any correspondence, even a familial one, letters inevitably are remains—of a relationship, of life experience. Yet, as Liz Stanley argues, the "present tense of the letters recurs—or rather occurs—not only in its first reading but subsequent ones too" (208). Within the continuum of the correspondence, each letter also forms an independent, self-contained unity, carefully and lovingly composed to uphold the bond between the sisters, strong enough to continue through years of vigilant censorship as well as discords and conflicts caused by increasing breadth between the two worlds inhabited by the sisters. Each time I remove yet another letter from the envelope and spread the many pages covered with my grandmother's firm, round handwriting looping over yellowish, poor-quality stationery or my great aunt's neat, regular hand filling sheets of elegant, semi-transparent air mail paper, I feel invited to share a bit of their epistolary world. As a third party, I cannot and should not be part of their exchange, but living a "secondary" epistolary life, creating a new life narrative, I feel part of an (epistolary) family bond.

## Acknowledgements

The chapter was supported by the Estonian Ministry of Education and Research (IUT22–2), and by the European Union through the European Regional Development Fund (Centre of Excellence in Estonian Studies).

## Notes

1. The two sisters—Helga (b. 1911) and Aino (b. 1922)—grew up in Tartu and attended the first Estonian-language gymnasium for girls in that city. Helga studied law at Tartu University, graduating already during World War II, the period of German occupation of Estonia. She married while still a student and had two sons (born in 1938 and 1945) and a daughter (my mother, born in 1943). Considered unemployable by the Soviet regime for political reasons, she finally found work in the field of the Soviet equivalent of real estate law. Aino left Estonia in the fall of 1944, during the great wave of emigration to the West and first settled down in the United Kingdom. After reuniting with her husband, who had been a prisoner of war in the Soviet Union for six years, she moved to the United States in 1958 and eventually settled down in Maryland. For more than thirty years, Aino worked at the Library of Congress in Washington, DC.
2. For other features making migrant letters an essential resource for studying migration, see Cancian and Wegge (352); Cancian (2012, 176). Migrant correspondences (dominantly the letters of migrants) that, according to Elliot, Gerber, and Sinke, form "the largest body of the writings of ordinary people of the past that historians and other researchers possess" (3) have been the subject of considerable scholarly attention over the recent decades (for an overview, see, e.g., Cancian 2010 6–9, 153–155), making the migrant letter perhaps the most thoroughly studied type of letter within the genre.
3. For a more detailed analysis of different strategies of building an emotional bond in the correspondence, see Kurvet-Käosaar (2015).
4. For a contrasting example, highlighting difficulties in maintaining an epistolary bond in migrant correspondences and of "feeling lost in that 'space of letter writing'", see Khanenko-Friesen (104).

## Works Cited

Barton, David, and Nigel Hall. "Introduction." *Letter Writing as a Social Practice*, edited by David Barton and Nigel Hall. John Benjamins, 1999, pp. 1–14.

Cancian, Sonia. *Families, Lovers, and Their Letters: Italian Postwar Migration to Canada.* U of Manitoba P, 2010.

———. "'My Dearest Love . . .' Love, Longing, and Desire in International Migration." *Migrations: Interdisciplinary Perspectives*, edited by Michi Messer et al. Springer, 2012, pp. 175–186.

Cancian, Sonia, and Simone A. Wegge. "'If It Is Not Too Expensive, Then You Can Send Me Sugar': Money Matters Among Migrants and Their Families." *The History of the Family*, vol. 21, no. 3, 2016, pp. 350–367. *Taylor & Frances Online*, doi:10.1080/1081602X.2016.1147372.

Cockin, Katherine. "Ellen Terry, the Ghost-Writer, and the Laughing Statue: The Victorian Actress, Letters, and Life Writing." *Journal of European Studies*, vol. 32, nos. 2–3, 2002, pp. 151–163. *Sage Journals Online*, journals.sagepub.com. ezproxy.utlib.ut.ee/doi/pdf/10.1177/004724410203212505.

Couser, G. Thomas. "In My Father's Closet: Reflections of a Critic Turned Life Writer." *Literature Compass*, vol. 8, no. 12, 2011, pp. 890–899. *Wiley Online Library*, onlinelibrary-wiley-com.ezproxy.utlib.ut.ee/doi/10.1111/j.17414113. 2011.00847.x.

Gerber, David A. "Epistolary Masquerades: Acts of Deceiving and Withholding in Immigrant Letters." *Letters Across Borders: The Epistolary Practices of International Migrants*, edited by Bruce S. Elliot et al. Palgrave, 2006, pp. 141–157.

Hannah, Martha. "A Republic of Letters: The Epistolary Tradition in France During World War I." *The American Historical Review*, vol. 108, no. 5, 2003, pp. 1338–1361. *JSTOR*, doi:10.1086/529969.

Jolly, Margaretta. *In Love and Struggle: Letters in Contemporary Feminism.* Columbia UP, 2008.

Jolly, Margaretta, and Liz Stanley. "Letters as/Not a Genre." *Life Writing*, vol. 2, no. 2, 2005, pp. 91–118. *Taylor & Frances Online*, doi:10.1080/ 10408340308518291.

Khanenko-Friesen, Natalia. *Ukranian Otherlands: Diaspora, Homeland and Folk Imagination in the Twentieth Century.* U of Wisconsin P, 2015.

Kurvet-Käosaar, Leena. "The Epistolary Dynamics of Sisterhood Across the Iron Curtain." *Life Writing*, vol. 12, no. 2, 2015, pp. 161–175. *Taylor & Frances Online*, doi:10.1080/14484528.2015.1022929.

Lejeune, Philippe. *On Diary.* U of Hawaii P, 2009.

Maybin, Janet. "Death Row Penfriends: Some Effects of Letter Writing on Identity and Relationships." *Letter Writing as a Social Practice*, edited by David Barton and Nigel Hall. John Benjamins, 1999, pp. 151–178.

Popkin, Jeremy D. "Life Writing in the Family." *a/b: Auto/Biography Studies*, vol. 25, no. 2, 2010, pp. 172–185. *Taylor & Frances Online*, doi:10.1353/ abs.2010.0038.

Stanley, Liz. "The Epistolarium: On Theorizing Letters and Correspondences." *Auto/Biography*, vol. 12, 2004, pp. 201–235.

# 11 Life Narrative Methods for Working With Diaries

*Kylie Cardell*

The diary is an iconic autobiographical form with a long and diverse history of practice, and it is a genre that is hybrid, dynamic, and evolving. For scholars in a vast range of disciplines, the diary is a distinctive method of research, a tool used to elicit serial qualitative data in relation to experiences, feelings, and motivations of individuals over time (Bartlett and Milligan). For life narrative scholars, diaries are also interpretable as texts and understood as a mode of literary practice that engages with aesthetic and formal limits in relation to genre and reveals intention in relation to authorial self-expression. While very many overtly literary uses of diary forms exist, diaries are also and crucially "ordinary writing" (Sinor). They demand responsive reading strategies and creative, flexible critical approaches.

This discussion explores some of the methods that scholars working with diaries might encounter and might practice. Diaries can be highly aesthetic, complex, and very literary, but they are also equally as often ephemeral or "ordinary" and can resist easy categorisation in terms of value or meaning. Life narrative scholars working with diaries need to negotiate assumptions about intention and crafting that are perhaps less urgent or visible to scholars working with more overtly literary modes of life writing. The digital context draws such issues of value into view and also in conjunction to ethics: given the vast array of life writing automedia that uses or redeploys the serial, personal point of view in the contemporary moment, and given the efflorescence of diverse and evolving technologies for serial self-representation, what does diary offer in terms of an interpretative or responsive framework? What are the benefits of this approach, and what are the limits or concerns? It is clear that diaristic writing is still more often seen in conjunction with certain kinds of subjects; are there problems here? What is subverted or made new, and what is a diary now?

## What Is a Diary? Value, and Ethics

For scholars who work with diaries, definition is often a foundational encounter: "what *is* a diary" can be a significant question, for example, in justifying or valuing certain kinds of ongoing and everyday self-representative practices or in attending to where and how "ordinary" discourse and modes of communication are being emphasised. It can also denote value in a different kind of way, or as a detriment: diaries are still quite often constructed as potentially shameful or as incidental versus deliberate modes of communication. The diary is valued for its potential as an "outlaw" genre, a form through which marginalised or overlooked voices can be heard. But it is equally often derided as too personal or ephemeral to be taken seriously. This is also very often a gendered issue (Cardell *Dear World*). For example, a scholarly recuperation of women's life writing has demonstrated that diary is itself a key methodology through which subjects excluded from more public or literary modes of address have been able to recount and record experiences otherwise left out of the public record. In the contemporary context, acts of ongoing, serial representation such as those carried out over social media have often been considered negatively. Seen within an evolving etymology of diary-keeping, however, such acts also speak to the particular strategic and rhetorical power of the diary as a mode of testimony, witnessing, and documentation—and this is important.

Scholars who work with diaries are often called on to negotiate competing frameworks of value. This complexity is perhaps particularly visible in working with new media and online contexts, where serial, personal modes of representation are proliferating. Lee Humphreys et al.'s content-analysis argument in relation to Twitter, for example, relies mostly on crafting a seamless transition between pre-digital, material cultures of diary practice with contemporary contexts of online communication. An emphasis on historical precedents in relation to the privacy (or not) of the diary form sustains this analysis. Seeing Twitter as a diary, however, might lead the life narrative scholar to questions that Humphreys et al. do not address: why is diary-style narration persuasive (and why is it not) in a digital, online context? What kinds of subjects are recognised as performing "diary" in this context, and who is left out of this ascription? What new ideas about privacy and personal disclosure are visible in a shift to diaristic style discourse in online spaces? Seeing Twitter as "like a diary" because it replicates certain formal aspects of diary texts, or resembles certain communities of historical diary practice, may end up eliding the ways in which new communication technologies are genuinely evolving and transforming existing rhetorical features of diaries. The scholar in this context must work carefully to recognise both the "newness" of diary online as well as what persists in terms of form or convention. There are rich insights to be gained, for example, in exploring how Twitter or Instagram function in relation to diaries historically, and there are also important benefits to engaging responsively with the ways in which contemporary subjects are deploying and subverting assumptions or cultural stereotypes in relation to autobiographical practice (Cardell et al.).

Diary writing is a cultural practice that is seen as available to broad communities, including those who would not usually consider themselves "writers" or as public voices, and it is a method for capturing and facilitating and coaxing this kind of subjective narration. This is significant because diaries are very strongly imagined in popular culture. For example, the diary both imagined and manifested as a "locked book" amplifies a cultural discourse around the diary as a private or secret form of knowledge. However, not all diaries are books, or private, or even chronological (something Judy Nolte Temple, for example, has explored in detail). This has been an important point for researchers exploring the diary in online spaces, where the overt presence of an audience has sometimes been seen as precluding a status as "private" discourse. Of course, there are many ways to be "private" online and that replicate a sometimes legally enforced definition of this status (for example, through instating controls that prevent or limit audience), yet the diary as "private" also speaks to a kind of discursive subjective stance: the diary is a distinctive form for recording and documenting experience, and it is associated rhetorically with both the everyday and the private sphere and the personal voice. The diary can be used as a technology to organise or represent experience or other personal data, and it can be used as a position from which to speak of this experience or data in a particular way.

Scholars who work with historical diary texts may be working with records of life from people who are not otherwise at the centre of the historical record, or they may be encountering diary material that provides a supplementary account for figures very much in the public eye. These accounts are interesting for what they might tell us of "ordinary" lives, or the lives of people who are marginalised, or the "private" life of a public figure. As a life narrative scholar interested in contemporary life writing practices, and in a moment when the capacity to represent one's own life is available in unprecedented ways, I have been interested to know where diary texts might "be" given new understandings of privacy or appropriateness attached to self-representative practices that are defining the current context. For example, attending to discourse or forms overtly presented as a "diary" account is equally as important as noticing the kinds of representation that invoke diary as an implied mode in intent or reception; the diary intersects with discursive and formal issues of privacy in various and ongoing ways.

While it is now generally accepted that a view of the diary as simply or only a "private" text is naïve, and must ignore a good deal of historically documented practice in relation to diaries and audience to be convincing, the diary retains a strong association with personal, private voice and, in a public or broadcast context, can be understood to signal an *intention* to share personal or "private" material. A good example of this is sexblogs, which I have argued are often used by their authors as a deliberate rhetorical mode in which "diary" is both seduction and disclaimer (Cardell *Dear World*). In other contexts, a diary form (what Aimeé Morrison usefully discusses in the digital context as an "affordance", an idea equally applicable to material diary objects) can be recognised as eliciting or coaxing a particular kind of narration or representation—to what ends and in what contexts are subjects coaxed to produce daily, ephemeral, and autobiographical communications online? What parameters for self-knowledge does a pre-formatted self-help diary workbook (or device) literally instate for the reader/user? These questions, for example, were crucial for me in my work with self-help diaries (*Dear World*) or in thinking about wearable activity trackers, like the Fitbit in relation to diary as affordance and culture ("Is a Fitbit a Diary?") Ultimately, the diary as a mode of self-surveillance that might expose its author through sharing or disclosure, through its archival affordances and personal, autobiographical emphasis remains significant and may be heightened online.

## Conclusion

When working with diary texts, or in presuming and interpreting diaristic acts within various contexts, issues of ethics and agency remain central. Where diary is an overt claim in relation to self-representation requires a different scholarly approach than where genre is implied or identified. For example, in a recent discussion of the Iranian asylum seeker Behrouz Boochani's "Diary of a Disaster", published online in the *Guardian* newspaper while he was still incarcerated in the Australian government's Manus detention facility, Gillian Whitlock is highly attentive to how Boochani's use of documentation in relation to daily, ongoing indignities and trauma mobilises the rhetorical affect of the diary form. Here the diary is both an embodied act of witness and testimony and a tool deployed with specific affect. Elsewhere, acts of serial self-representation acquire weight and significance through accumulation and context: archives of social media can become read as legacy in the wake of tragedy. The social media of teenage girls, the series of selfies, status updates, and YouTube videos, otherwise regarded as "noxious self-indulgence", become testimony after crisis: "the recording of daily minutiae, are the things we look for when unexplainable tragedy hits" (Koul). Is this production also a diary? An obvious and implicit ethical tension here is productive for scholars who wish to consider the ongoing ideological resonances of serial self-representation in relation to ideas of privacy and public in the digital age.

Diary writing is a dynamic cultural practice that, at various historical moments, and sometimes connected to particular historical forms, is valued or understood in particular ways. This is important because, as cultural theorists like José van Dijck have observed, autobiographical memory is not simply reliant on *what* is remembered but also on *how*.

The kinds of cultural scripts, personal experiences or subjective percep-
tive choices that affect, for example, the story a parent might narrate
to a child about developmental milestones is part of "a complex set of
recursive activities that shape our inner worlds" (van Dijck 5). Exploring
why, when, and how diaries are visible or implied as forms for documentation, or as modes that coax narration and other practices of individual
self-representation, is an interpretive method for analysing the shifting
cultural significance, pressures, and assumptions that attend the personal
and the private in autobiographical discourse.

Analysis of the diary as medium, and so of the limits and potential of
the form's affordances and particularly in relation to digital contexts, is
one crucial way in which scholars now engage with the diary as a genre:
how does the diary as medium respond to shifting cultural invocations
around privacy, personal disclosure, and as an everyday, "ordinary"
mode of discourse? In turn, this asks questions of intent and aesthetic:
when subjects self-consciously make a diary "public", whether through
traditional publishing or as a deliberate positioning online, they are inviting a specific kind of audience engagement and claiming a particular kind
of rhetorical and subjective position. When is diary a strong and powerful position from which to speak and represent? When is diary used to
disparage or discredit, seen as an act of excess or a confession or naïveté?
While diary writing has been considered a private practice at various
points in history, but not always, the contemporary era represents a context within which ideas of privacy are being contested and reshaped. The
diary as it appears online, for example, considered as a Twitter or Instagram account, contests long-established ideas of the diary as a mostly
private and confessional mode, which certainly characterised scholarly
perceptions of the genre in the nineteenth and twentieth centuries.

The diary as written and intended for an audience is now a prominent
contemporary form, visible in the vastly increased publication of diaries
by their living authors, both in print and online. This means that the
methods used in relation to the scholarly story of diary texts and practices must similar flex and adapt. What is clear is that personal acts of
narration by "ordinary" people are now proliferating, and diaries are a
form and genre of visible significance in this. A flexible, responsive methodology for working with diary texts that is attentive to ethics and to
shifting and diverse contexts for "private" or "personal" representation
is crucial in adequately dealing with the variety of discourse that occurs
within and around the diary as genre.

## Works Cited

Bartlett, Ruth, and Christine Milligan. *What Is Diary Method?* Bloomsbury,
2015.
Cardell, Kylie. *Dear World: Contemporary Uses of the Diary.* U of Wisconsin,
2014.

———. "Is a Fitbit a Diary? Self-tracking and Autobiography." *M/C Media Culture Journal*, vol. 21, no. 2, 2018. http://journal.media-culture.org.au/index.php/mcjournal/article/view/1348.

Cardell, Kylie et al. " 'Stories': Social Media and Ephemeral Narratives as Memoir." *Mediating Memory: Tracing the Limits of Memoir*, edited by Bunty Aviseon et al. Routledge, 2018, pp. 157–172.

Humphreys, Lee et al. "Historicizing New Media: A Content-Analysis of Twitter." *Journal of Communication*, vol. 63, 2013, pp. 413–431.

Koul, Scaachi. "The Instagram Obituaries of the Young Manchester Victims." *The New York Times*, 27 May 2017. www.nytimes.com/2017/05/27/opinion/sunday/the-instagram-obituaries-of-the-young-manchester-victims.html.

Morrison, Aimée. "Facebook and Coaxed Affordances." *Identity Technologies: Constructing the Self Online*. The U of Wisconsin P, 2014, pp. 112–131.

Sinor, Jennifer. *The Extraordinary Work of Ordinary Writing: Annie Ray's Diary*. U of Iowa P, 2002.

Temple, Judy Nolte. "Fragments as Diary: Theoretical Implications of the Dreams and Visions of 'Baby Doe' Tabor." *Inscribing the Daily: Critical Essays on Women's Diaries*, edited by Suzanne L. Bunkers and Cynthia Huff. U of Massachusetts P, 1996, pp. 72–85.

van Dijck, José. *Mediated Memories in the Digital Age*. Stanford UP, 2007.

Whitlock, Gillian. "Diary of a Disaster: Behrouz Boochani's 'Asylum in Space.' " *European Journal of Life Writing*, vol. 7, 2018. http://ejlw.eu/article/view/269/542.

# 12 Autoethnographic Life Writing
## Reaching Beyond, Crossing Over

*Sally Ann Murray*

Much of my scholarly work has involved forms of autoethnographic life writing, based on my sense, as a then-young scholar in a dramatically changing South Africa, that it was important to explore the unsettled and unsettling relations of self not only to historically supposed others, but to received bodies of academic knowledge. Here, I set out to consider how years of training in literary studies could (or could not) be brought to bear upon "othered" forms of knowing, such as malling (1997), walking (2005), gardening (2006), poetry (2011) and unusual forms of local fiction (2009). In this para-academic undertaking, the range of registers is telling, mixing the vivacity of colloquial idiom with normative citation; the personal reveal with dispassionate rhetoric, flights of imaginative narrative fancy with the authoritative gravitas of Historical Fact. In time, I began to extend these minor transgressions into pieces where, as poet and fiction writer, I wrote about my practices and processes, actively creating, as have influential women writers invested in experimental forms, a critical discursive context for such writing, where one was lacking. Autoethnography found me, whether by chance or necessity, before I had the word for the method. I simply knew the longing to write into being an academic life that did not require me, as a woman, to live only in what was narrowly construed as "the mind", relegating "the body" and its complexities to the margins.

In this chapter, I focus on autoethnography as a mode of life writing in research practice. Here, I acknowledge that autoethnographic impulses intersect with forms of autofiction, fictionalised autobiography, memoir, and personal essay (Boldrini and Novak). I understand autoethnography as an embodied disposition or a sensibility (Butz) in academic writing, one which accommodates the processual melee of the writer's vulnerability, flaws, partialities, blind spots, emotions, and conflicted positions in relation to her subject, rather than purporting to enter the terrain of knowledge from a vantage of knowing authority and systematised analysis. Autoethnography as a method in scholarly writing charts ideas in the process of discovery (and thwarting), insisting on the messy, convoluted connections between the cerebral and the visceral. It's not a matter of writing up your "findings", but of using the writing itself as grounds of inquiry.

There is no checklist, or inventory of methods: autoethnography is a shape-shifter, "a heuristic device, a metaphorical learning tool", not a set of rules. This is aptly implied in variants of the "term—auto-ethnography, auto/ethnography, auto*e*thnography (with a dash, with a slash, with the wink of an eye)" (Butz 138). The effort of seeking to find alignments of "auto" with "ethnography", rather than assuming commingling sans gap or slant or mistake, generates productive disruption about what "we" supposedly know to be true and valid. G. Thomas Couser notes that autoethnography "is a slippery, ambiguous, but useful, indeed indispensable, term" (126). If, as he says, the term reverberates differently in different disciplines, the methods are, usually, more personal in their originating impulses than academic discourse is accustomed to accommodating, and "the term's ambiguity is a function of its broad interdisciplinary utility" (126).[1] The methods are highly situational, responding both to the erratic irruptions and the perdurable, ongoing constraints that make "one's" life but a life, one life, lived in forms of proximity to (and distance from) the lives of many other people, creatures, and things in mediated social structures and infrastructures: the neighbourhood, the family, the highway, the mall, the classroom, the garden, the poem, the TV series. . . . Autoethnographic methods entail creative-conceptual risk, all in the hope of inventive knowledge-makings, combinations of poetics and politics, "guestures" where bodily doing and mental processes blur, being asked to hold unsettling forms. Sometimes, these forms of mind–body meeting resolve into the hospitable and convivial. At other times they remain prickly, suspicious, even hostile. In this, error is not only to be expected but also welcomed as a method of discovery. Is autoethnography, then, idiosyncratic? Yes. But is it generalisable? The extent of that extent is discovered—*is to be discovered*—en route, part of the speculative process of learning the limits and possibilities, the complexities and complicities, of autoethnographic extrapolations from a particularised self in a particular culture. (As could also be pointed out: it is precisely in visibly *exercising* such constraints, in performing their ambit, or otherwise, that autoethnographic life writing reveals the sleights and fabrications of what have often been considered the universal methods and concepts upon which normative academic knowledge is premised.)

An autoethnographic life writer's methods, from the outset, are usually not imagined as being willed by an eventual arrival at indisputable certainty, or the mapping of a surveyed territory from preconceived coordinates. Rather, working as a means not to an end but in the service of process, the desire is likely to be to explore, procedurally, the always less-than commensurate measures from which any academic autoethnographer's living, thinking, and writing proceeds in the difficult becoming of the relational. The methods of autoethnographic writing in scholarly articles include, without embarrassment or apology, modes that can seem discomfortingly personal, or creative, or affective, or experimental, in the more sober company of traditional scholarly discourses premised on analysis and critique.[2] Anecdote, extended conversation, poetry, dialogue snippet, recurrent questions, dramatic vignette, image, ekphrasis, story fragment, personal account: all of these are methods that frequently feature, and have value. While anecdote, for instance, as brief narrative, may be viewed sceptically by methodological purists who eschew relativism and assert the importance of knowledge as reproducible authority, the very particularity and specificity of an anecdote can give memorable distinction to what might otherwise remain abstraction. An anecdote (and its companion methods), may serve not as mere ephemera or personalia, but as tentatively representative, illustrative of larger research questions.

> . . . a black youth glimpsed down at the harbour. Dusk. Hunkered in a dark hoodie. In his hand, a book. And unprompted, in the blurred connections of the fading light, he turned the cover towards you: *How to get the love you need.*
> . . . early morning. The determined sound of a man (in blue overalls) hauling a handmade cart alongside the road. Tireless pram wheels. A seat attached to a wooden pallet. He pauses, bends down. Only then do you notice: blanketed into this contraption is a very small bundle. He has stopped to feed a baby, from an infant's feeding bottle filled with milk.
> . . . the new Vice Chancellor of Stellenbosch University stands at the crossroads of a major urban intersection. Around him, student protesters swell. His address does not carry. He sheds his suit jacket. Rolls his shirtsleeves. Up-ends a municipal dirtbin to use as a raised platform. Uneasily, he mounts. Looks across the crowds.

Such memoried moments may not initially announce themselves as evident features of your larger methodological conceptualising of an academic autoethnographic project. Yet en route, a memory may come to mind; in doing so, it may prompt others. Such clusters can become invaluable nodes of method, as your thinking develops:

- What is your subject, in every sense of the word? (Topic, individual, collective. . . . Are there central and subordinate subjects, and how and why have you elected to establish these?)
- Thinking creatively: who—or what—are the central characters, and how do you imagine them as variously different *and* interrelated elements of your research focus?
- Where do events take place and what are the implications? (Are there other locations that become important, as your thinking gathers?)

- What about the *whens*? (Time matters . . . and timing. Think wider historical context and social movements, but also about your daily routines, and the variously generative and disruptive power of moments of interruption.)
- Where are "you" *in* all of this, or in relation to this? (Is "your self" and the associated "person" and point of view imagined as constant, or necessarily shifting?)
- What about "person" as a grammatical positioning: first person, second person, third person? (Each has associated proximities and distances, levels of assumed trust and questioning, that in the context of scholarly autoethnographic life writing a writer may use, and unsettle.)

These are just a few of the questions that could guide your method, when you use forms such as anecdote. The point is: academics engaged in auto-ethnography as a mode of living research need to be open to the gifts of everyday experience as prompts. The mundane can suddenly materialise differently than ordinariness and custom have schooled us to expect. If the word "mundane" means banal, it also refers to "of the world", meaning that *we* as autoethnographers can act as agents, in life writing, to imagine into being the very connections we wish to make, actively *making them materialise* rather than just marshalling "the material". It's not a matter of excavating or uncovering, but of making, of poiesis, in which description, as much as critique, can be a powerful methodological tool. (On that note: when using autoethnography as a method in my academic life writing, I hope it's clear that I recommend we don't privilege the "life" or "lives" at the expense of the *writing*, giving attention to treatment, style, and voice precisely *as* elements of method, rather than stylish additions or decorative flourishes. The effect is one of both polish and spontaneity, of care and improvisation: I favour methods of autoethnographic life writing that enable me to craft experiments in thinking and writing that honour, not *capture*, unusual encounters in the identities of self and relationality. The writing often aims to be a performative enactment of the ideas, creating *in language*, rather than relegating language to a conduit for conveying "meaning". This can work. And yet I must always guard against falling so deeply into the allure of language that the piece gets too clever, too tricksy, and becomes a performing monkey. I don't always succeed.)

The everyday moments that might become useful anecdote and similar autoethnographic life writing resources are ephemeral and can quickly disappear. Unless you practice imaginative awareness across the senses, *noticing*, these little serendipities are not likely to collect into a repertoire or informal archive on which your efforts at autoethnographic life writing in the context of academic scholarship can draw. Moments like these can help you not only to form your ideas but also to enact them, enliven them. They create the effect of life, in the discourse of your academic life writing, giving a vitalising life-likeness that is often missing in a routinised, habituated academese. The additional recognition, then, is that moments like these offer not only stirring evocation and description but also *embodied* conceptual spaces for analysis and for engagement with received bodies of thought, giving complex human textures to scholarly abstractions.[3] I am not, myself, presently writing on complications of hegemonic masculinities. But if I were: what excellent, intersectional nodes of engagement the three preceding anecdotes could offer, at once "poetential" *and* critical potentialities that reach beyond the level of poetic effect (and affect), towards a democratising politics. Indeed, as Chawla and Atay remark (2018), autoethnographic life writing has the capacity not only to represent othered life stories and histories, but also to shift understandings of method and concept. While there is no clear sense, yet, of the possibilities of and impediments towards the developing of a "decolonial autoethnography", for example, it is important to begin to imagine what such a field and associated methods might "look, sound, and feel like" (3), so that we can explore "what it means to write the self in and out" of existing cultural–political frameworks.

This means taking care with ethics, even while walking fine lines. Often, the most powerful personal writing digs deep, probing wounds, disrupting received mythologies about family, race, gender. This writing may be therapeutic for the writer. It may have wider social value, in debunking established "truths". But since such writing does not set out to be "pleasing", there are many who won't be pleased by the intrusion into privacy, among them your relatives, or intimates. As a student reminded members of our class recently, "Your life is not only your own". I know. Sometimes, in my work, I am not sure where that leaves me. I use both verifiable, checkable facts about people, and also a range of fictionalising filters, hoping to respect the rights of others, in my writing, to forms of privacy (see Murray "Writing Like Life").

While first person writing can easily be trashed as emotional, confessional, not appropriately academic (and in a few strokes silencing the noisy, multiplying, minoritised practitioners of these ostensibly mediocre minor modes), autoethnographic life writing is not, as some aver, inherently synonymous with solipsistic self-referentiality. Yes, the "auto" element of autoethnography can congeal into a first person first self-centredness. But the first person can also be powerfully revelatory of previously unthought, or under-considered, links between the personal and the political, which makes it a compelling site of embodied, democratic scholarship, engaging positions and bodies not historically welcomed by normative academic languages and conventions. The methods of autoethnographic life writing proceed from the corrective premise that a self is not a given, but *always* a contested becoming, relationally situated. The scholar who turns to autoethnographic life writing as a research method is usually interested in locating her own participant voicings in the text, rather than (as in traditional genres of cultural ethnography) situating her confidently superior self "outside" or "above" the subordinated cultural subjects being subjected to her indisputable observing authority.

Still, given the many detractors of autoethnographic forms of research writing in academic life, it is a good idea for those of us interested in developing the (best) practice to avoid entrenching its possibly limiting features. Quite often, for instance, I notice we're inclined, in our writing, to unpack every minutiae of an occurrence, the vagaries of every turn of thought, each call and response of an illustrative conversation. We shouldn't. No method can ever capture lives in their entire lived complexity; any method is but suggestive. Which means that comprehensive writing practices belabour. A helpful move, working by analogy, is to borrow from fiction writers. In a novel, when a novelist wants to get the character into another room, she won't relay every step—the colour of the door, the turning of the door handle, the texture of the carpet. Instead, she will deftly use combinations of detailed "scene" to draw a reader into developing events and emotions, revealing back-story and ideas through gesture and implication, and then, at other points, she will rely on strategic "summary" to move things along, quickly shifting time frames or contexts. Overall, in terms of method, the writer is getting a reader where the reader needs to be, in order for the next phase of the narrative (or emplotment) to ensue. So, there are valuable methods to borrow from creative writers. In addition, we can also shake up several of the adages: Write What You Know. Yes, but unless this is to become another version of navel-gazing, for the autoethnographic life writer, it's necessary to be willing to make leaps of imaginative–empathetic faith in writing oneself in relation to the lives of others, and to combine these with careful background research and ethical attempts not to appropriate experiences and voices. Similarly: if we just accept the instruction to "Show, Don't Tell", we might miss out on the very tactical moves offered by the power of overt explanation at one point in our writing, and more sensuous description at another. As I'm always re-discovering, in writing a variety of experimental academic autoethnographies, I must manage the modulation, the momentum; the moments of surface and depth, in the critical life accounts I sky-build and heart-rend and ground-swell. Accumulated details don't speak for themselves. Neither does intimate narrative. It's the writer's agency that has to make it possible for something of consequence to happen in the autoethnographic life writing text, and then possibly in the imaginative life world of a reader. It's not social impact. It's not critical interrogation. And that, to my mind, is good. For when it comes to handling method, that is reassuring, as I am not being (automatically) written by superstructures and institutional machineries, which in contemporary academic culture are so often alienating. Metrics. Outputs. Productivity. If I can use autoethnographic life writing methods to create a little space within, *from within*, the machine, I can persuade myself that my work has the power, possibly, to invigorate deathly instrumentalisms, to claim human being, to create surprising, supple pathways of connection between critical and creative practice.

## Notes

1. Indisciplined though I am in literary-cultural studies, I scarcely have to think of autoethnography as a *qualitative* alternative to quantitative or more positivist methods for academic life writing. Such meta-reflexivity, however, may be demanded of scholars who use autoethnographic methods in contexts like the social and health sciences. (See Watson.)
2. Choose your journals carefully. Familiarise yourself with those that welcome academic writing that demonstrates autoethnographic inflections. Not all will discern method in what might be perceived as your questionable madness.
3. Autoethnographic life writing in the scholarly context means that "your" "experience" also encompasses your experience of reading the writing of others, or of encountering their art and performances. Here, whether through deliberate focus or the glancing inattention of peripheral vision, your imagination selects, adapts, grows overt and latent relations. These relations may be "citable" according to academic conventions of acknowledgement, but they may also percolate subliminally, erratically, sometimes constituting less "a method" than a personal mythodology.

## Works Cited

Boldrini, Lucia, and Julia Novak, editors. *Experiments in Life-Writing: Intersections of Auto/Biography and Fiction.* Springer, 2017.

Butz, David. "Autoethnography as Sensibility." *The SAGE Handbook of Qualitative Geography,* 2010, pp. 138–155.

Chawla, Devika, and Ahmet Atay. "Introduction: Decolonizing Autoethnography." *Cultural Studies↔ Critical Methodologies,* vol. 18, no. 1, 2018, pp. 3–8.

Couser, G. Thomas. "Disability and (Auto) Ethnography: Riding (and Writing) the Bus With My Sister." *Journal of Contemporary Ethnography,* vol. 34, no. 2, 2005, pp. 121–142.

Murray, Sally Ann. "An Academic Milling Around 'The Mall': (De) Constructing Cultural Knowledge." *Critical Arts,* vol. 11, nos. 1–2, 1997, pp. 153–176.

———. "En Fuite, on Foot, in Thought: Making the Metropolis Elusive." *Current Writing: Text and Reception in Southern Africa,* vol. 17, no. 2, 2005, pp. 102–124.

———. "The Idea of Gardening: Plants, Bewilderment, and Indigenous Identity in South Africa." *English in Africa,* vol. 33, no. 2, 2006, pp. 135–158.

———. "Ivan Vladislavić and What-What: Among Writers, Readers and 'Other Odds, Sods and Marginals'." *Current Writing: Text and Reception in Southern Africa,* vol. 21, nos. 1–2, 2009, pp. 138–163.

———. "Lyric↔ L/language: Essaying the Poetics of Contemporary Women's Poetry." *Scrutiny2,* vol. 16, no. 2, 2011, pp. 12–31.

———. "Writing Like Life? 'Life-Like' Relation, Femaleness and Generic Instability in *Small Moving Parts.*" *Agenda,* vol. 28, no. 1, 2014, pp. 72–84.

Watson, Julia. "Autoethnography." *Encyclopedia of Life Writing: Autobiographical and Biographical Forms.* Routledge, 2013, pp. 83–86.

# 13 Telling Life Stories Using Creative Methods in Qualitative Interviews

*Signe Ravn*

## Introduction

Studying people's life stories using qualitative interviews is a well-established approach in the social sciences and beyond, whether in the form of actual biographical interviews or through a focus on select parts of individuals' lives and the stories they tell about this. Such methods, and their resulting representations, have also been subject to critique from sociologists, perhaps most famously Pierre Bourdieu's famous critique of the traditional life history as "a biographical illusion" (Bourdieu). According to Bourdieu, the life history makes the chaos of "life as lived" *look like* a chronological and straightforward trajectory with a clear purpose or project; but this is an illusion. As Margaretha Järvinen writes, "a biography is a story put together with the help of culturally available instruments and ingredients" (372). A central task for the life writing sociologist is therefore also to shed light on these "cultural instruments", or in other words, to illuminate the broader socio-cultural context in which a certain life story is told to build an understanding of how this shapes the story that emerges. This can also make us aware of the constructed character of such life stories, a construction that the method in question itself is part of. With this in mind, we can think of creative methods as holding the potential to construct *other* stories. Thus, using creative methods in research interviews can be one way for life writing scholars and those writing auto/biography to discover alternative, or otherwise untold, life narratives.

In recent years, the literature on qualitative methodologies has developed significantly as participatory and creative methods have experienced immense popularity among researchers. While the motivations for applying such methods differ, they can be seen as part of a general attempt at breaking away from "the standard interview" (cf. Bagnoli) and exploring the potential of other methodological approaches. They are often also embedded in attempts to address and shift the power dynamics inherent in the research encounter. Helene Hjort Oldrup and Trine Agervig Carstensen differentiate between neo-realist approaches and constructivist–interactionist approaches to the data that these methods produce. That is, scholars either apply creative methods to get "closer" to the experiences of the topic under study or to approach the topic under study from a *different*, but not better or more "true", perspective. In line with the sociological reflections on the status of biographical data mentioned above, I approach creative methods from a constructivist point of view, as methods that allow us to inquire into *other* dimensions of people's life stories. Giving a full overview of the broad range of creative methods lies beyond the aims of this chapter. Instead, I will focus on three broad types of such methods—life charts, mapping methods, and music-focused methods—to illustrate the potential of each of these for studying life narratives. As Kuzmics put it, "representing life history/biographical narratives through art forms can create multi-vocal, dialogic texts which make visible emotional structures and inner experiences as sensuous knowledge" (Kuzmics 9, cited in O'Neill and Hubbard 47). Hence, the focus of this chapter is on how creative methods can assist interdisciplinary life narrative researchers in bringing forward *other* aspects of life stories than those favoured by the traditional, biographical interview.

## Life Charts

The creative method that comes closest to a traditional life history or biographical interview is what is known as life charts, sometimes also called life grids or timelines. Life charts are used in qualitative interviews to visually represent the participant's biography, or aspects thereof. Depending on the epistemological approach, the life chart can be used as a means of uncovering factual events in a person's life, getting an overview of the chronology of such events, or even "validating" information from other sources (e.g., Berends); or it can feature as a way of investigating what individuals see as the key events in their lives. This latter approach is often underpinned by analytical concepts such as turning points (Elder) or critical moments (Thomson et al.), i.e., events that are seen as having impacted one's life trajectory or sense of self. Life charts have been used across disciplines and for a number of purposes, not necessarily related to biographical research, for instance, youth loneliness (Thomsen et al.), substance use (Berends), and weight loss (Sheridan et al.). In my current research project, a three-year study of the everyday lives and imagined futures of young Australian women who have left school early, I work with life charts to produce data on what the young women themselves see as important for how their lives look today. What comes through here is that this task not only captures "traditional" life course events (cf. Elder) such as marriage, parental illness, or leaving the parental home, but also events such as going to see a musical or meeting a new friend for the first time. Embedding such events in a biographically oriented project, the central analytical question that comes to the fore is why these events, and not others, have made it onto the life chart, how they sit in relation to the broader biography, and how they shape the participant's identity today. What must also be kept in mind, though, is how life charts are likely to give prominence to a certain "biography", as they are likely to produce data on ruptures and changes rather than continuity and stability. This should be taken into account when interpreting the charts—by approaching it as an "organising principle" (cf. Adriansen) in itself—but also ideally be picked up on in other parts of the interview to gain perspective on what has happened between these turning points or critical moments. In other words, life charts may be most productive when designed as one element of a longer, qualitative interview, allowing the researcher to probe further into the resulting life chart.

## Mapping Methods

Mapping methods is an umbrella term for a range of methods that are used across different disciplines. One cluster of mapping methods focuses on social networks and seeks to map, for instance, the quantity and quality of an individual's social relations, or social capital. This is the case, for example, with what is termed the "hierarchical mapping technique" (Antonucci), which involves different variations of locating family, friends, and acquaintances in concentric circles that are closer or further away from the participant, depending on the nature of the relation. While these can have a longitudinal or life course dimension to them (e.g., Pahl and Spencer), they are typically not used for generating biographical data. Another cluster of mapping methods is more concerned with maps in a geographical sense and uses mapping methods to create a visual representation of, for instance, uses of urban spaces (Duff; Clark; Travlou et al.), or to produce data on spaces that are hard to access for the researcher (Ravn and Duff). At a first glance, this method is also not linked to analytical interests in biographical aspects of the participants' lives. However, it can be designed to produce insights into life stories that, while not fitting traditional formats, can yield significant insights into how biographies relate to space and place (e.g., Taylor; O'Neill and Hubbard). As an example, in my current research described above I am asking the participants to first draw a map of their neighbourhood, including places they pass through or in which they spend time. Second, I ask them to attach sticky notes with two different colours, one for places they like and one for places they do not like. The dialogue that comes from this task not only concerns their sense of belonging in the present but also traces this back in time, for instance through talk of places where they used to spend time (e.g., as kids), places that have changed, and places that hold certain memories, whether negative or positive. Depending on the population in focus of the research, one can also imagine how this approach can touch on family relations and family histories in relation to place.

## Music

Creative methods involving music are yet to be further explored and developed. The uses of music so far seem to be parallel to uses of photos, i.e., music is either brought by the researcher and used to stimulate discussion in the interview ("music elicitation") or music is brought by the research participants who have chosen this to tell a certain story ("music voice"). Nicola Allett's research on Extreme Metal fans in the UK is an example of the former (Allett). By making participants listen to pieces of metal music in the context of the interview, she aimed to study how music featured in their everyday lives. While Allett's interests were not life histories or biographical experience, her research did produce insights into the feelings and memories that the music brought to the fore in the interview situation. In contrast to Allett's study, "music voice" as a method was used in a more recent study of transitions to adulthood among young people who had grown up in out-of-home-care in Denmark.[1] Inspired by the work of Sarah Wilson and Elisabeth-Jane Milne, participants were asked to bring a piece of music that was important to them to the second interview (Ravn and Østergaard). Using music in research with an interest in biographical experience rests theoretically on the argument made by Tia DeNora that music is not only a central part of our everyday lives in the present but also that "music is a medium that can be and often is simply paired or associated with aspects of past experience" (48). Music is closely linked to memory (van Dijck), and while not biographical in a chronological sense, using music as a method can in that sense be seen as a form of memory work (McLeod and Thomson). This was also the case in the Danish study, where the music brought by participants facilitated stories about growing up, (troubled) family relations, and identity formation (Ravn and Østergaard). This study, however, had its primary focus on the role that music played in the everyday lives of the participants— for instance as a "technology of the self" (DeNora 53) to help manage difficult emotions—rather than the biographical components. Hence, there is scope for innovative designs that draw on the capacities of music and link this to life histories.

## Summing Up

The aim with this brief chapter has been to suggest some alternative ways of exploring life stories through the use of creative methods in the setting of qualitative interviews. These methods are not meant to replace the conventional qualitative interview but are rather to be used in the context of such interviews. While not in any way suggesting that the traditional life history interview should be "retired", the purpose of this chapter has been to suggest ways of supplementing the life stories this produces with other stories. The research findings we get depend on the methods we use; hence, using new methods might help us produce new findings; or add nuances to the findings we get from the conventional qualitative interview. The creative methods presented in this chapter are by no means extensive, and neither are the uses of them described here. For researchers to use any such methods, there are multiple ways of moving forward and adapting these to the research questions and aims of single projects.

## Note

1. The Danish study is part of a three-country comparative research project on young people leaving care entitled "Against All Odds", comprising Norway, England, and Denmark. The music component was only used in England (PI Professor Janet Boddy, Sussex University) and Denmark. For more information about the project, see Boddy.

## Works Cited

Adriansen, Hanne K. "Timeline Interviews: A Tool for Conducting Life History Research." *Qualitative Studies*, vol. 3, no. 1, 2012, pp. 40–55.

Allett, Nicola. "Sounding Out: Using Music Elicitation in Qualitative Research." NCRM Working Paper Series 04/10. Morgan Centre, 2010. http://eprints.ncrm.ac.uk/2871/1/0410_music_elicitation.pdf.

Antonucci, Toni C. "Social Support Networks: Hierarchical Mapping Technique." *Generations*, vol. 10, no. 4, 1986, pp. 10–12.

Bagnoli, Anna. "Beyond the Standard Interview: The Use of Graphic Elicitation and Arts-Based Methods." *Qualitative Research*, vol. 9, no. 5, 2009, pp. 547–570.

Berends, Lynda. "Embracing the Visual: Using Timelines With In-Depth Interviews on Substance Use and Treatment." *Qualitative Report*, vol. 16, no. 1, 2011, pp. 1–9.

Boddy, Janet et al. "Navigating Precarious Times? The Experience of Young Adults Who Have Been in Care in Norway, Denmark and England." *Journal of Youth Studies*, Early online, 2019.

Bourdieu, Pierre. "The Biographical Illusion." *Identity: A Reader*, edited by Paul Du Gay et al. Sage, 2000 [1986], pp. 297–303.

Clark, Alison. "Multi Modal Mapmaking With Young Children: Exploring Ethnographic and Participatory Methods." *Qualitative Research*, vol. 11, no. 3, 2011, pp. 311–330.

DeNora, Tia. "Music as a Technology of the Self." *Poetics*, vol. 27, 1999, pp. 31–56.

Duff, Cameron. "On the Role of Affect and Practice in the Production of Place." *Environment and Planning D: Society and Space*, vol. 28, no. 5, 2010, pp. 881–895.

Elder, Glen H., Jr. *Children of the Great Depression: Social Change in Life Experience*. U of Chicago P, 1974.

Järvinen, Margaretha. "The Biographical Illusion: Constructing Meaning in Qualitative Interviews." *Qualitative Inquiry*, vol. 6, no. 3, 2000, pp. 370–391.

McLeod, Julie, and Rachel Thomson. *Researching Social Change*. Sage, 2009.

O'Neill, Maggie, and Phil Hubbard. "Walking, Sensing, Belonging: Ethno-Mimesis as Performative Praxis." *Visual Studies*, vol. 25, no. 1, 2010, pp. 46–58.

Pahl, Ray, and Liz Spencer. "Personal Communities: Not Simply Families of 'Fate' or 'Choice'." *Current Sociology*, vol. 52, no. 2, 2004, pp. 199–221.

Ravn, Signe, and Cameron Duff. "Putting the Party Down on Paper: A Novel Method for Mapping Youth Drug Use in Private Settings." *Health & Place*, vol. 31, 2015, pp. 124–132.

Ravn, Signe, and Jeanette Østergaard. "En anden fortælling? Musik som metode i interviews med udsatte unge [A Different Story? Music as Method in Interviews With Vulnerable Youth]." *Metoder i ungdomsforskning* [*Methods in Youth Studies*], edited by M. Pless and N. Soerensen. Aalborg UP, 2019.

Sheridan, Joanna et al. "Timelining: Visualizing Experience." *Qualitative Research*, vol. 11, no. 5, 2011, pp. 552–569.

Taylor, Stephanie. "A Place for the Future? Residence and Continuity in Women's Narratives of Their Lives." *Narrative Inquiry*, vol. 13, no. 1, 2003, pp. 193–215.

Thomsen, Rannva et al. "Tidslinjer som metodisk greb i studiet af vendepunkter i unges livsforløb" [Timelines as methodological approach in studies of critical moments in young people's life course]. *Visuelle tilgange og metoder i tværfaglige pædagogiske studier [Visual Approaches and Methods in Interdisciplinary Pedagogical Studies]*. Frederiksberg: Roskilde Universitetsforlag, 2013, pp. 283–308.

Thomson, Rachel et al. "Critical Moments: Choice, Chance and Opportunity in Young People's Narratives of Transition." *Sociology*, vol. 36, no. 2, 2002, pp. 335–354.

Travlou, Penny et al. "Place Mapping With Teenagers: Locating Their Territories and Documenting Their Experience of the Public Realm." *Children's Geographies*, vol. 6, no. 3, 2008, pp. 309–326.

van Dijck, José. "Record and Hold: Popular Music Between Personal and Collective Memory." *Critical Studies in Media Communication*, vol. 23, no. 5, 2006, pp. 357–374.

Wilson, Sarah, and Elisabeth Milne. *Young People Creating Belonging: Spaces, Sounds and Sights*. U of Stirling, 2013.

# 14 Performing and Broadcasting Lives

## Auto/Biographical Testimonies in Theatre and Radio

*Gunn Gudmundsdottir*

As testimonial and auto/biographical acts spread across an ever-wider field of media, the critic's task becomes ever more complex. It seems one needs to be an expert in many different fields—such as in new media, performance studies, social studies and history, literary and autobiographical theory, and so on—to contend with contemporary practices. But perhaps scholars of life writing, due to the transgeneric nature of their subject matter, and the interdisciplinary nature of their academic field, are in fact particularly suited to this task.

The three sites of auto/biographical acts and performances that I will briefly look at in this chapter are theatre, radio/podcasts, and the interview. These could seem like three distinct modes that might better be viewed separately, but here I would like to investigate the overlaps, interactions, and transactions between these three different modes. In order to do so I interviewed the writer/director María Reyndal (theatre/radio/television); the choreographer/director Ásrún Magnúsdóttir (theatre/dance); and radio producer Þorgerður E. Sigurðardóttir (radio/podcasts), who have all worked with documentary and/or auto/biographical material in recent years.[1] The purpose of the interviews, of looking behind the scenes, so to speak, is to see if creative practices and methods reflect the theoretical and critical methods of the scholar's work. What can we learn from radio producers and theatre practitioners by investigating their methods in testimonial, documentary, and/or auto/biographical productions? Do their practices and experiences address and reflect similar issues and concerns as those faced by the critic or theorist?[2]

There are three key issues which I will focus on here; first, form—the crucial question of how life stories are given different form in different media, and the importance of analysing those formal qualities; second, process—how the creative and the critical process must in some sense leave the individual and "real events" behind, or more to the point, allow the work/performance/broadcast to become a distinct and independent entity; and finally ethics—our responses as writers and readers to the life stories of others, not least when centred on trauma.

## Form and Process

In the radio series *Sendur í sveit* ("Sent to the farm", Icelandic National Broadcasting Service, RUV, 2016),[3] the writer and journalist Mikael Torfason travelled around the country and interviewed people at farms where he had spent his summers as a child. The series is a mixture of an audio diary, interviews, and reportage from a road trip. When Torfason was growing up, it was common practice for parents to pay farmers to take care of their children during the school holidays. Some were sent to relatives, but many were sent to strangers, and their experience has for the most part not been told or heard to any great extent in Icelandic cultural memory. Torfason was sent to the country every summer for ten years from the age of 6 to six different farms. Each episode focuses on one farm and interviews with the current inhabitants as well as Torfason's attempts to find out what those summers were like and, not least, trying to find out if and/or how the people remembered him. The editor and producer of the series was experienced radio presenter and producer Þorgerður E. Sigurðardóttir, who had previously edited documentaries in a similar vein, such as *Flóð* (Flood, RUV, 2015)—a series based on interviews with people who survived a deadly snow avalanche in the western part of Iceland in 1999 and broadcast in conjunction with a play by the same name premiered at the Reykjavik City Theatre at the same time.

Such transmedial practices are more and more common, with radio spreading through digital media, as well as life performances, and listening clubs, as Maura Edmond elucidates in her article on contemporary radio. As she explains, "following the advent of new audio delivery formats, radio has undergone another period of profound aesthetic reflection" (1568). And such series/podcasts as *Sendur í sveit* and *Flóð* are very much in that vein, also echoing the trend elsewhere, where documentary and auto/biographical material is very prominent.[4] These new forms call for different approaches; the theorist needs to identify the changes, the break from tradition, the narrative capacities of each form and media type. We also, however, need to bear in mind that many are based on older forms, such as the interview, the diary, and theatre, and the interaction between the old and the new can bring with it innovative ways of talking about the self and the past. When Torfason, for instance, mixes the audio diary and the interview, he draws attention to the differences between these forms and how, when juxtaposed in one setting, the narratives can clash and therefore generate new meaning.

The role of the producer can be crucial in those instances where different narrative forms are edited and mixed together, as the editing can have a profound effect on the narrative, as is well known in film studies. Sigurðardóttir finds that in radio documentary-making there are many overlaps and convergences with artistic practices and stylistics. Cutting and editing make it possible to play with the form and structure, using turning points, parallels, contradictions, and irony. But, of course, working with documentaries also means that the producer/editor has a responsibility not to take things out of context unless signposting that in some way, and not to alter the material to such an extent that it has become fictional. In radio, it is possible to manipulate the material in all kinds of ways, for instance by creating particular situations that then serve as the base material for the broadcast. This is what Torfason does in his series. He creates particular conditions by driving around the farms and meeting people without knowing the outcome of the encounters beforehand. In his case, it turned out that what people told him was often contrary to his expectations, and therefore ultimately changed the theme of the series; the process itself generated a different meaning, different memories, from what he expected. At the centre of his self-perception and his "story" of himself is an angry child and adolescent who had the whole world against him. The memories many of the people from the farms convey is of a happy and friendly boy, a hard worker, and great company. I believe a theoretical analysis of such works benefits greatly from making use of narratology and genre theory, and that borderline cases, transgeneric instances, transmedial works, can shed light on the formal properties of self-expression in many different media.

Torfason's focus shifts as his series become not only his childhood reminisces of a difficult and fraught period in his life, but also reflect farming conditions in Iceland in the 1980s, and the lives and tribulations of the individual farmers themselves. The outcome is therefore surprising and gives voice to many more experiences than those of Torfason and his family. The interview, in itself, thus reflects the transactional nature of auto/biographical representation, the significance of the relationship between the author and reader/listener, between practitioner and subject.

The changes to self-expression or the spreading out from its literary origins is not only tied to new media. Auto/biographical performances in the theatre have been very prominent in recent decades, as Alan Filewod asserts: "It is not too far a reach to say that life writing or life staging is one of the formative conditions of postmodern theatrical performance" (3). In the interview I conducted with María Reyndal and Ásrún Magnúsdóttir, we discussed the perils, challenges, and rewards of working with other people's lives.

María Reyndal has, in many of her works, kicked off the creative process by interviewing groups of people with particular backgrounds and life experiences, such as immigrants in Iceland (*Best í heimi*, The World's Best, 2006)[5] and victims of sexual violence in *Mannasiðir* (Common Courtesy 2017, 2018).[6] For the play *Sóley Rós ræstitæknir* (Sóley Rós, cleaner), premiered in Reykjavik 2016 by Reyndal and Sólveig Guðmundsdóttir, the story of "Sóley" and her experience of losing a child in pregnancy as told to the authors is performed on stage.[7]

The question of form proved challenging during the creative process. How will this taped interview be transformed into artistic form? Reyndal explains that it took them a very long time to find the right form; the move from interview to a performed piece is a big leap. But in that leap, it also became more removed from the individual in the interview. For *Mannasiðir*, Reyndal used an interview form for the victim's voice, staging her testimony in police questioning and her writings on social media. There the challenge was to let the documentary and the fictional work together. "Sóley" told her story in a very particular way, in a way that made her the hero of her own life; out of the traumatic experiences in her life comes triumph—individual triumph over circumstances. The creators of the play were very aware of this—they hear her story already mediated, and they have to balance "Sóley's" narrative with their own theatrical interpretation.

With works of this nature, the analysis must focus on the staging. How is the documentary material revealed? Is the interview in one way or another still present or has it been glossed over with scene settings? What are the implications for the overall interpretation of the play?

Choreographer and theatre practitioner Ásrún Magnúsdóttir has worked with teenagers and children in some of her performances.[8] In *Grrrrls* (2015), she created a dance piece with a group of 14–16-year-old girls, and in *Hlustunarpartý* (Listening Party, 2017), she works with a group of teenagers of both sexes. Both pieces were premiered at the dance festival *Everybody's Spectacular* in Reykjavik. The performers are not professional dancers, and some have very little dance training, but they are asked to bring their own stories, their own narratives, into the performance through dance and music. They use their own names, and thus are not playing characters in the usual sense but rather are presenting a version of their self, their identity.

Magnúsdóttir agrees with Reyndal that the most challenging task is finding form. In her work, the focus is on the group rather than the individual, and the form is found during the creative process with the group's participation. Nothing is decided beforehand; she has at most a theme, and she has to find a way for the members of the group to discover the way forward. For her, the process is often more rewarding and more interesting and thought-provoking than the final outcome. They are not narrative pieces, but narratives are nevertheless born out of the teenagers' performances.

The theorist's work is also a process that brings its own set of challenges and rewards. We all know the importance of rereading the material—or re-listening, as now made possible with podcasts, and how that changes our perception and therefore our analysis of a work. Our theoretical stance must also regularly be revisited and rethought, which makes our analysis and interpretations richer and more nuanced. And a central part of the process, and not least valuable in working with transgeneric or transmedial material, is disentangling the various discourses and traditions at play in the works to deepen our understanding of them.

## Ethics

Reyndal tells me that the woman the character Sóley is based on had a very strong voice of her own and had already given form and meaning to her story. According to Reyndal, she was an impressive story-teller, so they were in fact "given a story" they could use as they pleased. She is herself far removed from the cultural elite as a cleaner in a small town in the north of Iceland. What Reyndal and her co-creators had to ask themselves was: could they take this voice, this story, this testimony, and produce a performance, a play, a work performed in public? So, the ethical questions were immediately raised and became a particularly thorny issue when it concerned the stories of other people implicated in Sóley's story. She has given her permission, but they have not. The theorist's role is not necessarily to ask the same questions as the work's creators, but an awareness of the documentary nature of works calls for another type of listening, not least in trauma narratives.

Sigurðardóttir explains that in making radio documentaries it is vital that everyone whose voice is heard in the program is aware that the material will be broadcast publicly. She notes that there are exceptions, as in investigative journalism, but for the type of series she works on, consent is vital. In the series *Flóð*, where the interviews were originally recorded during the actors' preparation for the play, but not for the radio, everyone had to be contacted after the fact and asked for permission. Consent, an agreement that their voices, experiences, stories can be used, is an ethical concern, which highlights the fact that "using" other people's lives is a sensitive issue. Not least when the stories recount a trauma, as in *Flóð*, based on events where many lives were lost. Witnessing another's testimony always carries with it a responsibility; it has a particular status as a narrative, which fiction and life writing have of course long grappled with.[9] It is that responsibility Sigurðardóttir describes, which scholars of autobiographical representations must also constantly be aware of and negotiate.

Both Reyndal and Magnúsdóttir have given voices to groups that are not necessarily often heard. Reyndal, for instance, has given a platform to immigrants in Iceland, where they could be heard with their different accents and experiences; and Magnúsdóttir has included young people in her performances who are usually on the margins of society. This platforming of marginal voices is reminiscent of feminist practices in performance; as Jenn Stephenson describes, the "consciousness-raising project of feminism, of bringing the quotidian into view through autobiographical acts, is simply to create visibility and awareness, to say, 'I exist. This is my life'". And this can be said as well of groups represented in the performances mentioned here. She goes on to explain:

> However, the public telling of self-stories quickly moves beyond mere description or demonstration to take on a profoundly performative quality. Autobiographical performance provides [. . .] a vehicle for the creation of identity, a way to speak oneself into being. The act of performance itself becomes a strategy to grant self-possessive agency to the performing subject thereby avert objectification and marginalization.
>
> (10)

When asked if the participants would experience their participation in the performances as a therapeutic process, with Magnúsdóttir as the therapist, she explains that she consciously rejected that role. It is something that they might discover for themselves, but this is first and foremost a creative practice rather than a therapeutic one, although having them on stage, having them develop their performance, and asking them to give their voices and bodies to it, gives them agency and power, which teenage girls do not necessarily have. And both are aware, and wary, of the possibility (or perhaps the inevitability) of influencing the lives of others through creative practice.

The question of agency and authorship is one that the theorist has to pay attention to, and here feminist theories are of great value, not least in identifying the line between giving agency and exploitation. It brings us back to form; over-dramatisation, melodramatic performances, and sensationalistic staging are all possible pitfalls when telling a traumatic past. But at the same time—and this is the crux of the contradiction life writing theorists are faced with—we have to move away from the individual or particular subject and remind ourselves that what we are analysing is not an unmediated reality but a representation, a mediation, and a remediation of a self, of a past.

One of the central conclusions, I believe, is that one cannot underestimate the importance of form, nor the importance of the process that led to the final broadcast/performance/play. It is essential to pay attention to it, and to remind us of the move from "experience", from "life", from the past, from events, to testimony, to interview, to writing, to stage, to radio, to podcast and, with the ethical questions raised here in mind, to analyse and investigate the form we give to life stories and how the qualities of each medium influence that form and the reception of those stories.

## Notes

1. The interview with Reyndal and Magnúsdóttir was conducted in Reykjavik on 11 June 2018. The interview with Sigurðardóttir was done by email in August 2018.
2. The interview in itself is an interesting auto/biographical practice as is made clear in the latest issue of *Biography* (2018)—and will therefore also deserve

our consideration here. As the editors, Anneleen Mascchelein and Rebecca Roach, state in the introduction to the journal: "Highlighting difficult questions around the status of authorship, collaborative practice, reading strategies, aesthetic production, and the function of institutions, networks, and disciplinary boundaries, examining interviews compels us to face issues that are central to contemporary research and have only become more urgent in the digital moment" (169).

3. The six-part series was broadcast weekly from 20 August–21 September 2016 and was made available as a podcast.
4. Popular NPR podcasts such as *This American Life* are examples of this.
5. Premiered in Reykjavik in 2006, written by Hávar Sigurjónsson, María Reyndal, and the cast. Performed as a radio play in 2013.
6. Premiered on radio in 2017, then turned into a two-part television series for Icelandic National Broadcasting Service, RUV, and broadcast in April 2018.
7. A trailer for the play is available on Vimeo: https://vimeo.com/282946534.
8. Further information about Ásrún Magnúsdóttir's work can be found on www.asrunmagnusdottir.com/.
9. For a further discussion on the role of the listener/reader in trauma testimony, see for instance Cathy Caruth. *Unclaimed Experience: Trauma, Narrative, and History*. Johns Hopkins UP, 1995; and Aleida Assmann. "History, Memory and the Genre of Testimony." *Poetics Today*, vol. 27, no. 2, Summer 2006, pp. 261–273.

## Works Cited

Edmond, Maura. "All Platforms Considered: Contemporary Radio and Transmedia Engagement." *New Media & Society*, vol. 17, no. 9, 2015, pp. 1566–1582.

Filewod, Alan. "'The Experience Being My Own': Identifying Life Writing in Plays by Canadian Veterans of the Great War." *Biography*, vol. 41, no. 1, Winter 2018, pp. 71–90.

Masschelein, Anneleen, and Rebecca Roach. "Putting Things Together: To Interviewing as Creative Practice." *Biography*, vol. 41, no. 2, Spring 2018, pp. 169–178.

Stephenson, Jenn. *Performing Autobiography: Contemporary Canadian Drama*. U of Toronto P, 2013.

Torfason, Mikael, and Þorgerður E. Sigurðardóttir. *Sendur í sveit*. Icelandic National Broadcasting Service, RUV, 2016. http://podcast.ruv.is/sendur_i_sveit/podcast.xml.

# 15 Big Data and Self-Tracking
## Research Trajectories

*Julie Rak*

Big data poses a big problem for life writing research methods and methodology. The field of life writing has developed a sophisticated set of problematics in the last forty years, articulating positions about ethics, identity, memory, truth claims, and genre, to name just a few. But the methods used to study problematics at the present time mostly come from literary studies, critical theory, history, and (more rarely) the study of rhetoric. As Laurie McNeill explains, when she teaches life writing texts to students, "we analyze the texts for the choices writers make about how to represent experience: we are not studying experience itself—and that's a disciplinary difference" (McNeill np). What makes this a different kind of analysis from literary criticism is that life writing has adapted its own set of interpretative frames—but not research methods—more suited to its non-fictional objects of study. Sidonie Smith and Julia Watson highlight this tendency when they argue that "the analytical frames and theoretical positions of scholarship on life writing can provide helpful concepts and categories for thinking about the proliferation of online lives" (71). Smith and Watson are not making a case that the study of digital media should involve using a life writing method. Rather, life writing problematics and theory—which come from humanist approaches to the study of representation—have something to offer the study of digital life.

There is no doubt that life writing scholarship as it exists, including Smith and Watson's provision of an analytical toolkit, has much to offer other fields approaching the study of online life. But the study of big data poses special problems that most life writing methods cannot yet address. In *We Are Data*, John Cheney-Lippold forcefully makes the point that no matter what we might think about our agency and autonomy in the offline world, when we enter the online world, a few swipes of a finger or clicks of a mouse provide multinational companies with reams of data about our habits, our desires, where we live, and what we purchase. Those same companies do what they can to get us to provide more data about ourselves, all the time, whether we know it or not. Through algorithms, those companies create predictive pictures of digital users that may or may not accurately map onto the offline lives those users lead. In other words, "online you are not who you think you are" (Cheney-Lippold 6). And, in the latest appearance of Baudrillard's simulacrum, the pictures of ourselves that algorithms paint can replace other versions of ourselves. The way statistical analysis parses behaviour according to sets of rules has the potential to act epistemically, creating "algorithmic identities" that may or may not map onto other parts of our lives (Cheney-Lippold 14). Online, we "become" our data as we interact with websites, social media networks, and more, and that determines how—increasingly—systems outside our knowledge or control decide to treat us. Online, "we are temporary members of different emergent categories" such as high-risk, low-income, or even terrorist (Cheney-Lippold 12) because of what algorithms decide a statistical analysis of our online behaviour means. The work of big data is the work of bio-power, the name Michel Foucault gave to "an explosion of numerous and diverse techniques for achieving the subjugations of bodies and the control of populations", beginning in mediaeval times in Europe as way to control the spread of the Plague, then continuing on a larger scale during the eighteenth century with the advent of statistical data collection and analysis, among other methods, to elicit assent from the populace (Foucault 140–141). In the contemporary world, widespread use of the internet as a way to gather statistical evidence furthers the purpose of biopower, particularly when algorithmic analysis is used by corporations or nation-states.

What does all this have to do with the study of life writing? Throughout its history, the field of life writing has taken the idea of the individual life as its subject, examining how lives are constructed, shaped, and received in autobiographies and biographies as well as a host of other forms. Most of that scholarship accepts that individuals have forms of autonomy and either create or record—or, others do that work with or for them—the story of their lives on paper or on a screen. We can study these individual "lives" in detail, asking questions about the connections between representation and experience through an appeal to specific types of evidence. Although there are now post-humanist approaches in life writing studies and sociological and anthropological approaches to life writing are beginning to make their way into the field, assumptions within humanism about the nature of subjectivity and what it means to be an individual continue to inform life writing scholarship. Big data, however, does not work with detail of this kind or with this kind of subtlety. Big data, in the words of danah boyd and Kate Crawford, is the following:

> A cultural, technological and scholarly phenomenon that rests on the interplay of:
>
> (1) Technology: maximizing computation power and algorithmic accuracy to gather, analyze, link, and compare large data sets.
> (2) Analysis: drawing on large data sets to identify patterns in order to make economic, social, technical, and legal claims.

(3) Mythology: the widespread belief that large data sets offer a higher form of intelligence and knowledge that can generate insights that were previously impossible, with the aura of truth, objectivity, and accuracy.

(663)

The elements of technology and machine analysis for patterns lay the groundwork for the belief, held by practitioners of big data methods and analysis, that bigger is better: the larger the dataset, the more possible it becomes to "know" with accuracy who people are, where they are, and what they want.

The precepts of big data are part of what boyd and Crawford call "the computational turn", where what constitutes knowledge is re-framed entirely as the product of machine collection and even machine analysis, and that analysis is assumed to be correct simply because there are so many elements in the dataset (665–666). Obviously, the elements of a mathematical model may leave out important questions or, as Cheney-Lippold points out, lead to wildly incorrect assumptions about identity, with sometimes humorous and sometimes frightening results (55–56). The methods of life writing scholarship at the present time would seem to be opposed to the methods of big data. And yet, the object of big data collection and analysis, human lives and online identities, is becoming increasingly important to the work of life writing scholarship. But the methods of life writing study have not yet been matched to this object of study.

They need to be, because life writing scholarship is poised—as Smith and Watson point out—to address the ethical dimension of big data. Who is big data for, who is it about, and most importantly, how is the quantification of identity by machines affecting us all? What is a life and what counts as life within and despite data? Is data evidence of experience? How can we address ethical problems with the ownership of personal data, in an age of surveillance and online social life? Such problems with the assumptions of big data, boyd and Crawford say, need to be posed by humanists because mathematical models themselves are not innately ethical (670–671). But how to pose them in the wake of the computational turn, in terms of the methods we should use? The methods of literary studies may not work for thinking about lives in the wake of big data. Franco Moretti's endorsement of "distant reading" as a way to see the big picture because a machine can "read" the details for us might be one way to respond (Moretti 1). Lisa Gitelman has suggested that studying the historical media and its inventors is also a way to bring data, which she sees as the flow of information, down to size and to resist the tendency to think that media has no history (10–11).

Another response could be to historicise the operations of big data. Biopower is a historical phenomenon, as Foucault has pointed out. It is only the speed and scope of collecting data and classifying it with machines that is new, not the impulse to do so, particularly when we think about how collective biography developed in the English-speaking world a century ago. The idea of amassing many exemplary lives as examples to inspire readers was central to the enterprise of Victorian-era collective biography in Britain and the United States. Alison Booth has discussed in detail the complexities of understanding this type of "big data" collection, since it involves collecting hundreds of accounts and interpreting them (Booth 3–4). Laura Marcus has read national biographical collections of the nineteenth and early twentieth centuries as evidence of cultural history of the self connected to developments in psychoanalysis and an interest its editors and readers had in the idea of individual genius (59).

Yet another way for life writing scholars to study big data is to think about the work of data input, particularly via the practice of biodata collection and self-tracking. Such approaches can move research away from the grand scale of big data in order to bring into view the complexity of individual users and specific communities, in order to address ethical questions about data and its uses. Olivia Banner, for example, has used a case-study approach about online patient networking sites to show how data works on and works through the construction of a specific patient subjectivity that she identifies as "biosociality" within an informatics discourse created by drug companies (199–200). I looked at ancestry.com as a case study about big data, because ancestry.com is engaged in an effort to collect all of the world's personal and genetic data and monetise it (Rak 493–495).

In *Self-Tracking*, Gina Neff and Dawn Nafus make a case for understanding self-tracking of data about one's health or habits—often done with the help of a smartphone or computer—as a dynamic practice that can show "how data can be useful, powerful, tedious, pleasurable, underwhelming, wrong, or just beside the point in a variety of everyday contexts" (2). For Neff and Nafus, self-tracking is a practice that can be quotidian, but it also can be managed and monetised by corporations or nation-state apparatuses. For them, examining the motivations and beliefs of self-trackers is key to understanding whether subjects have agency or not as they track. They also point out what scholars of life writing already know: self-tracking is not a new phenomenon, because it is related to the maintenance of European identity during the advent of industrialisation and modernisation, and its roots run older and deeper than the advent of modernity (15–18). Diary writing—a type of self-tracking—came about because older practices of letter writing and religious confession became connected to the invention of new technologies that facilitated the management of time and money, such as the railway table and the account book (Lejeune 51–53; Nussbaum 131). Benjamin Franklin was another self-tracker who reproduced his thirteen Virtues table as part of "the bold and arduous project of achieving moral perfection" in his autobiography as a way to show others the advantages of monitoring their behaviour through the collection of personal data (Franklin np).

Taking a cue from Benjamin Franklin, and from Philippe Lejeune, who researched diary writing by analysing his own diary-keeping practice (79–88) and even revisiting his old diaries and copying them (234–326), methods for studying data collection and self-tracking could start with life writing researchers themselves, with examples from the past, or with case studies in the present. There may be life writing scholars interested in using the methods of distant reading and data modelling from the digital humanities to critique the presence of the liberal subject, and get at what the proponents of big data are up to. Whatever the methods, there do need to be new ones developed and used that are suited to the unwieldy object of big data. Looking to other kinds of methods than those most suited to certain kinds of print texts, and changing our methodology to include ourselves and case studies in our research, could help life writing scholars interested in this area to understand the power, possibilities, and problems of big data, bringing it down to size to see how it is structuring our lives, online and offline.

## Acknowledgements

Thanks to Anna Poletti for helping me to frame the argument of this chapter, and for pointing me to the fierce work of John Cheney-Lippold. Thanks to Danielle Fuller for helping me to articulate the central questions posed here.

## Works Cited

Banner, Olivia. "'Treat Us Right!' Digital Publics, Emerging Biosocialities, and the Female Complaint." *Identity Technologies: Constructing the Self Online*, edited by Anna Poletti and Julie Rak. U of Wisconsin P, pp. 198–216.

Booth, Alison. *How to Make It as a Woman: Collective Biographical History from Victoria to the Present.* U. of Chicago P., 2004.

boyd, danah, and Kate Crawford. "Critical Questions for Big Data." *Information, Communication & Society*, vol. 15, no. 5, 2012, pp. 662–679. Web. 11 Aug. 2018. doi:10.1080/1369118X.2012.678878.

Cheney-Lippold, John. *We Are Data: Algorithms and the Making of Our Digital Selves.* New York UP, 2017.

Foucault, Michel. *The History of Sexuality: Volume 1 an Introduction.* Translated by Robert Hurley. Pantheon Books, 1978.

Franklin, Benjamin. *The Autobiography of Benjamin Franklin.* Edited by Frank Woodworth Pine. Henry Holt & Co., 1922. ebooks Adelaide. Accessed 11 Aug. 2018.

Gitelman, Lisa. *Always Already New: Media, History, and the Data of Culture.* MIT P, 2006.

Lejeune, Philippe. *On Diary*. Edited by Jeremy D. Popkin and Julie Rak. Translated by Katherine Durnin. U of Hawaii P, 2009.

Marcus, Laura. *Auto/Biographical Discourses: Theory, Criticism, Practice*. Manchester UP, 1994.

McNeill, Laurie. "Conceptual Impasses: Strategies for Supporting Students in Life Narrative Courses." *European Journal of Life Writing*, vol. 7, 2018, pp. TL3–TL10. Accessed 11 Aug. 2018.

Moretti, Franco. "Conjectures on World Literature." *New Left Review*, vol. 1, Jan.–Feb. 2000. Accessed 11 Aug. 2018.

Neff, Gina, and Dawn Nafus. *Self-Tracking*. MIT P, 2016.

Nussbaum, Felicity A. "Towards Conceptualizing Diary." *Studies in Autobiography*, edited by James Olney. Oxford UP, pp. 128–140.

Rak, Julie. "Radical Connections: Genealogy, Small Lives, Big Data." *a/b: Auto/Biography Studies*, vol. 32, no. 3, 2017, pp. 479–497.

Smith, Sidonie, and Julia Watson. "Virtually Me: A Toolbox About Online Self-Presentation." *Identity Technologies: Constructing the Self Online*, edited by Anna Poletti and Julie Rak. U of Wisconsin P, pp. 70–98.

# Frameworks

# 16 Another Story

*Jeanine Leane*

This chapter shares some of my experience of writing voices, spaces, silences, and collective memories. And of listening to the hush of women who raised their children on stories and secrets. How can such anecdotes, which are orally encrypted over generations, be contained on a page and told by the written word?

I am Wiradjuri. I was born in the middle of the fresh water cradle of south-eastern Australia. I grew up on Country as one of three generations of Aboriginal women—parts of whose histories of place and times were the foundation of and inspiration for my writing. My Nanna was born in 1887, the eldest of the two Aunties in 1909, the other in 1923, and my Mother in 1937.

*Purple Threads*[1] (a short story cycle) tells why and how my Nanna, two unmarried Aunts, my Mother and my sister and I were living on a small piece of Wiradjuri Country—our Country. And why my Grandmother came to marry my grandfather; and why my Aunties remained unmarried and cared for animals and other people's children; and why my Mother had no patience with me as a child; and how I was told the histories of the Wiradjuri matriarchs who raised me. *Dark Secrets*[2] (a poetry cycle) is based on my Nanna's story as bits and pieces of her early life were told to me as a child and young adult; it also represents incidents retold to me from my Grandmother's memory of her Mother, my great Grandmother.

It is not my intention here to write about my poetry or prose or offer any textual analysis. I want to reflect on the process of writing that weaves together some of the threads of an intergenerational story through a series of micro-stories that revolve around significant people, places, times, and events.

Both works are grounded in a sense of place—the upper Murrumbidgee River as it bends through rocky slopes and ridges at Gundagai, before swinging further inland, leaving the hill country and heading west through Wagga Wagga, then Narrandera, across the flatlands where water cuts though clay and red gum to the Hay plains, then Balranald before joining the Murray—Mother of the inland river system. And the people—my Nanna, my Aunties, my Mother, my sister, and myself.

But the story of this writing, like the stories it is based on, begins in the middle. I am not working with diaries, letters, journals, certificates, media, or reports—when I did decide to write, I was writing of voices and from voices. I was writing from story. It takes a long time to learn a whole story. There are parts I still don't know.

It was September 2003. And I wasn't there when Aunty Boo passed. I was in Kambera where I had spent the last twenty years of my life with my partner raising our family and working. In early spring, Kambera is a swirl of pollen and petals. Daffodils, tulips, hyacinths, crocus, and freesias amass in splotches of yellow, red, blue, pink, purple, and orange across the fenceless front gardens.

She grew flowers—beds and beds of all sorts of bulbs and shrubs—both native and introduced, alongside herbs and vegetables. My sister and I played jungle games in her garden while she worked. She liked to feel the dirt, she said. She often worked barefoot and loved nothing better than the heat of high summer in the western Riverina, working in the sun. I didn't know it then, like many things that were told to me bit by bit and I didn't get the full picture until I was older; but the garden wasn't just pretty; it was, like many other things the women in my life did that seemed so benign at first glance, an act of rebellion; and a space for women to talk.

My Grandfather, descendant of English protestants from Devonshire, died in 1967 on his 90th birthday—the same year I turned 6 and the year before I faced the western classroom. I grew up at the end of the reign of my grandfather, who like many other white men conducted their own personal eugenics/assimilation practices in the colonies.[3]

I have a clear picture in my mind of what he looked like in his dotage, but I was not subjected to his abusive strictness. It was the hush of him that I remember most. The Aunties and Nanna never spoke around him, save to acknowledge his bidding or answer a question. Not just because he was old—because they never had. Everything public about the house that I grew up in—the pictures on display from England, the family bible recording the births of twelve live children—eight daughters, much to his disappointment, the youngest of whom was my Mother; and four sons in whom he took some hope and was intent on raising white; the log-books recording livestock purchases, mainly of dairy cattle that his daughters tended and milked for no wages. Everything in the house told his story.

But the story I saw, hanging on the walls, or sitting on the mantelpieces or recorded in his log-books and journals, was not the one I heard. What appeared on the surface told nothing of the story underneath—appearance was not reality. I grew up from a very young age conscious of two stories—the public and the private—the spoken and the whispered—the outside stories and the home stories.

My sister and I were the lighter skinned children of a single Mother. While the reign of terror within the house had subsided, the one outside was still raging. We were born the middle of the assimilation policy, and the threat of authorities loomed ever present in our lives. I learnt quickly that maintaining external appearances was crucial to our survival—or more specifically was essential to our extended family staying together.

As children, we were regularly lectured about what "the welfare" will do if they think we are being neglected or "behaving badly". Every day, we were scrubbed from head to toe, our fingernails cleaned, hair pulled back, shoes shone and uniforms pressed before we went to school. At the suggestion of an older Aunty in the area, my Mother sent us to a catholic school run by Irish nuns. Beyond school, my Nanna and Aunties did their best to keep us out of the public eye.

I fell asleep night after night to the sound of my Aunties yarning. I love voices, and listening. They were both night-owls and while ever I was content to listen, curled up beside my sister on makeshift bed of arm-chairs in the kitchen, they talked on into the night, long after I lost the battle with sleep. When I asked them why they stayed up so late, they said they liked to yarn in peace; and listen to ghosts and things you only hear when it's quiet—and still.

We lived just out of town, on the road to Gundagai, on a few acres that were the remnants of the once larger dairy farm of my grandfather. In winter 1969, Nanna slipped and broke her arm on a grassy slope while she was collecting firewood by the creek. The Aunties became concerned after that about her wandering about on her own as she had done all her life. They invested in a second-hand television to keep her occupied and indoors, especially during the winter months.

I was the one assigned the task of sitting with or "minding", as the Aunties said, Nanna after school from then on, almost every day until I was 15, while the Aunties did their chores and cooked. The TV played as a backdrop, catching her attention only every now and again. Mostly, she talked about people long gone and times past—Cobb & Co-coaches, bushrangers; the sad story of brave Captain Moonlite; and of the last women hanged in Goulburn jail—a story passed down from her own Mother of the condemned making the hangman wait until she fed her baby before she mounted the gallows.

As time passed through years of long and once wet winters, the talk shifted from the world outside to family; her life as a child and young woman, and *some* early stories of her own Mother. Some of her stories chilled me to the core despite the raging fire. She talked in hushed tones, then, as she stared at the flames. Sometimes she spoke so softly, I had to lean in from the wood-box where I sat to hear her.

My Grandmother passed in 1980 at home, surrounded by all of her eight daughters, my sister, and me. That same year I finished school and left home to go to university. I was away for most of the eighties, visiting the Aunties only over university and work holidays.

It was in the 1990s when I had my own children that I began to come home again. Aunty Betty, the younger of my two Aunts, had begun to put together photo albums—mainly of my sister and I as children and our many cousins that she'd taken on an old box-brownie—and to compile scraps books of snippets from newspapers she'd collected over the years. They were mainly births, deaths, and marriages of family members: a picture of me graduating from university; a large family gathering to celebrate Nanna's 90th birthday. Other clippings related to significant events in the area—times when the Murrumbidgee rose and swallowed the town; long dry spells and heat waves; large celebrations, like the settler centenary of Gundagai; and the tragedies—the farm and road accidents, and the triple murder suicide that sent tremors through the whole community.

When Aunty Boo passed away in 2003, the loss and the emptiness was overwhelming and overpowering. I went home to mourn her and, with my sister, to oversee her final wishes for her passing. She was laid to rest without ceremony, with just a few words of goodbye said by family in an unmarked plot in a local cemetery—no tombstone erected by request. She wanted to return to the earth and leave no material sign to mark the ground. She left no visual sign to commemorate her 93 years. Just stories, memories—and the sound of her voice in my head.

When Aunty Boo passed, Aunty Betty's sense of urgency for me to pass on the stories of our place and our people was all consuming. The years between 2003 and 2009 were some of the busiest of my life. I had three children in school, I worked full-time, and I completed a PhD in Australian literature.

While I'd kept journals and diaries from an early age, as Aunty Betty encouraged me to, I'd never written any of the stories I'd heard growing up—they were stored in my head in the circular and entangled way that I heard them, the same way the Aunties and Nanna had committed our stories to memory.

I tried writing the stories of the women in the years following Aunty Boo's passing, in between visits to Aunty Betty. She was eager to talk; to walk me back over stories I'd heard; explain the significance of unlabelled photos and uncaptioned clippings in the newspapers, albums, and scrapbooks; and remind me that some stories are unfinished. She recalled, during those last visits, of something I'd said after a particularly harrowing day at school. It was about writing another story—one that wasn't in my school books.

Aunty Betty passed early in 2009. She was cremated as requested and her ashes scattered on a hill summit she loved. She left nothing to mark the ground. Like my older Aunty and my Nanna, she left only stories and memories.

Beyond the grief and the emptiness, I felt the responsibility to write the other story. I struggled with the way the stories I heard might look on the page under the clumsy convention of words. Western genres crowded my head and froze me out—non-fiction, life writing, autobiography, biography—but the women's story could not be contained within any of these. For me such genres did not address questions of the responsibility I felt, in trying to represent the women respectfully. How could I write the silences? The snippets and gatherings of stories spanning three generations? Nanna's secrets? The individualism of the genres could never tell the stories of the collective memory that I wanted to write. I abandoned several attempts to write our story chronologically and in a way that a conventional piece of life writing might look like. I was paralysed.

But that "other" story haunted me. The voices of the women pulled at me from the inside like an understory struggling to rise. I thought of Nanna's stories about the Murrumbidgee—the deep undertow that tugs at the surface.

It was not until I came across Alexis Wright's seminal essay "The Politics of Writing"[4] on the power of fiction that the paralysis lifted. Her words resonated:

> fiction penetrates more than the surface layers and probes deep into the inner workings of reality . . . fiction would allow me to create some kind of testament, not the actual truth, but a good portrayal of truth which I see.
>
> (13)

With this in mind, I thought about the fragments and arcs of the women's lives I had stored in my head—the micro-histories that needed to surface and the power of poetry and short prose or episodic story to reflect this. I thought of the circular and entangled way that I first heard the stories; and the way I heard bits and pieces of the same story from different family members at different times. The circularity, interweave, incompleteness, and the movements of the stories were integral to the telling. I thought, too, how my imagination had been informed by the lives and memories of the women before me; and how I could use my informed imagination to write parts of the story that I didn't know. Or, in the case of my Nanna's story, told through poetry in *Dark Secrets*, that it was all right to leave some gaps untold and some incidents as unresolved, as is the reality of my family history.

I was fortunate due to life circumstance to become the medium for these stories, which are a testament to the resilience of Aboriginal women, and in acknowledging this it was very important for me to remain the de-centred character that I was as a child hearing the stories. Retrospectively, it was easy for me to look back and read the agency of the women in many of the things they did; to read the black feminism in their fierce independence and firm belief that women were the future. With hindsight, it is clear to me that I was being groomed to "go out into the world" and bring the master's tools back to the houses of women and use them to build a safer, more solid dwelling of our own. But I didn't see it at the time and so, to be faithful to the story, it was important to write it as I heard it, not as I later interpreted it—to write the voices as I heard them at the time and in the contexts in which I remembered them.

I had to put the present out of my head and let the voices come. I thought about my Aunties' late-night conversations—the way they yarned long into the night and let the conversations taper from hushed whispers to silence. I recalled my Nanna's stories by the fire. As their words rose up in me, so too did their faces, gestures, and expressions. I left the silences to speak for themselves and unfinished business as unresolved when I wrote it as it was when I heard it.

When I started writing down the gatherings of Nanna's story, I realised that it looked like poetry—fragmented and broken, yet vivid and tactile and layered with deeper meanings and secrets. I also realised that poetry centred the protagonist—Nanna, not the narrator/writer—me. *Dark Secrets* was Nanna's story alone and as such was only fitting that the sequence of poems that emerged centred her experience and, as much as possible, her voice and memory, channelling through me.

When it came to writing the voices of all three women, though, the nature of the story changed. Such a story had to focus on dialogue, conversation, and episodes and the cyclic rhythm of storytelling where different arcs of the same story are told by different people at different times; or, where stories started by one person are taken up and continued by another. *Purple Threads* is a series of arcs rather than a single thread—it is a short story cycle where each story is both complete and incomplete at the same time and can either stand alone as an arc, or be read as a smaller part of a bigger cycle.

To finish on, I'd like to reflect on the role of the "informed imagination"—my term to explain a technique I used in writing where I knew some stories, I understood the role of secrets as an adult; and, most importantly, I knew the people I was seeking to represent. And as a way of reflecting back on the threads that wove my life; and the secrets; and the stories that are woven through the body into the soul, stored in the memory-baskets of the mind to become intergenerational history. And, first and foremost, as a testimony and tribute to the continuing role of women as gatherers of all things that sustain the life of a clan—the physical and emotional substance food and stories to nurture and nourish future generations.

## Notes

1. Leane, *Purple Threads*.
2. Leane, *Dark Secrets After Dreaming: AD 1887–1961*.

3. Kim Scott's 1999 novel *Benang: From the Heart*, set in Western Australia in the aftermath of A.O. Neville's "breed out" eugenics, depicts an extreme example of this among settler men and Aboriginal women and its legacy of intergenerational trauma for future generations.
4. Wright 10–20.

## Works Cited

Leane, Jeanine. *Dark Secrets After Dreaming: AD 1887–1961*. Berri: Presspress, 2010.

——. *Purple Threads*. St Lucia: U of Queensland P, 2011.

Wright, Alexis. "The Politics of Writing." *Southerly*, vol. 62, no. 2, 2002, pp. 10–20.

# 17 Reading Digital Lives Generously

## Laurie McNeill and John David Zuern

In 2015, we joined forces to co-edit *Online Lives 2.0*, a special issue of the journal *Biography*. Coming twelve years after the journal's original *Online Lives*, a collection John had edited and in which Laurie had published an article, our "2.0" issue sought to survey the critical and cultural terrain of digital life texts, terrain that had changed considerably since the earlier project. In designing and distributing our call for proposals, we made a concerted effort to invite scholars working with these texts, practices, and platforms from a wide range of disciplinary positions and linguistic, geographical, and cultural interests. How were scholars from outside as well as inside auto/biography studies thinking about the now-ingrained practices of representing our own and others' lives online? How were they approaching these questions, using what methods? What could we in the field learn from others about how to tackle the challenges—such as scale, scope, privacy, and ephemerality—that the study of digital lives presents? What could we offer other fields in analysing how individuals, groups, and indeed networks were using digital media to make meaning of lived experience?

Like many ideals, our hopes of bridging the disciplinary and other divides in the study of digital life were largely unrealised: though we received many friendly and supportive rejections from those we invited, clearly few scholars saw their research agendas reflected in the description of *Online Lives 2.0* and what it wanted to consider. But our issue did reflect the efforts of those in (or at least nearer to) auto/biography studies to think about what we in this field are doing when we study "online lives" and how we go about it. For example, Julie Rak's groundbreaking analysis of *The Sims 3* challenged the default reading of digital representations through a narrative framework, Gillian Whitlock analysed asylum-seekers' cell phone documentaries, and Patricia Lange reflected on her ethnographic study of young YouTube producers. These projects engage the amateur and often ephemeral auto/biographical acts that characterise so many of the digital texts we now seek to understand. The work of that special issue, and the considerable scholarly output in the field since that time, have underscored for us what auto/biography studies, with its enduring emphasis on the mediation of lived experience, can bring to other disciplines' efforts to understand how digital media are reshaping subjectivity, social relations, and political processes. In this chapter, we draw on our own experiences as researchers and editors to outline some of the methodological approaches we can use to pursue the interests of our field while addressing some of the most compelling research challenges in the study of digital lives. We also reflect on aspects that in their relative newness and complexity continue to ask us to think in different ways about how and why we study these materials.

## Generous Reading

In our own research, we have adopted and adapted methods from our own discipline and others appropriate to the subjects of our research. In particular, we identify "generous reading" as a shared praxis, one that has the potential flexibility, rigour, and curiosity to analyse digital life texts and to foster critical openings rather than foreclosures. Generous reading straddles our professional responsibilities as critics and teachers; we take inspiration from Mimi Ito's call to augment "a research agenda that is about describing and critiquing" with "an educational agenda that is about supporting productive forms of engagement and literacy" (Jenkins et al. 99). In composition studies, Tiane Donahue has described generous reading as a pedagogical practice that takes student writing "as legitimate text, with the assumption that it does make sense, carries its own internal logic, is justifiably studied as any other text, literary or expository" (323). Within the context of auto/biography studies, generous reading similarly rejects the hierarchies of literariness inherent in traditional models of close reading but retains its attention to the choices creators make in representing their experiences, and it brings from cultural studies, rhetoric, and genre theories a commitment to take seriously "ordinary" texts composed by "amateur" people as well as professionals, instances of digital "everyday autobiography", just as feminist and post/colonial scholars argued in the case of life narratives in print.

This practice extends from our disciplinary training in literary and comparative studies: both of us started our careers as readers of words on paper. In the early 2000s, as we each began to work with born-digital texts, we brought the methodologies of qualitative literary studies to bear on those emerging forms, yet each of us had to develop new critical "reading" practices that could account for the role of computation in the production of meaning. Laurie's research on digital lives grew out of a genre study of diaries, which led her to examine the blog as extending the diary in response to the new rhetorical situation of the internet. A framework based in rhetorical genre studies guided her questions about how form, audience, and occasion are embedded in historical, social, and technological contexts of production that inevitably shape our representations of ourselves and others. In his work on electronic literature, John has argued for a comparative approach that acknowledges continuities between digital literary texts and their counterparts in other media, such as print and drama, so as to better appreciate how our aesthetic and moral experiences of literary artefacts are conditioned by the material affordances and constraints of the media through which we encounter them.

Our subsequent engagement with scholarship on self-representation in digital forms, both as writers and as editors, has shown us that the choice of a particular methodological framework not only dictates the questions researchers ask about digital lives but can also limit their perception of what counts as a digital life in the first place; as Johanna Drucker notes, "what is considered meaningful will vary depending on the model of research" (629). Even as we affirm the benefit of our familiar qualitative practices, we recognise that our grounding in textual analysis and genre theories might predispose us to ask comparative questions about digital auto/biographical production—how is a blog like a diary (McNeill "Teaching")? How is Instagram like a memoir (Cardell et al.)?—and that such questions could hamstring as well as facilitate our critical projects.

That recognition means that, even as generous readers, we must be alert to potential misreadings—or even outright failures to read—that qualitative literary analysis can bring about. We concur with Julie Rak and Anna Poletti's assertion in their introduction to *Identity Technologies* that auto/biography studies can produce more expansive and insightful analyses of online lives by engaging with methodologies in other disciplines, in particular media studies (5). Likewise, we recognise how ethnographic and autoethnographic approaches are well suited to shedding light on people's lived experiences in digital environments rather than foregrounding scholars' interpretations of the materials they produce about those experiences. Surveys of young people's activities on social media like danah boyd's *It's Complicated* and Patricia Lange's *Kids on YouTube* demonstrate how such methods can access the dynamics of *participation* within social networks, a key dimension of online life that examinations of particular posts and videos doesn't always capture (see Jenkins et al.). Situating the researcher as an active participant in the on- and offline activities of social groups, "digital ethnography", as John Postill and Sarah Pink describe it, "shift[s] the methodological emphasis from models of network and community to a focus on routines, mobilities and socialities" (124) and offers auto/biography scholars a model of scholarship that attempts to capture the everyday dynamics of living *with* but not always *on* the internet. Similarly, Sidonie Smith and Julia Watson's call for "backyard ethnography" (*Getting* 17) can frame analysis of auto/biographical acts produced in the course (and constraints) of daily digital living. The digital humanities, for their part, offer quantitative methodologies, such as data mining, distant reading, and what Alison Booth has proposed as "mid-range reading"—an idea she illustrates with the "documentary social networks" generated by the biographies of the nineteenth-century writer Mary Russell Mitford (621)—that can generate insights into collective online auto/biographical practices on a larger scale than qualitative methods focused on smaller sets of texts can encompass.

At the same time, the questions that auto/biography studies has traditionally asked continue to serve as methodological guideposts. How do subjects engage verbal and visual semiotic systems to make meaning of their experiences for themselves and for others in dialogic encounters? How are subjects themselves produced within semiotic systems and social interactions in which power relations are rarely symmetrical? What is ethically and politically at stake in representing a life? Keeping such questions in view as we engage digital media allows auto/biography scholars not only to weigh the advantages of the methods we borrow from other fields but also to appreciate how our own disciplinary perspectives can inform those fields. "Life-writing approaches", Rak observes,

> tend to assume that lives matter and have a politics of representation. These approaches could be helpful within new-media studies because some of that scholarship runs the risk of being overly descriptive of online phenomena or of interviewing users without thinking of the epistemological lines that create users, avatars, or virtual worlds.
>
> ("Derailment" 165)

Our methodological choices, then, reflect our disciplinary ways of knowing. But they can also enact resistance to dominant hierarchies that might not accept that the "mundane fragments of self-narratives" (Schmitt 11) bear up under close reading. As Kate Douglas has demonstrated in the case of selfies, such a reading can bear theoretical fruit, helping scholars better understand these traces of online lives as products of cultural and aesthetic practices with sometimes serious ethical and political ramifications. As auto/biography scholars turn as well to methodologies that can more readily address the distinctive characteristics of digital life texts, it is important to maintain our disciplinary centre of gravity. Doing so can be especially challenging when our inquiries run up against the potential stumbling blocks we identify above: scale, scope, privacy, and ephemerality. In what follows, we share strategies to take up the traditional questions of auto/biography studies in ways that also attend to the contexts of digital cultural production.

## Scale

The question of scale looms up when we try to account for the shaping influence of the online platforms on which most of us craft our digital lives. Online auto/biography, in whatever form it takes, is now almost always embedded in systems its author cannot fully control (and often does not fully understand). This recognition calls our attention to the contexts of production and reception, with close consideration of the technological (and corporate) apparatuses within which digital self-representations are created and shared. In some ways, such questions extend the practices of paratextual analysis to think about both what the author produces themselves and about how they are produced by other agents engaging with that content, for purposes that may align with or be independent of the author's. As Aimée Morrison and Laurie McNeill have each explored, the appearance, "affordances" (Morrison 125–127), and culture of such sites "co-produce" (McNeill, "There Is No 'I'" 71) users' self-representations, acting as human and algorithmic "coaxers, coaches, and coercers" (Smith and Watson, *Reading* 64). Similarly, acknowledging the structure of a WordPress site, for example, and how its layout, comments stream, and aesthetics contribute to how lives are produced and consumed reminds us to think about the material conditions of these life texts.

Given that many life narrators and narratives unfold simultaneously across different, linked platforms, it is possible to consider the differences in presentation and engagement afforded by these different sites as well as pathways of circulation, performing the kind of "intertextual" analysis of "everyday" life materials produced across multiple contexts that Anna Poletti's work with zines (36–43) and Emma Maguire's analysis of YouTube star Jenna Marbles' online personas (84–85) aptly demonstrate. Another example is Brandon Stanton's *Humans of New York*, which exists as a blog while distributing the same content on Facebook, Twitter, and Instagram. However, the presentation differs as mandated by each site's layout: on the blog and Instagram, for example, readers see multiple story tiles at once, while Twitter and Facebook foreground individual portraits in separate posts, and readers have different, site-dependent opportunities to respond to or share this material. Recognising these large commercial platforms' powerful shaping influences on the production and reception of digital lives might encourage "paranoid" readings of the kind Eve Sedgwick has critiqued. A more generous—or what Sedgwick calls a "reparative" (146–150)—reading of the interchanges between platform and auto/biographical subject aims to understand both the "active, creative characteristics of individuals and groups" who use these sites "as well as the structuring or conditioning powers of social processes" that shape how they use them, as Mark Cieslik and Donald Simpson have argued youth research must consider (43).

## Scope

The question of scope arises when, reading generously and inclusively, we shift our attention from "professional" autobiography in online forms to "amateur" practices or producers—keeping in mind, as Axel Bruns has argued, that since web 2.0 the roles of consumer and creator have commingled (21–23), and, as Arnaud Schmitt notes, millions of people are now documenting their lives online, and few of them are professional content creators (13). What becomes a representative example when we are analysing potentially thousands of texts? How do we choose one blogger from the myriad options, knowing the constant risk that another instance might be more fitting or more indicative? (Qualitative researchers must also suffer "FOMO".) Rodman Gilbert's observation about "the inevitable incompleteness of any given research project" on popular culture applies here: "There is no definitive popular culture canon, no easily delimited set of textual artifacts, no final point at which an analysis has accounted for everything that needs to be considered" (388). In the face of this inevitability, we adapt our research practices: we continue to look for patterns, whether in a book-length memoir or in posts on social media, and we are explicit about how we have identified those patterns. We attend to what we identify as distinctive features of texts and consider how these make meaning in the context of production and consumption. We articulate our rationale in selecting particular subjects or stories to discuss: users with a high degree of influence, measured in number of followers and media coverage; channels or posts with high (or low) response rates, followers, reposts, or "likes", and so on. While these choices may be imperfect and necessarily limit the wider applicability of our findings, they are some ways that we make qualitative analysis ethical and productive within those limits. They are also methods that we can model for our students, helping them conceptualise and implement research projects on digital life narratives.

## Privacy and Ephemerality

The privacy and ephemerality of many online auto/biographical acts limit the researcher's access to "primary texts" and demand methodologies that do not necessarily rely on the techniques of close reading. We find an instructive recent example of such strategies in Kylie Cardell et al.'s study of Snapchat and Instagram, both platforms that facilitate the private exchange of very short-lived posts and "stories". In the absence of durable and readily accessible concrete documentation of auto/biographical acts in these systems, Cardell et al. turn to tech journalism, scholarship from sociology and communication studies, Snapchat's support pages, and their own painstaking explanation of how users deploy the platform's features to build up a "thick description" of the dynamic social context of those acts. On platforms like Instagram and Snapchat, they argue, "the value of the autobiographical image is lodged in its (however brief) *circulation*, and the value of trace and preservation that has so long been associated with practices of self-life writing is subordinated"

(169). In our view, this study exemplifies a generous reading practice that rises to the challenges we have identified. It is capacious its attention to the constraints and affordances of the large-scale systems that shape the amateur auto/biographical acts the researchers seek to understand, and it is inventive—and respectful—in its strategies for coping with the privacy and ephemerality of conventionally "legible" documents of those acts. It also emphasises the crucial role of time-sensitive interpersonal participation characterising these and many other modes of online self-representation, a feature that can elude critical approaches that depend on such evidence.

When we ask what methodologies might be optimal—or at the very least adequate—for the critical analysis of auto/biographical acts in digital media, we acknowledge that these acts are to some significant degree different from their counterparts in other formats. Those perceived differences are usually what inspire our inquiries, as they appear to bear witness to the transformative influence of digital technologies on the ways people are documenting their life experiences and sharing them with others. Identifying what those distinctive features actually are and, even more crucially, recognising the challenges they pose to our particular investigations are the first steps in determining which methodologies can best support a rigorous, responsible analysis of whatever manifestation of "digital life" we are seeking to understand. Our advocacy for a generous critical engagement with digital lives welcomes methodological approaches from other disciplines and, at the same time, reaffirms the ongoing commitment of auto/biography studies to take a broad, inclusive view of what counts as a "life" and what signs of life—however transient, fragmentary, and enigmatic they may be—we are willing to learn how to read.

## Works Cited

Booth, Alison. "Mid-Range Reading: Not a Manifesto." *PMLA*, vol. 132, no. 2, 2017, pp. 620–627.

boyd, danah. *It's Complicated: The Social Lives of Networked Teens*. Yale UP, 2015.

Bruns, Axel. Blogs, *Wikipedia, Second Life, and Beyond: From Production to Produsage*. Peter Lang, 2008.

Cardell, Kylie et al. " 'Stories': Social Media and Ephemeral Narratives as Memoir." *Mediating Memory: Tracing the Limits of Memoir*. Routledge, 2017.

Cieslik, Mark, and Donald Simpson. *Key Concepts in Youth Studies*. Sage, 2013.

Donahue, Tiane. "Cross-Cultural Analysis of Student Writing: Beyond Discourses of Difference." *Written Communication*, vol. 25, no. 3, July 2008, pp. 319–352.

Douglas, Kate. "Youth, Trauma and Memorialisation: The Selfie as Witnessing." *Memory Studies*, 2017. doi:10.1177/1750698017714838.

Drucker, Johanna. "Why Distant Reading Isn't." *PMLA*, vol. 132, no. 3, 2017, pp. 628–635.

Jenkins, Henry et al. *Participatory Culture in a Networked Era: A Conversation on Youth, Learning, Commerce, and Politics*. Polity, 2016.

Lange, Patricia. *Kids on YouTube: Technical Identities and Digital Literacies*. Routledge, 2014.

———. "Vlogging Towards Digital Literacy." *Online Lives 2.0*, special issue of *Biography*, edited by Laurie McNeill and John David Zuern, vol. 38, no. 2, 2015, pp. 297–302.

Maguire, Emma. *Girls, Autobiography, Media: Gender and Self-Mediation in Digital Economies*. Palgrave Macmillan, 2018.

McNeill, Laurie. "Teaching an Old Genre New Tricks: The Diary on the Internet." *Online Lives*, special issue of *Biography*, edited by John Zuern, vol. 26, no. 1, 2003, pp. 24–47.

———. "There is No 'I' in Network: Social Networking Sites and Posthuman Autobiography." *(Post)Human Lives*, special issue of *Biography*, edited by Gillian Whitlock and G. Thomas Couser, vol. 35, no. 1, 2012, pp. 101–118.

Morrison, Aimée. "Facebook and Coaxed Affordances." *Identity Technologies: Constructing the Self Online*, edited by Anna Poletti and Julie Rak. U of Wisconsin P, 2014, pp. 112–131.

Poletti, Anna. *Intimate Ephemera: Reading Young Lives in Australian Zine Culture*. Melbourne UP, 2008.

Poletti, Anna, and Julie Rak. "Introduction: Digital Dialogues." *Identity Technologies: Constructing the Self Online*, edited by Anna Poletti and Julie Rak. U of Wisconsin P, 2014, pp. 3–22.

Postill, John, and Sarah Pink. "Social Media Ethnography: The Digital Researcher in a Messy Web." *Media International Australia*, vol. 145, no. 1, Nov. 2012, pp. 123–134.

Rak, Julie. "Derailment: Going Offline to Be Online." *a/b: Auto/Biography Studies*, vol. 32, no. 2, 2017, pp. 164–165.

———. "Life Writing Versus Automedia: The Sims 3 Game as Life Lab." *Online Lives 2.0*, special issue of *Biography*, edited by Laurie McNeill and John David Zuern, vol. 38, no. 2, 2015, pp. 155–180.

Rodman, Gilbert B. "Notes on Reconstructing 'the Popular.'" *Critical Studies in Media Communication*, vol. 33, no. 5, 2016, pp. 388–398.

Schmitt, Arnaud. "From Autobiographical Act to Autobiography." *Life Writing*, 2018. doi:10.1080/14484528.2018.1478598.

Sedgwick, Eve. "Paranoid Reading and Reparative Reading, or, You're So Paranoid, You Probably Think This Essay Is About You." *Touching Feeling: Affect, Pedagogy, Performativity*. Duke UP, 2003, pp. 123–151.

Smith, Sidonie, and Julia Watson. "Introduction." *Getting a Life: Everyday Uses of Autobiography*. U of Minnesota P, 1996, pp. 1–24.

———. *Reading Autobiography: A Guide for Interpreting Life Narratives*. 2nd ed. U of Minnesota P, 2010.

Whitlock, Gillian. "The Hospitality of Cyberspace: Mobilizing Asylum Seeker Testimony Online." *Online Lives 2.0*, special issue of *Biography*, edited by Laurie McNeill and John David Zuern, vol. 38, no. 2, 2015, pp. 245–266.

# 18 Reading the Life Narratives of Children and Youth

*Kate Douglas*

When my collaborator Anna Poletti and I wrote our book *Life Narratives and Youth Cultures*, we wrote a short section to conclude the introduction titled, "A Brief Note on Method and the Ethics of Studying Youth". In this short statement, we carefully and self-consciously explained how our study of young people's life narrative would work at the intersection of different disciplines, namely, literary and cultural studies and childhood and youth studies. We explained that overt discussion of research methodologies was expected in research on childhood and youth because there are always ethical questions surrounding, for instance, the appropriateness of studying children and youth. We acknowledged that even though ours was not qualitative or quantitative research of child subjects, engaging with the life narratives of young people requires ethical methodologies, and, more particularly, ethical strategies for the reading and analysis of and writing about youth-authored works.

Young people are subject to much public surveillance; their self-representation is often judged according to the norms and values of the time and ideas about what sorts of public discourse is appropriate for children and youth. For instance, while social media activists like Pakistani blogger Malala Yousafzai and Syrian tweeter Bana al-Abed are largely lauded by mainstream media for the positive political work that they do, other infamous social media influencers such Danielle Bregoli (Bhad Bhabie), Alissa Violet, or Jake and Logan Paul are given major media attention and constructed as frivolous, banal, and dangerous. These are, perhaps, the most extreme examples; but this also makes my point. It is most often "spectacular youth" that gain the most media attention (Douglas and Poletti 30). But, in reality, there are many young life narrators, across various media, who offer self-representations that cover a diversity of experience, including the everyday.

As these texts circulate, scholarly responses to young people's life narratives come with a series of significant challenges. For instance, any research "on" or "with" children and youth has potentially significant power imbalances attached to it, however well intentioned the research might be. The first questions should (of course) involve permissions.

Then, there is also the question of who benefits from the research: does the research have the capacity to boost the child or youth author in some way, or is its purpose to merely elevate the research status of the adult professional researcher? Does the research pose any risk to the child/ youth subject? For instance, sometimes research into children and youth that has the intention to celebrate or empower youth subjects is instead co-opted and used to judge (Bennett et al. 4).

This is challenging work; but we need to be creative and brave as we work towards inclusivity. Life narrative scholars have long played a role in bringing marginal voices and texts into public view; it makes sense that scholars would be interested in the work of young life narrators who bring new forms and subjects into life narrative's view. In my research, I have worked on close reading methodologies for reading different types of childhood life narrative: published books (autobiographies, memoirs, and diaries), mediated anthologies, unpublished archival documents, documentary media, public performance or speeches, and online texts, particularly those from social media sites such as Instagram and Twitter. It is not within the scope of this chapter to discuss each of the different methodologies that I, and my collaborators and I, have engaged in. And I do not want to conflate methodological approaches or downplay the significantly different approaches required for reading literary texts and texts from social media. This research requires recognition of and commitment to the diversity of life narrative texts by children and youth, and a desire to engage respectfully.

This discussion circles back to what I think is the core methodological question for reading childhood texts across different genres: ethical reading and writing practices. In the section that follows, I discuss some practical examples from my own research that I think address ethical reading methodologies, including some success, some failure, and some suggestions for future research.

## The Life Narratives of Children and Youth: Ethical Reading and Writing Practices

Ethical research involves questioning and reflection, and a deep consciousness of why the research is being done and how, and with the highest respect for the subjects. In the section that follows, I contextualise these ideas in proposing five steps towards an ethical reading and writing methodology for life narrative texts by children and youth.

### Ask Yourself: Why Do I Want to Research This Group?

It is very common for life narrative scholars to engage with texts, authors, and subjects "on the margins"—texts that testify to inequality or trauma (for instance) and work towards social justice. I have followed influential

auto/biography scholars such as Leigh Gilmore, Margaretta Jolly, Kay
Schaffer, Sidonie Smith, Julia Watson, and Gillian Whitlock. They have
considered the vital role that life narrative genres have played in circulating testimony, impediments to the circulation of testimony, and the
effects of testimony on those readers and witnesses who receive it. Reading testimony has the power to change lives and attitudes, to raise consciousness, to suggest complicity, and to promote ethical reading.

But when we engage in research on the life narratives of vulnerable
groups and subjects such as children and youth, our motivations in doing
so need to be made clear, and scholars (such as those listed above) are
highly self-reflexive in their scholarship, in explaining and exploring
what brought them to their research texts and subjects, and what makes
this research important.

In my paper on African child soldier memoirists Ishmael Beah and
Emmanuel Jal, I reflect on my desire to find text-appropriate methods
and the various challenges in researching texts by young authors. It is
often difficult for young people to participate in culture, so a scholar's
role can be one of recognition and boosting: the possibility of "productive dialogues" (274). Scholars,

> like writers, journalists, critics, and policymakers (to name just a
> handful of stakeholders), are cultural commentators, offering per-
> spectives and interpretations, and acting as interlocutors or conduits
> among scholars, students, and the broader community, depending on
> the reach of the scholarship, for the reception of texts and the issues
> they represent.
>
> (273)

Response to young people's public-sphere activities are inevitable.
These responses will come from a range of discourses, and the tenor
of these responses will be diverse. This is where scholarly interventions
can play a significant role.

### *What Contextual Information Do I Need to Know Before I Can Adequately Read These Texts?*

It would be impossible to read and understand children's and young people's contribution to life narrative genres without a solid understanding
of the text's cultural archaeology: the myriad socio-political, cultural, and
historical contexts within which these young writers came to construct
their work. For instance, in *Life Narratives and Youth Cultures*, Anna
Poletti and I wrote a chapter on Pakistani blogger and activist Malala
Yousafzai and Brazilian school girl activist Isadora Faber. Recently
I wrote on Syrian Twitter activist Bana al-Abed; and Kylie Cardell and
I are currently preparing a paper on the #NeverAgain movement activists

in the US, led by charismatic public speaker Emma Gonzalez. These are the diverse authors, subjects, and spaces occupied by contemporary life narrators. This writing is happening across the globe, across cultures, classes, age groups, genders, and sexualities, and, vitally, across genres (a point I return to in the next section). It is perhaps axiomatic to life narrative scholars that close reading methods, though very important, provide an incomplete picture.

In analysing these texts ethically, we need to gain as much biographical information as we can about the authors. For instance, in researching the abovementioned young life narrators, I spent hours trawling news articles to locate background information on these authors and their authorial aims, the production of their texts, and I often had to draw on Google-translate to access information. I watched YouTube clips of television profiles and interviews. Considerable secondary research is often required, for instance, into the literary and cultural traditions that these authors connected to, and the forms of life narrative they were working within (activism, blogging, interviews, public oration, feminist testimony, Ted Talks, Twitter). And lengthy web-based research is required to gain a comprehensive picture of the texts' reception (and again, Google translate may be required). We need to be prepared for contradictory information and points of contention in the interpretation of the texts (for instance, this was a significant issue in research on Malala). Ethical reading practices involve engaging with diverse knowledge and perspectives, but reaching strong, ethical conclusions in our own analysis.

Those researching other types of contemporary literatures will present a similar picture: a wealth of materials to wade through to generate often small amounts of writing. But there are great rewards from such research because we are working towards a complex, nuanced, "big picture" contextual analysis.

## What Theoretical Knowledge Do I Need to Do This Reading Justice?

Life narrative research is characterised by interdisciplinary approaches; as suggested above, we are never "just" reading books. When working with texts about and by children and youth, it has been necessary to immerse myself in the scholarship of childhood and youth and to familiarise myself with important concepts such as those in the subtitle of Anna Poletti's and my book: "representation, agency, and participation". These theories inform the textual analysis in important ways: providing a checklist of "things to look for" when reading the texts and a framework for the analysis that locates the work across disciplines (which can potentially accelerate its impact).

We called on the work of influential scholars in cultural studies and sociology working in childhood and youth (including: Andy Bennett, Amy Best, danah boyd, David Buckingham, Henry Giroux, Allison

James, and Henry Jenkins). Working within cross-disciplinary theoretical spaces offers a means to "open up" our analysis and to avoid reductive approaches. For instance, working interdisciplinarily allows us to bring together different types of texts and consider the cultural work these texts might do, for instance, challenging the problematic representations of children in culture and the marginalisation of children's voices in culture. It allows us to contextualise our analysis within broader cultural debates and constructions of childhood and youth.

### What Are the Risks and Benefits of Undertaking This Research (for the Subjects, for the Researcher)?

The risks and benefits are particular to the research and fast changing, so commitment and awareness are crucial here. G. Thomas Couser's concept of "vulnerable subjects", central to the discipline of life narrative studies, is a very good place to start. "Vulnerable subjects" are "persons who are liable to exposure by someone whom them are involved in an intimate or trust-based relationship but are unable to represent themselves in writing or to offer meaningful consent to their representation by someone else" (xii). Young people are sometimes, perhaps often, vulnerable subjects in culture and in research (Cockburn; James; James and James; Liebel). Tom Cockburn explains, "children's contributions to society continue to be belittled and devalued, and not accorded the respect and recognition of being involved in mutual esteem and solidarity" (201). So, we must be mindful of the power imbalances within our intellectual engagement (whatever form this engagement takes), and its potential to do more harm than good, for instance, to perpetuate negative stereotypes of young people, to romanticise or fetishise these young life narrators, to increase surveillance or draw attention inappropriately to young people.

For example, researchers studying young people's use of media (including social media) discuss and champion balanced, nuanced analyses that account for the complex relationship that young people have with social media. David Buckingham (2008) summarises,

> the needs of young people are not best served either by the superficial celebration of the exaggerated moral panics that often characterize this field. Understanding the role of digital media in the formation of youthful identities requires an approach that is clear sighted, unsentimental, and constructively critical.

> (19)

When working with texts authored by children or youth, one of my guiding principles is authorial intention: did the child author know that their text was in the public sphere, or fully understand the implications of their circulation? Do they want to be "studied"? Claire Lynch's idea of "the ante-autobiography" is helpful here. Ante-autobiographical texts are types of life writing that come before published auto/biography or perhaps were never intended to be public life writing. Lynch explains:

> Although only a small proportion of people will compose and pub-
> lish a full-length autobiography, almost everyone will, inadvertently,
> produce an archive of the self, made from public records and private
> documents. Here, such works are seen as providing access to writing
> both about and by children.
>
> (97)

Ante-autobiographical texts might include children's diaries, drawings, personal essays, or stories written for school. In her examples, Lynch talks about her own childhood texts (which, obviously, she has permission to write about, or does she? We might argue that as adults, we are a different self, a different version of "me" than we were as children. How can we approach our past lives and texts ethically? These are questions that deserve more scholarly attention).

In deciding to write about young people's life writing, our initial methodological question must be: can I study this text? Is it ethical to do so? Even if the life narrative exists in a public archive or is circulating in the public sphere, we cannot assume we can or should study it and write about it. If we do decide we can study the text, we go back to the do no harm principal. For example, Kylie Cardell and I recently wrote on Instagram selfies as travel narratives and some of the examples we used were by young people (Cardell and Douglas "Visualising Travelling Lives"). The texts were in "public" accounts, but just because something is "public" this does not mean this Instagram user anticipated our response to it. The journal we were writing for was unsure of the ethical protocols here. So, we followed the conventions of social media research and sought permission to include these selfies in our paper. In our correspondence with authors, we were careful to explain the focus of our paper, where it would be published, how it would be circulated and who would likely read it. We presented our intellectual position in requesting permission: that these selfies were testimonies of travel, and selfies were a significant mode of contemporary travel writing that combined. We only included and identified those we had permission to use.

In "Youth, Trauma, and Memorialisation", I wrote on young people's selfies taken at memorial sites. I engaged with examples of selfies that had already been criticised negatively by mainstream media. I attempted to reread these selfies through a more nuanced critical lens that contextualised these young authors within a cultural milieu that circulates mixed messages about social media use. I concluded that young people's selfies at trauma sites revealed new ways of witnessing for the twenty-first century.

There are many potential benefits of studying life narrative texts by children and youth, not the least of which is a recognition of the importance of these texts to the genre, and an acknowledgement of the authors' contribution to culture. Young people often produce life narratives at the margins of mainstream publishing, and, as Anna Poletti and I contend, "it is not productive to underestimate the individual agency and creativity at work in these life narratives" (Douglas and Poletti 31). But as Lynch argues, if we are working with archival texts of childhood, we need to find methodological approaches that are ethical but also attend to the poetics of the texts (97). It is this question of poetics that is the focus of the section that follows.

### How Will I "Critique" These Works?

It would be very easy to patronise young people's life writing in our scholarly responses to it, or to read these texts according to established methods used to assess literary quality or value. Neither approach would account for the complexities of young people's life narrative. When I wrote *Contesting Childhood*, I raised a series of issues throughout the book that might be used as "checks" for reading life narratives by or about children:

- Acknowledge the genres and cultural spaces that are available for young people to write into and considering what type of writing might be enabled and limited in these modes.
- Recognise the subject matter and the limits and affordances of writing about these subjects (for instance, trauma affects memory).
- Understand the power imbalances that might exist between author and reader.
- Consider reading these texts through interdisciplinary social justice frameworks.
- Recognise the potential for extending literary studies scholarship in reading and writing about these texts.
- Draw on existing methods for reading popular or genre literatures.
- Consider the politics of language use. Autobiographical writing is not always concerned with producing "beautiful" literature but is often interested in the potential of literature as a weapon, for instance, for identity negotiation, or for addressing trauma or injustice.
- However, autobiographical writing by or about children should not be denied a "literariness" just because this writing explores socio-cultural issues. Young people's life narrative, in its various forms, is often highly literary and crafted, and reflects a strong mastery of life narrative.

These approaches follow what Laurie McNeill and John David Zuern, in this volume, describe as "generous reading" practices. They write:

> Within the context of auto/biography studies, generous reading . . . rejects the hierarchies of literariness inherent in traditional models of close reading but retains its attention to the choices creators make in representing their experiences, and it brings from cultural studies, rhetoric, and genre theories a commitment to take seriously "ordinary" texts composed by "amateur" people as well as professionals, instances of digital "everyday autobiography", just as feminist and post/colonial scholars argued in the case of life narratives in print.

To summarise: we should not avoid critiquing life narrative texts by children and youth. But we need to engage with these texts within their cultural contexts.

## Conclusion

We are on challenging terrain when we re-contextualise "real lives" for academic research, but to ignore ethically challenging subjects is perhaps equally problematic (Douglas and Poletti; Patricia Yaeger). Social media and the public presence of social media authors add new variables that require consideration. These variables go beyond the domains of university and textbook ethics and thus require the sorts of reflections I am attempting here.

There are many issues to consider as we work across genres and through diverse authorship and contexts. But the reflective steps I suggest in this chapter might be useful in starting a conversation, and also in suggesting that ethics is always relevant to any discussion of life narrative and any discussion of children's cultural production.

If we choose to research children's or young people's life narratives, it should be because we value their experiences, what they think, what they care to write about and share with publics. We should want to hear their voices and engage with these authors if we sense this is what they themselves want. Researchers can act as facilitators, even cheerleaders for young people's life narratives, moving them into cultural and intellectual spaces that might bring further recognition and readership, and further show their vital contribution to life writing genres.

## Works Cited

Bennett, Andy et al. *Researching Youth*. New York: Palgrave Macmillan, 2003. Print.

Best, Amy, editor. *Representing Youth: Methodological Issues in Critical Youth Studies*. New York: New York UP, 2007. Print.

Buckingham, David. *Youth, Identity and Digital Media*. Cambridge, MA: MIT P, 2008. Print.

Cardell, Kylie, and Kate Douglas. "Emma González, Youth Testimony, Silence and Witnessing." Unpublished paper.

Cardell, Kylie, and Kate Douglas. "Visualising Travelling Lives in a Digital Age: Dark Tourism and 'The Selfie'." *Travel Writing and the Visual*, special issue of *Studies in Travel Writing*, 6 June 2018. https://doi.org/10.1080/13645145.20 18.1463843.

Cockburn, Tom. *Rethinking Children's Citizenship*. London: Palgrave, 2012. Print.

Couser, G. Thomas. *Vulnerable Subjects: Ethics and Life Writing*. Ithaca, NY: Cornell UP, 2004. Print.

Douglas, Kate. "@AlabedBana: Twitter, the Child, and the War Diary." *Textual Practice*. Published online: 16 Oct. 2018. https://doi.org/10.1080/09502 36X.2018.1533493

Douglas, Kate. *Contesting Childhood: Autobiography, Trauma and Memory*. New Brunswick, NJ: Rutgers UP, 2010. Print.

Douglas, Kate. "Ethical Dialogues: Youth, Memoir and Trauma." *a/b: Auto/ Biography Studies*, vol. 30, no. 2, 2015, pp. 271–288. Print.

Douglas, Kate. "Reading Malala Yousafzai: Reception, Mediation and the Limits of Radical Life Writing." *Life Writing*, vol. 14, no. 3, 2017, pp. 297–311. Print.

Douglas, Kate. "Youth, Trauma and Memorialisation: The Selfie as Witnessing." *Memory Studies*, 11 July 2017. https://doi.org/10.1177/1750698017714838.

Douglas, Kate, and Anna Poletti. *Life Narratives and Youth Culture: Representation, Agency and Participation*. London: Palgrave, 2016. Print.

Gilmore, Leigh. *The Limits of Autobiography: Trauma and Testimony*. Ithaca, NY: Cornell UP, 2001. Print.

James, Allison. "Agency." *The Palgrave Handbook of Childhood and Youth Studies*, edited by Jens Qvortrup et al. Basingstoke: Palgrave, pp. 34–45.

James, Allison, and Adrian L. James. *Constructing Childhood: Theory, Policy and Social Practices*. London: Palgrave, 2004.

Jolly, Margaretta. *In Love and Struggle: Letters in Contemporary Feminism*. New York: Columbia UP, 2010. Print.

Liebel, Manfred. *Children's Rights From Below*. London: Palgrave, 2012.

Lynch, Claire. "Ante-Autobiography and the Archive of Childhood." *Prose Studies: History, Theory, Criticism*, vol. 35, no. 1, 2013, pp. 97–112.

Mama, Amina. "Is It Ethical to Study Africa? Preliminary Thoughts on Scholarship and Freedom." *African Studies Review*, vol. 50, no. 1, 2007, pp. 1–26. Print.

Schaffer, Kay, and Sidonie Smith. *Human Rights and Narrated Lives: The Ethics of Recognition*. New York: Palgrave, 2004. Print.

Smith, Sidonie, and Julia Watson. *Reading Autobiography: A Guide for Interpreting Life Narratives*. Minneapolis, MN: U of Minnesota P, 2001. Print.

Whitlock, Gillian. *Soft Weapons: Autobiography in Transit*. Chicago: U of Chicago P, 2007. Print.

Yaeger, Patricia. "Consuming Trauma; or, the Pleasures of Merely Circulating." *Extremities: Trauma, Testimony and the Community*, edited by Nancy K. Miller and Jason Tougaw. Urbana: U of Illinois P, 2002, pp. 25–51. Print.

# 19  Negotiated Truths and Iterative Practice in Action

## The Women in Conflict Expressive Life Writing Project

*Meg Jensen and Siobhan Campbell*

> I have come to believe that human rights work is, at its heart, a matter
> of storytelling [. . .] the most important act of rescue [. . .] is not deliver-
> ing supplies but asking questions, evaluating answers, and pleading with
> those of us who observe from a distance.
>
> (Dawes 394)

As James Dawes argues here, storytelling is central to the advancement
of human rights in our time. But how these stories are elicited, by whom,
using what protocols, and under what conditions are at least as important to the success of that humanitarian project as their dissemination.
This chapter focuses on the research, collaborative development, and
delivery of the *Women in Conflict Expressive Life Writing Project*, which
investigates the complex relationship between storytelling and human
rights through an intervention at the site of the interview. The aim of this
project is to test the use of expressive life writing workshop methodologies with survivors of sexual violence in conflict as an ancillary approach
to evidence-gathering that might move beyond "do no harm" by supporting recovery from traumatic experiences. By doing so, the *Expressive
Life Writing Project* interrogates current best practice guidelines on the
documentation and investigation of rights violations and suggests adaptations to existing protocols for the interviewing process.

As we shall explain, the methodology as well as the key research questions raised by this work has been to large extent iterative: our enquiries,
theories, and procedures have been shaped by extensive and ongoing interaction with local stakeholders, by practical application, and,
of course, by the interviewees themselves. That is perhaps our clearest
learning outcome: research on best practice in interviewing begins and
must proceed with intentional, active, responsive listening that leads to
an ongoing reiterative feedback of lessons learned and experiences shared
into new, flexible, and collaboratively achieved solutions.

In the pages that follow, we outline the initial research development,
further iterative research, adaptation, and finally the implementation of

150 *Meg Jensen and Siobhan Campbell*

the project, which was developed with the support of *Beyond Borders Scotland*, a not-for-profit organisation facilitating international cultural exchange, and INMAA, a non-governmental legal aid organisation based in Kirkuk Governorate, Northern Iraq. INMAA currently deploy a team of Mobile Human Rights Defenders to document instances of sexual violence in conflict. Both this documentation project and our research were generously funded by the UK Foreign and Commonwealth Office (FCO), Human Rights fund.

## Background

Through our joint work as mentors for the John Smith Memorial Trust (JSMT), a UK non-governmental organisation that supports human rights in developing democracies, we began working with young leaders from the Middle East and North Africa in 2010, helping them develop strategies for rights campaigning using the power of life-storytelling. More recently, we were asked to mentor fellows of the *Women in Conflict Peace Initiative* developed by *Beyond Borders Scotland* and launched by First Minister of Scotland Nicola Sturgeon in 2015. These women, working to support civil society and rights defence in Syria, Yemen, and Iraq, spoke with us about their desire to run life storytelling projects with women in their regions, particularly with those who were victims of sexual violence. Campbell had recently completed a number of projects in which she developed and successfully tested a set of creative life writing methodologies to support UK combat veterans who suffered from stress-related disorders (REF case study 40629, The Military Writing Network). Subsequently she had adapted these materials for use with settled refugee groups in Jordan. The initial research question for our joint project, therefore, was: *would it would be possible for these materials to be further adapted for use by the Women in Conflict fellows in their local communities?*

As our discussions continued, however, it was also clear that the *Women in Conflict* fellows wanted more than writing exercises and workshop materials. They wanted access to the conclusions of the most recent research on the complex relationship between traumatic experience and life narrative and to hear more about traumatic injury and evidence-based treatments. They also wanted training in the best practice protocols for delivering these materials, to learn how best to conduct life storytelling workshops and interviews in such a way as to empower witnesses and survivors of rights violations to speak out and seek justice.

Much of Jensen's recent research had convinced her, however, that speaking out about trauma can be psychically dangerous even in relatively safe communities: the process of telling itself can re-traumatise the witness/victim (Jensen "Post-Traumatic Memory Projects"; "Surviving the Wreck"). Moreover, each of the communities the *Women in Conflict* fellows were returning to was very different: some were in the midst of long-term and ongoing conflict; others were new conflict zones or just at the start of a post-conflict recovery period. And the women to whom these materials might eventually be delivered were also widely diverse: some would be highly educated, multilingual city dwellers, others semi-literate women in rural communities—and, when working in Internally Displaced Persons Camps, a complex and changing group of mixed ethnic, religious, and educational backgrounds and experiences. Moreover, the needs of these women would necessarily be wide-ranging: while some would be victims of sexual violence in conflict, others might be seeking support for a friend or neighbour, or they might be survivors of domestic violence or other kinds of civil or criminal rights violations. Our second research question, therefore, was: *is it possible to research and develop a set of training and expressive writing and telling materials that could be adapted to suit the needs of diverse individual communities such as these?*

As we began to consider these initial questions, we came across a project under development by a former JSMT Fellow, Asmaa al Ameen. Al Ameen, a human rights lawyer, is now the General Director of INMAA, a legal aid charity in Kirkuk. Her project, entitled "Beyond Do No Harm", jointly managed with *Beyond Borders Scotland*, is a training program for the INMAA team that takes as its overriding principle the UK FCO's directive to "do no harm" to victims in the investigation and documentation of sexual violence in conflict (*Protocol* 6). As the title of the project suggests, however, INMAA and *Beyond Borders* wanted to do more than avoid harm: they wanted a program that actively supported survivors of trauma.

## The International Protocol

In 2014, the FCO published best practice guidelines for the documentation of sexual violence as a crime under International Law (hereinafter *Protocol*). In the section on interviewing and collecting testimony, the *Protocol* offers interviewers practical tips aimed at ensuring the justiciability of the evidence gathered by these means. It begins by reminding interviewers to be sure to obtain the witness' "informed" consent to participation:

> Explain clearly that the survivor/witness has a choice whether or not to speak to you, and that s/he can exercise this choice before, during and after the interview.
>
> (114)

Likewise, they are told what equipment might be useful to them during the interview process and they are warned about the volatile potential of such materials:

> Have sketch paper and pens available. Bring a camera and a ruler in case you need to take photographs of the injuries. (Be careful, however, not to show a survivor/witness any diagram or photograph or video which would lead them to alter their evidence).
>
> (114)

The interviewers are given a template requiring more than twenty elements of information to be collected from the survivor/witness before the process of documenting rights violations can begin. (See the Appendix.) And those 20-plus questions are just the start. The interviewers are given a further set of advice and warnings about the questions that can and should be raised in determining the facts of the case:

> Make sure to cover the "who", "what", "where", "when" and "how" of the crimes (while remaining wary about asking the survivor/witness any "why" questions, so as not to apportion blame to the survivor/witness).
>
> (114)

As those of us who have studied the complex relations between trauma and life narratives will know, a survivor/witness will likely encounter many difficulties when trying to respond to questions presented in this form. While the pursuit of linear, chronological collection of data as outlined here might suit legal purposes, research has long demonstrated that traumatic experience disrupts normal memory processes, leaving victims with a fractured sense of their past. The reasons for this narrative disruption in post-trauma are complex and continue to be an area of intense debate among scholars in both biomedical and psychological arenas.[1] But the felt effect on survivors of trauma is clear.

As we read through the FCO material it was equally clear that because of this disruption of linear life narratives, the *Protocol*'s suggested interview approach was neither practical in terms of the collection of data nor beneficial to victims. By using such methodologies, interviewers may unknowingly be "doing harm" as they push witnesses to recall terrifying experiences in a manner that is either re-traumatising or simply impossible to remember or recount in the ways elicited by the interviewer. Moreover, while the *Protocol* advises interviewers to avoid any considerations of "why", there is much evidence to support the view that victims of trauma cannot begin to heal until they are able to construct some narrative of "meaning" for their experiences.

For most persons, "life stories" provide space for the reflection upon and the processing of experience, enabling the production of meaning. As Sophie Nicholls has argued, much of the current research on the therapeutic potential of expressive writing for trauma survivors employs the notion of a "holding space," a space in which we can feel both sufficiently free and sufficiently sage to let go and begin to access increasingly felt, bodily material [. . .] the page itself can provide some of this holding.

(Nicholls 174)

The exercises developed for the *Expressive Life Writing Project* draw upon the work of James Pennebaker, Celia Hunt, Antonio Damasio, Kathleen Adams, and Nicholas Mazza, among others, to elicit responses that provide just such a "holding space".

A fuller overview and examination of the various literary/cultural, biomedical, psychological, and neurochemical sources of this project can be found in the *Expressive Life Writing Handbook*. For the purposes of this chapter, however, it is sufficient to note that the most recent therapeutic modalities in the treatment of traumatic disorders concentrate in a variety of ways upon the complex relationship between memory and narrative.

## Best Practice in Interviewing

In a recent extensive overview of all published research on psychosocial interventions over the past two decades, Duncan Pedersen and his colleagues reached the following conclusions in determining the best practices in "medical and humanitarian assistance programmes" dealing with traumatised people in conflict and post-conflict settings:

(a) a primary concern in identifying those persons at risk (screening)
b) an implicit commitment to avoid inflicting further damage [. . .]
(c) gaining in-depth insight, identifying specific cultural resources at the local level [. . .] d) building on the existing endogenous resources [. . .] and e) promoting empowerment [. . .] where the community of actors and survivors is involved from the early stages.

(18)

These key elements for best practice (screening, do no harm, awareness of local resources and contexts, use of local actors and stakeholders, promoting empowerment) have been embedded into the development of the *Expressive Life Writing Project* in a number of ways, most notably in our partnership with INMAA.

INMAA travels to mainly rural, traditional communities in Northern Iraq, holding informal, informative town meetings, usually attended by the men of the community in the first instance. In this context, where there is a cultural assumption of men's responsibility for "vulnerable" dependents, INMAA uses local knowledge and sensitivities to foster an atmosphere of empowerment among key stakeholders. These visits also serve another purpose, however. As the INMAA pamphlets are taken home, they begin to circulate among community members. Sometimes these initial visits elicit a flurry of phone calls to INMAA—women calling in, often secretly on a borrowed phone, to report a range of difficulties, criminal and civil, domestic and conflict-related.

The staff of INMAA have, over the past several years, logged over two thousand such cases, all of them beginning with a phone call or visit and all leading to a crucial initial interview.

The *Expressive Life Writing Project* intervenes at the point of the initial interview with prospective clients, by utilising an "implicit commitment to avoid inflicting further damage to those at risk", to use Pedersen's phrase. We have done do so by developing materials and training interviewers in the relationship between life narratives and traumatic experience and in the use of expressive writing and telling methodologies in the collection of those rights violation narratives.

Pedersen's review stresses the importance of making use of local resources and knowledge (18). The approach of the *Expressive Life Writing Project* builds on "existing endogenous resources" and promotes empowerment of those resources. It does so by collaborating with local stakeholders on the development of tools for gauging the emotional impact of rights violation on the one hand, while on the other hand enabling the witness/survivor to produce and integrate into their whole-life stories a narrative of that violation that supports a sense of agency and detachment, thus benefitting their recovery.

Perhaps the most important of Pedersen's recommendations is that of the necessity for inbuilt flexibility:

> The collected qualitative evidence [. . .] reiterates the need for psychosocial interventions to remain flexible and adaptable to the prevailing social and cultural context and specific circumstances of the massive traumatic experience.
>
> (20)

This imperative is echoed in a related recent study of "capability gaps" in the implementation of post-conflict reform initiatives ( Andrews et al. 2012). That research argues that such reforms often fail when those implementing them aim to reproduce *external* top-down solutions considered "best practice in dominant agendas" using predetermined "linear" processes (9). The study further posits that "capability traps" can be avoided by aiming to solve "particular problems in local contexts"; creating an "authorising" local environment that enables "experimentation"; involving the "iterative feedback" of lessons into "new solutions" and creating sustainable programs that are "politically supportable and practically implementable" (10).

What we found in our project, working closely with local stakeholders, was precisely the necessity of challenging conventional wisdom, the need to listen as well as speak. Perhaps most importantly we realised the necessity of ongoing reiterative feedback of lessons learned into new solutions, collaboratively developed through a problem-driven-iterative-adaptation—or what might more helpfully be called listening, learning, and reacting by adapting.

## Challenges, Solutions, and Opportunities

In developing the set of expressive writing exercises with reference to how they would be used by the INMAA human rights defence teams, we encountered several challenges. It was the continual reiterative approach that allowed solutions and opportunities to be discovered. The resulting adapted exercises bear direct relationship to descriptions of good practice outlined by Pedersen, especially flexibility, agility, and the cultivation of local capacity and agency.

Practical questions we faced when drafting the expressive life writing exercises for the Kirkuk pilot included:

A.  How to manage the apparent tension between the juridical aims of the initial and subsequent interviews alongside using these to first introduce and then implement the options for expressive writing or telling?
B.  How to reflect the hard-pressed nature of the situation of those initial and subsequent interviews where women may not reliably have the ideal amount of time to be in the interview situation and while they may be under outside pressures while present?

## Writing or Telling

The first meeting between an INMAA team member and a client is used to record the details of an incident or incidents that might lead to a juridical process. This initial interview was to now be used to fulfil a second aim of offering an expressive telling or writing option to that client. The move to include "telling" as well as possibly "writing" was indicated as essential by INMAA to reflect the diversity of their clients. Whereas many women would be educated, literate, and articulate, others would not and, moreover, some would feel more comfortable giving their stories orally rather than in writing. This new information necessitated the adaptation of a set of exercises into a complete unit for "expressive telling". The application of "telling" or "writing" is now designed as interchangeable, depending on the situation and the timing. We were grateful for the understandings that led to the development of this other set of expressive narrative options.

## Justice or Healing?

INMAA's own intake form had a section that already asked for a narrative of sorts, headed "Briefly describe the background to the case". The presence of this descriptive "background" question allowed us, in training the interviewer/facilitators directly, to suggest they make the links between their clients' "telling" and the potential for going beyond the aim of creating solely a record of incident at this point.

In discussion, it became clear that the option for expressive telling/writing could be seen as potentially useful even in relation to the juridical. If this adapted form of interview had the effect of helping an interviewee to understand herself as the expert in her own case as well helping her to feel more at ease, it might be less likely for her to drop out of the process (something that is always a concern due to family and other pressures). A developed ability in expressive telling might help the process at a later stage, as a plaintiff could *inter alia* be enabled to tell their story more fully for court appearance. Our partners agreed that the exposure to expressive telling or writing might enable a sense of agency or of self-worth among those who pursued this option. There was also the hope that in the same way INMAA knows that word of mouth from woman to woman is how many people hear of their services, these expressive elements could also enhance this onward telling, leading INMAA to more fully fulfil their aims.

## Flexibility and Contingency Guidelines

In answering B above, we built in a flexibility of approach that allowed for shorter and longer versions of exercises, depending on the time available. We provided a number of paths through the exercises, dependent on how the opening section has been received.

We supported this flexibility with extensive notes to facilitators outlining risks, solutions to commonly encountered problems, and counterindicators. Our approach was to empower the interviewer/facilitator by conveying (during training) some of the knowledge-from-experience we had built up but also to indicate that *they* were the expert in their own locale and that both the facilitator and client are considered experts in this regard.

## Resilience in Support of Justice

In addition to the potential therapeutic benefits associated with the elicitation of narrative or story, it became clear that by acknowledging the expressive as having a relationship toward the juridical, our work brought certain linkages clearly into focus. By building in adaptability to every stage of the story gathering, these approaches—while born out of necessity and reflecting the pressures on the ground—are actually in line with research that shows the potential for resilience-building and the development of "hardiness" (including an ability to draw on support) among participants in research interventions that elicit story. Here, we use "hardiness" as described by Leah East et al. in "Storytelling: An Approach That Can Help to Develop Resilience" (17:3:17–25).

Such hardiness, as a support for the capacity to draw on their services, was acknowledged as necessary and desirable by INMAA as part of the set of enabling factors empowering women to pursue the juridical. These rights defenders hope that by participating in these exercises, their clients might be enabled to exhibit that "hardiness" that could support the often fraught and time-consuming process of pursuing legal justice.

## Adaptations in Action

In our project, both approaches (telling or writing) allow for "starter exercises". These are designed to show that there is no wrong way to respond to this work and that everyone can do it. Starter exercises also have the effect of establishing a rapport between the facilitator/interviewer and the participants/client. Such exercises encourage associative thinking, which happens when one word or phrase stimulates another in the mind.

The focus of the primary stage of the expressive telling process is on enabling participants to begin valuing their own story, to appreciate that this is a safe place to tell that story, and to trust the facilitator will not make judgements on that story, even if it emerges as non-chronological and sometimes even contradictory.

Then, after word list/clustering exercises, participants are led through exercises designed to increase ability in identifying and describing feelings and experiences.

These exercises are broken into three "units". Each unit has a focus of operation while allowing flexibility of application. Unit 1 presents exercises designed to systematically induct the participant into ways of approaching expressive writing/telling. Unit 2 encourages writing that bridges the past into the present, while Unit 3 moves more explicitly towards identity and feelings, and allows for a fuller whole-life narrative to be expressed. *The Expressive Life Writing Handbook* outlines the full set of approaches and pathways, characterised by inbuilt adaptability.

The development of exercises to reflect the situation on the ground ensured we remained realistic in our aims for the project. Perhaps most importantly it helped us to understand that the best-case scenario (several weeks of either one-to-one meetings or group workshops) might not be readily applicable. We felt, however, that it was important to still build in a progression of approach through the exercise units, allowing for future use or use in other environments by those who had undertaken the training. To maximise effectiveness, however, while we retained the cyclical "return" of certain motifs and exercise riffs that we hoped would have incrementally been built upon during a writing or telling process, we designed the exercises to have identifiable outcomes whether attempted sequentially or in single repetitions.

## Conclusion

If James Dawes is right about the central relationship between "human rights work" and "storytelling", our work with INMAA and *Beyond Borders Scotland* has demonstrated the importance of flexibility and problem-driven iterative adaptation in collecting those stories. Our project adopted malleable approaches to achieving solutions that are in several ways akin to those outlined by Pedersen, while also fashioning expressive exercises for use among a culturally diverse population (including Kurd, Arab, and Turkmen, city dwellers and rural communities, the highly educated and the minimally so). The key generative factor in all such adaptations of course was the ongoing dialogue with our partners.

We were keen to ensure that the exercises and the variety of their implementations met readily with Pedersen's description of best practice in terms of this emphasis on the local as well as allowing for deviation/experimentation. We believed we had also allowed for ongoing iterative feedback as leading to new solutions. In relation to Pedersen's description of creating sustainable programs that are "politically supportable and practically implementable", there is more study required. As of this writing, we have completed training the INMAA team and they will begin now to collective expressive telling narratives from interested clients. Next, we will need to analyse those narratives as they appear on the INMAA database. Afterwards, we will be presenting our findings and recommendations to the Foreign and Commonwealth Office in the hope of influencing, and improving, the procedure for investigating and documenting crimes of sexual violence in conflict—for moving beyond "do no harm".

As noted, the exercises are currently being developed for use in multiple and disparate settings. Likewise, the participants in our project will need to continue to develop their own narratives—life stories flexible enough to accommodate a myriad of possible future stories. The exercises allow for capstone work with the umbrella title of *"Looking at Future Selves"*. The final exercise, a *"Letter to Your Future Self"*, invites the participant to address that future autobiographical self. Our own hope is that those who participate in the *Expressive Life Writing Project* may be enabled to approach that future with an increased sense of agency, an enhanced resilience, and a sense of how life story narratives can begin to help them find their own, flexible answers to the question *why*?

# Appendix

Annex 4: This is a list of basic information that practitioners should collect from a survivor/witness when conducting an interview:

1. Code [for security purposes].
2. Name of survivor/witness (first and last, and any previous or alternative names by which the survivor/witness is known).
3. Sex of survivor/witness.
4. Date of birth of survivor/witness.
5. Place of birth of survivor/witness.
6. Name of father of survivor/witness.
7. Name of mother of survivor/witness.
8. Languages spoken by survivor/witness (including the survivor's/witness' preferred language).
9. Language of Interview.
10. Current residence/address of survivor/witness.
11. Permanent residence/address of survivor/witness.
12. Phone number(s)/email(s) of survivor/witness.
13. Occupation/work of survivor/witness—current or former.
14. Family status (names, age, and location, if known, of any stated family members).
15. Nationality of survivor/witness.
16. Religion of survivor/witness (if relevant and contextually appropriate).
17. Ethnicity/tribal origins of survivor/witness (if relevant and contextually appropriate).
18. Date, place, and time of Interview.
19. Persons present during Interview and positions/roles.
20. Additional evidence provided by the survivor/witness in the context of the Interview (e.g., photographs, diagrams, maps, videos, medical reports, other documents, etc.) and coding of same.
21. Information regarding whether the survivor/witness agrees to be contacted again.
22. Information regarding whether the survivor/witness requires psychosocial support.
23. Information regarding whether the survivor/witness agrees to have her/his evidence shared with national judicial authorities (specify which).
24. Information regarding whether the survivor/witness agrees to have her/his evidence shared with international judicial authorities (specify which). (Protocol 118).

From: The International Protocol on the Documentation and Investigation of Sexual Violence in Conflict, https://assts.publishing.service.gov.uk/government/uploads/system/uploads/attachment_data/file/319054/PSVI_protocol_web.pdf, accessed 1 October 2018.

## Note

1. A number of recent works outline the complex relationship between trau-matic experience and life narrative disruption, including among the neuro-chemists Katy Robjant and Mina Fazel (2010); among the psychologists and narrative therapists Maggie Schaeuer et al. (2011); and among the scholars of therapeutic writing Celia Hunt (2013).

## Works Cited

Adams, Kathleen. *Expressive Writing: Foundations of Practice*. Plymouth: Row-man and Littlefield, 2013.

Andrews, Matt et al. "Escaping Capability Gaps Through Problem Driven Itera-tive Adaptation (PIDA)." Centre for International Development at Harvard U Working Papers, Cambridge, 2012.

Campbell, Siobhan M., and Meg Jensen. *The Expressive Life Writing Handbook*. TSRN/Beyond Borders, 2017.

Campbell, Siobhan M. et al. "The Military Writing Network: Creative Writing, Life Writing and Trauma." REF 2014 case study 40629. https://impact.ref.ac.uk/casestudies/CaseStudy.aspx?Id=40629. Accessed 1 Oct. 2018.

Dawes, James. "Human Rights in Literary Studies." *Human Rights Quarterly*, vol. 31, no. 2, 2009, pp. 394–409.

East, Leah et al. "Storytelling: An Approach That Can Help to Develop Resil-ience." *Nurse Researcher*, 17, no. 3, 2010, pp. 17–25.

Hunt, Celia. *Transformative Learning Through Creative Writing*. Abingdon: Routledge, 2013.

*The International Protocol on the Documentation and INVESTIGATION of Sexual Violence in Conflict: Basic Standards of Best Practice on the Documen-tation of Sexual Violence as a Crime Under International Law*. UK Foreign and Commonwealth Office, 2014.

Jensen, Meg. "Post-Traumatic Memory Projects: Autobiographical Fiction and Counter-Monuments." *Textual Practice*, vol. 28, no. 4, 2014, pp. 701–725.

———. "Surviving the Wreck: Post-Traumatic Writers, Bodies in Transition and the Point of Autobiographical Fiction." *Lifewriting*, 2016. Web. 16 Feb. 2016. doi:10.1080/14484528.2016.1141034.

Mazza, Nicholas. *Poetry Therapy: Theory and Practice*. New York and Hove: Routledge, 2004.

Nicholls, Sophie. "Beyond Expressive Writing: Evolving Models of Develop-mental Creative Writing." *Journal of Health Psychology*, vol. 14, 2009, pp. 171–180.

Pedersen, Duncan et al. "Searching for Best Practices: A Systematic Inquiry Into the Nature of Psychosocial Interventions Aimed at Reducing the Mental Health Burden in Conflict and Postconflict Settings." *SAGE Open*, Oct.–Dec. 2015, pp. I1–25.

Pennebaker, James W., and John F. Evans. *Expressive Writing*. Enumclaw: Idyll Arbor, 2014.

# 20 Researching Online Biographical Media and Death Narratives After the Digital Turn

*Pamela Graham*

In recent years, auto/biography studies has increasingly considered texts beyond the printed word. Online life narratives have become a particular focus of the field, with special issues of journals and conferences being dedicated to the topic.[1] In fact, Julie Rak recently observed that "the study of auto/biography . . . is poised at an important moment"—that of the "digital turn" (164). This digital turn is clearly revolutionising how we work with online auto/biographical texts. Yet, at the same time, because of the speed and scope of technological development, there are few explicit, established methods for studying online forms. This is perhaps not surprising, as a number of core textbooks suggest that methods and methodologies are frequently overlooked or under-articulated in cultural and literary studies.[2] Moreover, some of the literature has a tendency to conflate *methodology*—which is, as one scholar puts it, "the theoretical and philosophical principles" that underpin a research approach—with *method*, "the application of those principles" (Powell 45).

The digital turn draws attention to questions of methodology and method, but it has also revealed that these questions are inseparable from ethical issues that demand careful attention. A researcher has significant power, and so choices of selection and focus are vital when working with online auto/biographies. Whose lives should we be studying, and as a result drawing attention to? How do we treat material that was produced in an analogue context but is now digitised and available to a potentially global readership? (Moravec 195). How do we treat life narratives and other online ephemera that have been created by non-professional writers who perhaps never anticipated academic scrutiny?

These are some of the questions we should be asking when studying online *lives*, and perhaps even more so when it comes to the study of online *death* narratives. In what follows, I briefly discuss the recent emergence of online death narratives, before focusing on my experience of studying a digital obituary project. In consultation with relevant scholarship, I discuss how my research in this context prompted me to work through entanglements of methods and ethics, with a particular focus on the issue of privacy. I offer some questions researchers might consider asking when working with online death narratives, although the discussion here is not designed to provide definitive answers but rather to prompt further thinking about this new frontier of auto/biography scholarship.

In recent years, in addition to presenting their lives online, people have increasingly commemorated the deaths of loved ones. There are now myriad websites devoted to the biographical memorials of "ordinary" people: MuchLoved.Com, GoneTooSoon.org, and Legacy.com are three of the most prominent purpose-built sites. In addition, social media has inadvertently become a space for commemoration, as users on platforms such as Facebook pass away and auto/biographical pages become biographical memorials where friends and family leave tributes to the deceased person. The newspaper obituary, too, has been affected by the emergence of digital technologies, with many obituary pages now available online, potentially reaching a wide audience.

All of these biographical tributes are important cultural expressions. Like other forms of biography, they can provide insight into what and whom any given culture values at any given time. So, it is not surprising that scholars from a range of disciplines—anthropology, media and cultural studies, and auto/biography studies—would be interested in researching this form. However, many of these memorial expressions raise a number of urgent questions about how to approach this kind of online material. Websites generate data, which can be downloaded, saved, modified, taken out of context, and redistributed, and which can have a "life" of its own far beyond its initial posting. In addition to this, the relatively new digital space of death and commemoration brings with it a cultural expectation of sensitivity, which is often discordant with the robust public spheres of social media and the internet more generally. In order to discuss these issues in more detail, I now turn to my own experience of researching online obituaries.

## Researching Online Obituaries: The Case of Australian Broadcasting Company's *In Memory Of*

In 2015, the Australian Broadcasting Company (ABC) launched a new website project called *In Memory Of*. As part of the ABC Open crowd-sourcing initiative, designed to encourage community engagement, *In Memory Of* invited "ordinary Australians" "to share a story about a family member or friend who died in 2014". A few months later, after a submission and editorial process, the website launched with 194 obituaries—each consisting of a 300-word written piece and a photograph of the deceased person. In 2016, the project was repeated, with a further 143 obituaries being published, commemorating people who had died in 2015.

I was interested in what *In Memory Of* suggested about the evolution of the obituary, as a biographical form, as it migrated into online spaces.

In contrast with a death notice, which anyone can put in a newspaper, the obituary has a history of being exclusive, commemorating the lives and deaths of the "great and the good" (Fowler 4–5; Starck 268). So, its appearance online deserves academic attention, both because it is a politically significant biographical form and because of the possibilities for the democratisation of obituary practice (Graham). As I began my research, I immediately faced questions about how to proceed: how should I treat this kind of material—crowdsourced obituaries that were publicly available on a public broadcaster's website, yet whose non-professional authors may not have expected that their tributes to loved ones would be the subject of academic scrutiny? In other words, if I were to proceed with reading and interpreting these examples of biographical media, then I would need to be mindful of the ethical dimensions of my approach.

I initially consulted the Association of Internet Researchers' "Guidelines for Ethical Research" document, before turning to the work of scholars experienced in studying death and grief online. Heather Carmack and Jocelyn DeGroot are two academics whose writing on this topic was particularly useful in informing my approach. Carmack and DeGroot propose that six of the most "salient issues" for researching death online include:

1. privacy and anonymity
2. researcher lurking—a researcher being online, observing but not participating
3. language choice and changes—the need to respect and preserve the form of the original poster's language, which may be emotional, profane, and ungrammatical
4. topical sensitivity—being aware of issues of power and privilege when researching the sensitive topic of death
5. emotional impact on researchers
6. researcher responsibilities and obligations—dilemmas involving the disclosure of information that may have ethical or even legal implications.

(317)

All of these issues are potentially important for life narrative researchers working with online death narratives. However, focusing on the issue of privacy and anonymity, John David Zuern recently noted "privacy has always been a problem for auto/biography studies", and this issue is arguably evolving and transforming as life—and death—narratives migrate online (267). This is because the online environment is blurring the lines between public and private, and there is a lack of clarity about whether the internet is, as Carmack and DeGroot put it, "akin to a public square, where naturalistic observations can be freely conducted, or if the Internet should be treated as a private entity, requiring authorisation from those who post information online" (318).

Clearly, context is important here and memorial tributes on a mainstream media platform, like the ABC, will need to be treated differently to those on a semi-private Facebook page. Guided by Carmack and DeGroot, I decided that because the obituaries on *In Memory Of* were part of a project administered, and indeed promoted, by the national public broadcaster, they were squarely in the public domain and so could be treated in a similar way to newspaper obituaries. From the very start of the process, the ABC makes it clear that contributions to ABC Open will be public and may also be re-published across the broadcaster's other platforms. The terms and conditions, for example, state that while contributors own their work, they agree to grant the ABC the "non-exclusive right throughout the world" to use that content "in whole or in part to the public on any media platform", including the capacity for the broadcaster to "provide [the content] in any downloadable format for free from any ABC online service". In fact, on one of the first pages of the ABC Open website, this transferability and public exposure is framed as part of the attraction of contributing to the crowdsourcing project. Potential authors are offered "a chance to be showcased by other ABC websites, radio, and TV" ("Add Your Story").

Furthermore, all obituaries submitted to *In Memory Of* were subjected to a moderation and editing process to ensure that they complied with ABC Open Terms & Conditions and ABC Editorial Policies. Authors were actively engaged in this process and had to give approval before their work was published ("Email Correspondence"). Therefore, it is unlikely that a contributor would have proceeded to the publication stage unaware of the fact that their writing would be public and sharable once it was published.

Yet, despite the fact that the ABC was clear about the potential reach and public nature of the project, I was aware that the authors of the obituaries were not necessarily seasoned professional writers used to working in the public domain. With this in mind, I was more careful about how I discussed participants' contributions. At each point I asked: how would this author feel to see his or her work analysed in an academic paper? Of course, without asking each individual author, I couldn't know the answer to this question, but I reasoned that my broad methodological framework was one that demanded I treat all auto/biographical texts with dignity and care.

My paper considered five obituaries from *In Memory Of*, including the most viewed profiles on the site: a three-week-old baby who died after she was kissed by a relative who had a cold sore and a young woman who committed suicide after being cyber bullied. In my reading of these obituaries, I was guided by Leigh Gilmore's discussion of teaching traumatic content, where she reminds students to "talk as if someone who had experienced trauma is in the room" (369). I approached my discussion in a way that was mindful of this. I imagined an implied readership not just of academics but of all the stakeholders of the *In Memory Of* project. To avoid misrepresenting the sentiments of the obituary writers, I let the obituaries "speak" for themselves, by quoting the writers directly and extensively.

In addition, I made sure that my analysis was not critical of the obituary material itself but rather that my focus remained on assessing the evolution of the obituary form, including the possibilities for online technology to educate, or to encourage affective communities to form around and support grieving friends and family. In other words, my discussion aimed to honour the memory of those who had died, as well as the labour of the obituary writers, by keeping the focus on the broader social benefits that online technologies might offer.

Lastly, although the paper would have benefitted from screenshots or images of the obituary pages, each of which featured a photograph of the deceased, I chose not to include them. This meant that if loved ones did find my paper online, then they would not be immediately confronted by a photograph of the deceased person. Ultimately, there is no way to know how each individual author or loved one would feel to see their work represented and discussed in a new context. However, by constructing an implied readership, honouring the sentiments and tone of each memorial, and keeping the focus on the social benefits of the project, I hoped to be able to discuss the obituary as a significant form of biographical media, while also minimising harm to those involved in the *In Memory Of* project.

My research was also complicated by another factor relating to privacy. As Carmack and DeGroot identify, online memorial sites often involve a broader network of contributors around the author of the original post:

> Blogs or social network sites devoted to the chronicling of a dying individual or being used as a space to communicate grief do not always focus on one individual; rather, grief blogs and social networking memorial sites focus on two different groups: the deceased and the bereaved survivors. Scholars interested in studying online communication about death and bereavement must now consider the privacy of both groups.
>
> (318)

Although *In Memory Of* was not a blog or social networking site, it was interactive and did provide a space for visitors to comment on the obituaries. The capacity for interactivity in online obituaries contrasts significantly with analogue media, such as newspapers, and as such I chose to include an analysis of visitors' comments in my discussion. This meant a consideration of the privacy of those individuals as well as the obituary writers. Again, because of the context—on a public broadcaster's website—I decided that the comments were part of the broader publication and so were public rather than private. I chose not to anonymise the comments, and I took the same steps as I did with the obituaries in order to avoid misrepresenting the authors.

## Conclusion

In some social science disciplines, biography itself is a research method. In these disciplines, recording oral histories, interviews, and life stories are all methods that have been claimed as part of the "biographical turn", and there is an associated body of scholarship related to this (Roberts; Chamberlayne et al.; Clough et al.). However, scholarship about online biographical media in the context of memorialisation and death is less prevalent. Clearly, more developed thinking and articulation is needed. The reach and persistence of online personal information is a more significant issue than ever before and consequently demands more focused attention on the ethical dimensions of research methods.

G. Thomas Couser has argued that there is no universal way to deal with ethical problems in life writing, and his words could equally apply to online death narratives. He suggests researchers take a relativist stance and deal with each case in context (33). In other words, the entanglements of methods and ethics are not easily resolved, and this is especially so when researchers are dealing with a variety of continuously evolving online environments and technologies. For auto/biography researchers working with online death narratives, it is worth taking the lead from organisations such as the Association of Internet Researchers, and beginning a project by asking questions about rationale, ownership, benefits, and potential harm. How can I ensure that I am using research methods that are as considerate and respectful towards their subject as possible? Why am I choosing to read and write about particular death narratives? What is the context or platform on which the "text" sits? Would authors be comfortable with academic scrutiny of their contributions? Who is set to gain from my research?

This brief story of my research experience is a very small one, but in light of Carmack and DeGroot's insightful work and relevant auto/biography studies scholarship, hopefully it is one that stimulates discussion about thoughtful approaches to reading and analysing online death narratives. The questions I have faced about the entanglements of methods and ethics, especially with regards to privacy, will continue to be relevant as life and death narratives manifest in new ways, and as scholars are increasingly expected to pursue interdisciplinary work across media.

## Notes

1. See, for example, the "Online Lives 2.0" special issue of *Biography*, the *Identity Technologies* collection edited by Anna Poletti and Julie Rak, and the 2017 IABA Europe Conference, with the theme of "Life Writing and New Media".
2. For instance, see Gabriele Griffin, editor. *Research Methods for English Studies*. Edinburgh: Edinburgh UP, 2013, pp. 1–2; Michael Pickering, editor. *Research Methods for Cultural Studies*. Edinburgh: Edinburgh UP, 2008, pp. 1–3; Graeme Turner. *British Cultural Studies: An Introduction*. London: Routledge, 2003, p. 225.

## Works Cited

"Add Your Story." *ABC Open*. 2018. https://open.abc.net.au/projects?projectStatus=active&type=all&submissionType=all. Accessed 4 Oct. 2018.

Association of Internet Research. "Ethical Decision-Making and Internet Research: Recommendations From the AoIR Ethics Working Committee (Version 2.0)." 2012. https://aoir.org/reports/ethics2.pdf. Accessed 3 July 2018.

Carmack, Heather, and Jocelyn DeGroot. "Exploiting Loss? Ethical Considerations, Boundaries, and Opportunities for the Study of Death and Grief Online." *Omega: Journal of Death and Dying*, vol. 68, no. 4, 2014, pp. 311–331. https://doi.org/10.2190/OM.68.4.b.

Chamberlayne, Prue et al., editors. *The Turn to Biographical Methods in Social Science*. London: Routledge, 2000. Print.

Clough, Peter et al. *Researching Life Stories: Method, Theory and Analyses in a Biographical Age*. London: Routledge, 2004. Print.

Couser, G. Thomas. *Vulnerable Subjects: Ethics and Life Writing*. Ithaca, NY: Cornell UP, 2004. Print.

Email Correspondence with ABC Open Producer, Bronwyn Purvis. 23 Dec. 2016.

Fowler, Bridget. *The Obituary as Collective Memory*. Abingdon: Routledge, 2007. Print.

Gilmore, Leigh. "What Do We Teach When We Teach Trauma?" *Teaching Life Writing Texts*, edited by Miriam Fuchs and Craig Howes. New York: The Modern Language Association of America, 2008, pp. 367–373. Print.

Graham, Pamela. "Crowdsourcing Obituaries in the Digital Age: ABC Open's *In Memory Of*." *Media International Australia*, vol. 165, no. 1, 2017, pp. 51–62. https://doi.org/10.1177/1329878X17725916.

Griffin, Gabriele, editor. *Research Methods for English Studies*. Edinburgh: Edinburgh UP, 2013. Print.

Moravec, Michelle. "Feminist Research Practices and Digital Archives." *Australian Feminist Studies*, vol. 32, nos. 91–92, 2017, pp. 186–201. https://doi.org/10.1080/08164649.2017.1357006.

Pickering, Michael, editor. *Research Methods for Cultural Studies*. Edinburgh: Edinburgh UP, 2008. Print.

Powell, Alison. "Method, Methodology, and New Media." *SAGE Internet Research Methods*, edited by Jason Hughes. London: Sage, 2013, pp. 45–52. Print.

Rak, Julie. "Derailment: Going Offline to Be Online." *a/b: Auto/Biography Studies*, vol. 32, no. 2, 2017, pp. 163–165. https://doi.org/10.1080/08989575.2017.1287863.

Roberts, Brian. *Biographical Research*. London: Open UP, 2002. Print.

Starck, Nigel. "Posthumous Parallel and Parallax: The Obituary Revival on Three Continents." *Journalism Studies*, vol. 6, no. 3, 2005, pp. 267–283. Print.

"Terms and Conditions." *ABC Open*. 2018. https://open.abc.net.au/conditions. Accessed 5 Oct. 2018.

Turner, Graeme. *British Cultural Studies: An Introduction*. London: Routledge, 2003. Print.

Zuern, John David. "Privacy." *a/b: Auto/Biography Studies*, vol. 32, no. 2, 2017, pp. 267–270. https://doi.org/10.1080/08989575.2017.1288034.

# 21 An Epistemological Approach to Trans* Autobiography

*Sarah Ray Rondot*

*Time* magazine's 24 May 2014 issue features a bold and provocative image of Laverne Cox in a skin-tight, dark blue cocktail dress. Next to Cox's image, the text proclaims: "The Transgender Tipping Point: America's Next Civil Rights Frontier". *Time Magazine* portrays Cox, a trans*-identified actress and activist, as the symbol of a new era of gender politics. In her cover story, Katy Steinmetz suggests that because trans* images and narratives proliferate in contemporary media, the concept of "trans*" (transsexual, transgender, genderqueer, two-spirit and other non-binary and gender-diverse identities included in the term's asterisk) is becoming more understandable for nontrans* Americans.[1] From *20/20* exposés and talk shows, to reality television and bestseller book lists, trans* stories are much more visible than they were ten years ago. Though Steinmetz shows how trans* stories have become more mainstream, she doesn't analyse the types of representations available or the detrimental effects simplified and sensationalised stories can have on trans* people. Instead, Steinmetz erroneously suggests that heightened trans* visibility inevitably leads to heightened trans* acceptance. In reality, most mainstream representations of trans* people tell a homogenous and pathologising story. Popular representations reinforce a history of degradation by displaying trans* people as objects who exist for the consumption of nontrans* consumers. What's more, as Kristen Schilt and Laurel Westbrook show, simplified and sensational trans* representations can increase levels of real-world discrimination, violence, incarceration, and death. Though art may imitate life, it also strongly affects how individuals experience and navigate their world.

My emphasis on trans* autobiography, in several articles and in my current book project, *Radical Knowledges in Twenty-First Century Trans* Life Narratives*, harnesses the energy of our cultural "tipping point" yet takes up the immediate need for representations that foreground the diversity and viability of complex, realistic trans* lives. Although mainstream media tends to represent trans* people as one-dimensional and sensational, trans* people's life narratives tell a different story. I analyse trans* autobiography of a variety of genres (e.g., written autobiography, documentary film, and video blog) to explore our distinct cultural moment—a moment in which individuals are breaking from and reworking prevailing gender knowledges.

To show how trans\* autobiography disrupts and expands dominant ideologies of gender, I engage in several distinct yet interconnected practices: first, I outline *what* the dominant ideologies of gender are by analysing popular media, contemporary medical discussions, current events, language, and politics. With an emphasis on "wrong body" narratives, rather than a spectrum of trans\* subjectivities, dominant ideologies explain trans\* people as "trapped" within incorrect bodies, which must be "fixed" by medical technologies or, in the case of our current political climate, erased from political existence. Second, I examine exactly *how* contemporary trans\* autobiographers disrupt dominant ideologies and stray from the common twentieth-century emphasis on normalisation. In contrast to earlier narratives, twenty-first-century texts reconceptualise trans\* identity as viable with or without medical intervention. Rather than viewing themselves as in need of an external fix, many contemporary trans\* individuals also view social and political systems as in need of change. In addition, many trans\* autobiographers articulate a whole, continuous subject rather than one that is split between pre- and post-transition, and, unlike twentieth-century texts and dominant ideologies, many contemporary narratives do not mourn a "previous" self. Instead, they illuminate the ways that all individuals are constantly changing in personal and societal ways. The trans\* autobiographies I highlight refuse limiting male/female identifications and position themselves outside the binary's control. Rather than moving from one gender to another, radical trans\* texts articulate gender as fluid. In so doing, radical texts articulate visions of difference for future generations of trans\* people.

In my work, I aim to identify the moments when trans\* people resist dominant culture's sensationalising, pathologising rhetoric and document new and healthier ways to understand gender. Because, after all, trans\* people are already thriving and existing, whether or not dominant ideology recognises or comprehends their existence (the recent #WontBeErased campaign shows just how true this notion is). In addition to encouraging knowledge growth, autobiography allows contemporary trans\* life writers the ability to control their life narratives within a transphobic culture that seeks to pin down, simplify, or erase diverse trans\* stories. As Margo Perkins argues, identity-focused autobiography can "give voice to oppositional or counterhegemonic ways of knowing that repeatedly invite readers to challenge their own assumptions and level of comfort with the status quo" (xii). Similar to how Perkins addresses black women's writings within the Black Power era, I understand trans\* autobiography within contemporary trans\* movements as "tied to impending struggle" in ways that "bear witness" to historical realities and "build legacies" for future generations (xiii). In this way, autobiography can be a community-building tactic and political tool of personal and collective survival. As Deidre McCloskey explains in the preface to *Crossing: A Memoir* (1999), "cross-gender" individuals write stories so that they are "heard and talked about and might even be imagined as one's own" (xvi). Trans* life writing can be "the difference between shame and life" (McCloskey xvi), not only for the author but also for the reader who finds their story told for the first time. In addition, Paul John Eakin contends that "narrative is not merely an appropriate form for the expression of identity; it is an identity content" (*How Our Lives* 100). In Eakin's view, narratives do not merely describe selves but actually produce them. As more trans* people share their stories, and as representations become more realistic and diverse, cultural understandings of what it means to live a trans* life should and must expand.

Though autobiography incorporates "first-hand evidence" (Bates ix), it does not pretend to be either objective or subjective truth. Instead, autobiography is unique to the author's life and yet representative of the author's social position. It illuminates the author's standpoint *and* the author's cultural moment. In 1937, E. Stuart Bates imagined autobiography as a genre that could more appropriately represent minority voices. More than sixty years later, Linda Anderson echoes yet expands Bates' sentiment: "autobiography becomes both a way of testifying to oppression and empowering the subject through their cultural inscription and recognition" (104).[2] Autobiography's unique yet representative aspects attest to and magnify the writer's social position, particularly for minority and non-normative narrators.

Nevertheless, as Anderson purports, because canonical scholars (such as James Olney and Philippe Lejeune, among others) imagine the ideal autobiographical subject as universal, they assume "masculine—and, we may add, western and middle-class—modes of subjectivity" (3). In this view, the ideal autobiographical subject is male. Women autobiographers thus destabilise a coherent reading of the autobiographical text; their narratives' "multiplicity . . . cannot be captured within one and the same, the singular 'I' of masculine discourse" (Anderson 98). So, what do we make of autobiographies written, filmed, produced, and created by authors who do not identify as male or female, or who transition from one subject position to another throughout their lifetime? How might trans* autobiographers construct a different relationship between gender and autobiography so as to challenge universal understandings of the autobiographical "I" as inherently masculine? How might trans* autobiographers challenge dominant discourses of gender diversity in politically and culturally transformative ways? These and other questions are ones I consistently explore in my work on trans* autobiography.

## Standpoint Epistemology: What Is It and What Can It Do?

In my academic research, my primary goal is to search for and validate trans* people's perspectives on gender using *standpoint epistemology* as my framework. I draw attention to the ways that our dominant frameworks do not adequately take into account or acknowledge trans* and non-binary people's histories, stories, and lives. In addition, I work to expose and disrupt dominant epistemology to illuminate the ways that trans* autobiography tells a truer and more useful story of gender identity and gender expression. In this way, I look to trans* autobiographies in three ways: 1) as historical artefacts, which reflect the author's cultural norms and dominant knowledges; 2) as literary texts, which can be mined for meaning; and 3) as theoretical materials, which create and uphold new ways to see and understand gender. Trans* autobiographies tend to subvert dominant narratives but they do not necessarily create new discourses out of thin air. As such, rather than solely investigating what texts represent, I also use them to think about the cultural frameworks in which they exist.

Critics of my work might argue that because I do not identify as trans*, I am appropriating trans* people's stories for my own betterment, which continues the violent cycle I mean to question. This critique is valid, particularly because nontrans* individuals have spoken for and continue to speak for trans* people. At the same time, it is important to remember that while trans* people may be visibly "doing gender" work, everyone "does gender" (Lorber 125), and to imagine trans* liberation as a job for only trans*-identified people is disingenuous and tokenising. Although trans* experience is an integral part of gender destabilisation, "it is neither fair nor realistic to lay the task of being a revolutionary vanguard at the doorstep of those who are already marginalized" (Calhoun Davis 125). Anti-racist movements should not rely on people of colour to teach and help white people, just as trans* liberation movements should not expect trans* people to educate nontrans* individuals. In relation, in anti-racist movements, it is white people who need to take responsibility for and reject their unearned skin privileges. Similarly, I believe that it is nontrans* academics who must take responsibility for and reject privileges associated with being cisgender. My goal is not to co-opt the narratives I analyse but to draw attention to the systems that allow nontrans* people's benefits to continue at the expense of trans* individuals' lives. Nontrans* academics should question why trans* people bear the responsibility for "subverting the gendered status quo" when all people have the capacity to do so (Calhoun Davis 125). If more nontrans* scholars took up these goals, the burden of responsibility would not fall so heavily on the shoulders of trans* people.

To continue, epistemology is the study and theory of knowledge with particular attention to knowledges that we tend to imagine as truthful or valuable. It asks us to consider how a culture knows what it knows. Using an epistemological framework begs several questions: as a culture and community, what do we know? How do we come to value certain understandings of the world over others? How do we collectively decide what is fixed knowledge—which might exist outside of our ability to theorise it—and what is socially constructed? How do individual explanations and experiences influence collective knowledge and vice versa? By asking these questions, what it means—what we imagine it to mean—to narrate a gendered life becomes clearer. Standpoint epistemology—what bell hooks calls a "politics of location"—focuses in on how an individual understands themselves and their world from a particular perspective and vantage point. It emphasises how they know what they know, based on their cultural position and life experience. Using this framework, it is my contention that trans* life writers and cultural producers expand knowledges about gender, which, taken collectively, have the capacity to influence macro systems of control; in other words, these expanded gender knowledges have the capacity to change the wider cultural epistemology. Gender is thus a personal identity and a historical process, which is constantly open to investigation.

Standpoint epistemology highlights how an individual's experience relies on one's social position in a stratified society, which affords privileges to some at the expense of others—as well as how one identifies within that social system. Both macro and micro forces influence how individuals behave as well as how they are inculcated in a system that may or may not value their identities. Because of these factors, trans* autobiography illuminates the author or filmmaker or video blogger's standpoint as well as the social knowledges that circulate within their culture. As feminist philosopher Naomi Scheman explains, "knowledge is socially created, under historically specific conditions . . . [and thus] there can be no valid epistemology that is inattentive to the conditions [and] politics under which and in response to which knowledge is created and judged" (185). Following Scheman's claim, I document the knowledges trans* people create in order to illuminate the social realities and "historically specific conditions" that allow those knowledges to flourish, go unnoticed, or fail.

Finally, by centring standpoint epistemology, I question how trans* experience becomes known or recognised as valuable as well as who is able to influence the public conversation. In answering these questions, I turn away from a methodology that privileges the knowledges produced by medical and academic experts and mainstream media and towards one that privileges the lived experience of trans* individuals themselves. Experience and autobiographical narratives, in this framework, take precedence over cultural or even academic claims. Trans* autobiographers, after all, are the experts of their own lives and stories. In this way, the perspectives that trans* autobiographers document must influence our social and academic understandings of gender, rather than the other way around.

One distinct way trans* life writers illuminate new knowledges is by putting their gender-diverse identities into cultural context; in one example, S. Bear Bergman's second autobiography, *The Nearest Exit May Be Behind You*, displays this notion: "Gender is an à la carte arrangement, even though the macroculture rarely realizes this and doesn't usually act accordingly. We are all, I firmly believe, in charge of our own genders" (91). Within the same essay, Bergman complicates their original statement: "When we live in a world that leaves only the tiniest sliver of room for the least complicated among us, it's difficult to find a place for all our complexities" (94). Instead of reading Bergman's statements as contradictory—that gender is self-fashioned yet controlled by "macroculture"—I see these statements as demonstrating the complex ways twenty-first-century life writers negotiate mainstream recognition. Trans* life writers like Bergman expose how gender is externally imposed *and* internally created.

Another way trans* autobiographers reveal new knowledges is through rewriting familiar stories, which exposes cracks or openings within dominant epistemology. These resistant moments can be both devastating and transformative for those who experience them. These moments also illuminate how trans* people are inculcated within a system that does not recognise trans* identity as viable. For instance, a familiar life moment many trans* autobiographers recount is one in which one's elementary school teacher asks the class, "What do you want to be when you grow up?" Because most Americans who were born in and after the 1940s share this experience, the non-normative responses trans* autobiographers feature are profound. In her first autobiography, *Redefining Realness: My Path to Womanhood, Identity, Love & So Much More*, Janet Mock recalls this exact moment; as a young child who was socialised as a boy, when her teacher asked her this question in front of her classmates, she said she wanted to be a "secretary" (37). Similarly, in *The First Lady* (1974), April Ashley remembers when her first-grade teacher posed the same question; in this fraught moment, Ashley enthusiastically blurted out that she wanted to be a princess. Written forty years apart, Mock and Ashley's narratives similarly focus on how they did not know their responses were "wrong" until peers and teachers responded with laughter, in Mock's experience, and outright punishment, in Ashley's. These memories *become* resistant in relation to a culture that prescribes strict gender roles and punishes those who do not follow the system's epistemological rules. These moments of resistance theorise how US society limits individual expression by fixing what is socially "normal" or acceptable. Initially lacking cultural and linguistic models with which to identify, these experiences shock and humiliate Mock and Ashley. Rather than reinstating dominant paradigms or dwelling in sorrow or defeat, however, these resistant moments layer one upon another to produce a new epistemology of trans* identity—a new understanding of gender fluidity.

As indispensable as these new knowledges are, they do not necessarily reflect radical social change. US culture still subjugates, oppresses, and denies trans* people in systemic and institutional ways. US judicial systems still refuse to protect trans* people, thereby making an already vulnerable population even more vulnerable.[3] Trans* people are still more likely than nontrans* people to be arrested, spend time in jail, and experience police brutality.[4] Trans* people experience much higher rates of physical and sexual violence, and trans* people (particularly trans* women of colour) are much more likely to experience attempted or completed murder.[5] The medical institution still regulates trans* identity, unequally granting access to economically privileged individuals and those who fit wrong body models. These and other lived realities affect trans* people on a daily basis.

Marilyn Frye's metaphor of a "birdcage" is a helpful visualisation of how dominant US culture, popular media, and medical legitimation discourses work together to constrain trans* people. In this metaphor, Frye invites us to think about systems of oppression as a cage with interlocking bars. If we look at the cage up close, one or two bars may become apparent and we might ask, why doesn't the bird merely fly around those bars? If we imagine a birdcage as a metaphor for the oppression trans* people experience, it might be appealing to argue that if only media representations would change, or if only the medical field would expand its understanding, or if only politicians would champion trans* people, etc., then trans* people would be liberated. However, looking only at the micro aspects of the birdcage fails to account for how the bars reinforce one another on a macro level. If we take a step back and view the cage as a whole—as what Patricia Hill Collins calls a "matrix of oppression"—we more adequately see the reality of intersecting and interdependent oppressions. The combination of "individual prejudice" and "institutional power" that co-constructs the birdcage is often a "toxic" recipe (Tatum 6–7). However, I work to understand how trans* autobiographers epistemologically create new conceptualisations of gender that fundamentally change the shape of the oppressive systems in which they exist. To see the big picture, it is crucial to analyse trans* people's micro resistances in relation to macro systems.

In our contemporary moment, mainstream media like *Time*'s "Transgender Tipping Point" article tends to determine the horizon of what we know as a culture. According to pop culture scholar Joshua Gamson, mainstream media is "the sea in which we swim, and to a large degree it sets the terms and boundaries of imagination" (393). In other words, pop culture puts limits on cultural epistemology. However, it is my intent to use trans* autobiography to expand that limit and to spatially, theoretically, and socially remap understandings of gender identity, expression, and transition.

Trans* autobiographies reveal a moment in a history of change rather than an end point. Undoubtedly, it is unclear what new gender knowledges trans* activists, authors, filmmakers, and artists will produce in the coming decades; it is possible that future trans* narratives will prove early twenty-first century gender epistemology obsolete. As more trans* life writers produce life narratives, our cultural epistemology of gender must change and morph to incorporate it.

## Notes

1. New systems of knowledge require new systems of language. While individuals and discourses use the terms *transgender, transsexual, genderqueer, cross-gender, gender nonconforming, gender-variant*, and *gender-diverse* in different contexts to mean different things, I use *trans** as an umbrella expression that refers to all of these categories. I use trans* as a descriptor of one identity vector rather than a closed referent. As an identity category, trans* includes those who might be read by others as gender-diverse as well as those who do not express traditional forms of masculinity or femininity. The asterisk suggests that there are many ways to understand the term and that the term itself is historically and culturally situated in twenty-first-century America. For an extended discussion of language use, see my article "Bear Witness and Build Legacies: Twentieth and Twenty-First Century Trans* Autobiography." *Auto/Biography Studies*, vol. 31, no. 3, 2016, pp. 527–554.
2. As Susanna Egan, Irene Gammel, and Sidonie Smith demonstrate, definitions of the genre change over time as individuals narrate new lives and identities. At the same time, decades of scholarship show that the genre is fundamentally unstable: "definitions of autobiography are based on the impossibility to define it" (Lynch 217).
3. For a comprehensive look at US law, which prohibits discrimination based on gender, see transgenderlaw.org. As of October 2018, only sixteen states (and Washington DC) protect trans* people from discrimination.
4. In the National Coalition for Anti-Violence Programs' (NCAVP) 2013 report, of those who reported incidences of violence, "transgender survivors were particularly likely to experience physical violence at the hands of the police". What's more, NCAVP found that "transgender survivors were 3.7 times more likely to experience police violence . . . and 7 times more likely to experience physical violence when interacting with the police". Not only are trans* survivors of violence less likely to report, they are also more likely to get arrested when they do (NCAVP).
5. According to Alexandra Bolles, Communications Director for the Gay and Lesbian Alliance Against Defamation (GLAAD), gender-diverse people are 27% more likely to experience "physical violence". As Bolles claims, violence against gender-diverse people is on the rise, and 87% of this violence is committed against trans* people of colour. More specifically, according to the NCAVP's 2013 report, 72% of "homicide victims were transgender women and more than two-thirds (67%) of homicide victims were transgender women of color". Disproportionately, black trans* women are most likely to be assaulted or murdered: of trans* people of colour killed in 2013, 78% were black trans* women (AVP).

## Works Cited

Anderson, Linda. *Autobiography*. New York: Routledge, 2001. Print.
Ashley, April. *The First Lady*. London: John Blake P, 2006. Print.

Bates, E. Stuart. *Inside Out: An Introduction to Autobiography*. Oxford: Basil Blackwell, 1937. Print.

Bergman, S. Bear. *The Nearest Exit May Be Behind You*. Vancouver, BC: Arsenal Pulp P, 2009. Print.

Bolles, Alexandra. "Violence Against Transgender People and People of Color Is Disproportionately High, LGBTQH Murder Rate Peaks." *GLAAD*, 4 June 2012. Web. 15 Apr. 2015.

Calhoun Davis, Erin. "Situating Fluidity: (Trans)Gender Identification and the Regulation of Gender Diversity." *GLQ*, vol. 15, no. 1, 2009, pp. 97–130. Print.

Collins, Patricia Hill. *Black Feminist Thought: Knowledge, Consciousness, and Politics of Empowerment*. New York: Routledge, 2000. Print.

Eakin, Paul John. *How Our Lives Become Stories: Making Selves*. Ithaca, NY: Cornell UP, 1999. Print.

Egan, Susanna. *Mirror Talk: Genres of Crisis in Contemporary Autobiography*. Chapel Hill, NC: U of North Carolina P, 1999. Print.

Frye, Marilyn. *The Politics of Reality: Essays in Feminist Theory*. Trumansburg, NY: Crossing P, 1983. Print.

Gammel, Irene. *Confessional Politics: Women's Sexual Self-Representations in Life Writing and Popular Media*. Carbondale, IL: Southern Illinois UP, 1999. Print.

Gamson, Joshua. "Popular Culture Constructs Sexuality." *Introducing the New Sexuality Studies*, Third Edition, edited by Nancy Fischer and Steven Seidman. New York: Routledge, 2016. Print.

hooks, bell. *Yearning: Race, Gender, and Cultural Politics*. Boston, MA: South End P, 1990. Print.

Lejeune, Philippe. *On Autobiography*. Minneapolis, MN: U of Minnesota P, 1989. Print.

Lorber, Judith. *Paradoxes of Gender*. New Haven, CT: Yale UP, 1994. Print.

Lynch, Claire. "Trans-Genre Confusion: What Does Autobiography Think It Is?" *Life Writing: Essays on Autobiography, Biography, and Literature*, edited by Richard Bradford. New York: Palgrave Macmillan, 2010, pp. 209–218. Print.

McCloskey, Deidre. *Crossing: A Memoir*. Chicago: U of Chicago P, 1999. Print.

Mock, Janet. *Redefining Realness: My Path to Womanhood, Identity, Love & So Much More*. New York: Atria Books, 2014. Print.

National Coalition for Anti-Violence Programs. "Lesbian, Gay, Bisexual, Transgender, Queer, and HIV-Affected Hate Violence in 2013." *AVP.org*. New York: Arcus Foundation, 2014. Web.

Olney, James. *Studies in Autobiography*. Oxford: Oxford UP, 1988. Print.

Perkins, Margo V. *Autobiography as Activism: Three Black Women of the Sixties*. Jackson, MS: UP of Mississippi, 2000. Print.

Rondot, Sarah Ray. " 'Bear Witness and Build Legacies': Twentieth and Twenty-First Century Trans\* Autobiography." *Auto/Biography Studies*, vol. 31, no. 3, 2016, pp. 527–551. Print.

Scheman, Naomi. *Engenderings: Constructions of Knowledge, Authority, and Privilege*. New York: Routledge, 1993. Print.

Schilt, Kristen, and Laurel Westbrook. "Doing Gender, Doing Heteronormativity: 'Gender Normals', Transgender People, and the Social Maintenance of Heterosexuality." *Gender and Society*, vol. 23, no. 4, 2009, pp. 440–464. Print.

Smith, Sidonie. *Subjectivity, Identity, and the Body: Women's Autobiographical Practices in the Twentieth Century*. Bloomington, IN: IUP, 1993. Print.

Steinmetz, Katy. "The Transgender Tipping Point." *Time Magazine*, 29 May 2014. n.p. *TIME.com*. Web.

Tatum, Beverly Daniel. *Why Are All the Black Kids Sitting Together in the Cafeteria? And Other Conversations About Race*. New York: Basic Books, 1997. Print.

# 22  Genetics and Auto/Biography

*Pramod K. Nayar*

Auto/biography studies now need to account for the genetic make-up of individuals when the latter can easily procure, in the age of personal genomics, documentation about their chemistry. This means, methodologically speaking, a shift back to the corporeal, as I have argued elsewhere, when studying life writing (Nayar). Alice Wexler's *Mapping Fate* (1995), Masha Gessen's *Blood Matters* (2009), Steven Pinker's "My Genome, My Self" ( 2009), Misha Angrist's *Here is A Human Being* (2010), and Rebecca Skloot's *The Immortal Life of Henrietta Lacks* (2010) are examples of texts that document the individual's engagement with their genomic data, the ramifications of this discovery, or, as in the case of Skloot's biographical text, the racialised medical-capitalisation of living matter. In what follows, I offer three provocations by way of developing frames of reading the genomic auto/biography, with particular attention to their generic status, narrative characteristics, and role as memoirs of a special kind.

## Autobiology, Life Writing, and Predictive Biologies

The medicalisation of everyday life due to the extraordinary dominance of biomedical surveillance narratives—blood tests, ECGs, MRIs, monitoring apparatuses, and reports—constitutes a return to the corporeal–ontological as the foundational components of life writing. My ECG is a part of who I am, like my sugar or cholesterol levels. Genomics only adds an additional layer to such medical autobiographies. It is therefore time to consider genomic data as integral to life writing, alongside cultural training, familial relations, or the nutritional history of the individual.

Autobiographies with a significant genomic component may be termed autobiogenographies ( Nayar 2016). Here the individual discovers the genetic foundations of her/his life and documents it for the world in the form of this autobiogenography, a variant of the autobiography and the autobiology narrative. Autobiology, as Harris et al. describe it (2014), is a narrative of the self that displays an awareness of one's biochemical processes. When autobiology is dominated by genetic information and knowledge, it morphs into a subgeneric form that I have termed autobiogenography.

Autobiogenographies offer information, even knowledge, about the individual's past. As life writing, these texts have an epistemological component. Just as the autobiography reveals the growth of an individual, autobiogenographies document the biomedical growth of, and changes in, a life as linked to genomic data. Autobiogenographies are therefore about inheritances, lineages, and genealogies. They situate an individual within a genomic timeline, community, and their features. In many ways, autobiogenographies are travel accounts: they explain how traits, similarities and differences, and behaviour, among others, may be traced through the movements of genetic material, including mutations, and across gene reservoirs, geographical territories, and populations, determined by factors as diverse as wars, socio-cultural norms (around, say, marriage), and climate change.

However, autobiogenographies also constitute the anticipatory segment of writing one's life: what the future holds in terms of diseases and conditions as predicted by the genetic code. Predictive biological narratives speculate, via genomic data, where the *future* expressions and formations of biological matter of an individual may be read into genetic data, and which makes it integral to the *remainder* of one's life. In, for instance, Masha Gessen's memoir, she anticipates the breast cancer that she carries in her gene: cancer, she believes, *is* her future (2009). When considering a life narrative, then, with the information from genomic analysis, the individual composes a future plot, or narrative, one determined by the conditions "seen" in the genetic data. It is essential therefore to see life writing in the wake of genomics as directed at a specific narrative trajectory of one's future: the anxious expectation and the anticipation. Predictive biologies, instantiated in works such as Gessen's or Wexler's (*Mapping Fate*), are the narrative extrapolation of genomic data. They are object biographies (Hoskins 79), in a sense, of the chemicals, but examining the present and future ontological manifestation of these chemicals in the form of the individual's life.

Therefore, genomic data woven into one's life writing may be read as both analeptic and proleptic narratives, although the former might not fully explain one's life already lived, and the latter cannot accurately, or entirely, describe the future. The key point to be kept in mind here is: genomic data reveals aspects—chemical, biological—of one's life that were hitherto hidden (Couser 170–171). I therefore suggest that the autobiogenography may also be read as a discovery-and-disclosure narrative. The individual, having discovered the biochemical foundations of her/ his life, proceeds to document it for the world. In the age of biometric identification, the genomic data is one more example of the dominance of the biological identities of individuals in the narrative of their lives. This discovery-and-disclosure form of the autobiogenography may be examined in some detail for the paradigm shift they engender.

## Autobiogenography, the New Materialism, and Bioeconomy

The self-discovery here is no longer restricted to moments of introspective and reflective knowledge (made famous by William Wordsworth and Jean-Jacques Rousseau, among others). It is not even a disease narrative, in most cases. As a discovery narrative, the autobiogenography reinstates the somatic and its biochemical foundations. I propose that autobiogenography may be fruitfully read through the lens of the New Materialism advocated by, among others, Karen Barad, Rosi Braidotti, Elizabeth Grosz, Jane Bennett, and Vicki Kirby. However, this examination of the materiality of matter cannot be made independent of the new bioeconomy in which this matter appears, grows, matures, acquires value, and multiplies.

First and foremost, autobiogenography returns us to the materiality of bodies, lives, and existence. The texts in the genre also force us to comprehend the agentic nature of matter, such as even a molecule of carbon, in our bodies. As Diana Coole and Samantha Frost phrase it, "materiality is always something more than 'mere' matter: an excess, force, vitality, relationality, or difference that renders matter active, self-creative, productive, unpredictable" (9). Life and its dynamics are determined by matter and its vitality, just as inertia is also an effect of matter. In Elizabeth Grosz's words,

> Matter, inorganic matter, is both the contracting condition of determination and the dilating expression of indetermination, and these two possibilities characterize both matter in its inorganic forms and those organized material bodies that are living. As isolatable systems, fixed entities, objects with extrinsic relations to each other, the material universe is the very source of regularity, predictability, and determination that enables a perceiving being to perform habitual actions with a measure of some guarantee of efficacy.
>
> (150–151)

While this does not mean we abandon the historical, psychological, and sociological approach to auto/biography as a form, the genre of autobiogenography ensures that we concede foundational materiality, material agency, and agentic chemistry to our lives. It further alerts us to the power and influence of intra-actions among non-living, inorganic, and mineral matter, such as chemical bases. Matter performs, and the nature of this performance—for example, as mutation or combination—determines a host of *expressions* of this matter. This return to materialism is perhaps the most significant methodological innovation autobiogenography brings to auto/biography studies.

Second, it calls for attention to the ethical dimensions around this materiality. As Diana Coole and Samantha Frost remind us, "the emergence of pressing ethical and political concerns that accompany the scientific and technological advances [are] predicated on new scientific models of matter and, in particular, of living matter" (1). The diagnostics and manipulation of this matter is a cause, they argue, for discussion and debate, for example, in the case of genetically engineered babies, the alteration of the cell lines, and hybridisation of bodies. Critics have even called for a ban on cloning technologies. In an essay in the *American Journal of Law and Medicine*, George Annas et al. propose a Convention against cloning and genetic engineering since these constitute "crimes against humanity" because they are "techniques that can alter the essence of humanity itself" (153).

Third, autobiogenography, or genomic biography, an adjacent genre, documents the modes by which the vital matter—such as cells—is imbricated within "technologies of living substance" (Hannah Landecker, appropriating nineteenth-century biologist Joseph Loeb's phrase). Cultured cells and cells sourced from human persons grow outside the frame of the human body. In some cases, such as HeLa (the "immortal" cell line sourced from Henrietta Lacks in 1951 and subsequently the source of cell lines for research across the world—see Skloot), may serve as "proxy diagnostic bodies for the patients from which they have been extracted", as "living material base for contemporary life science", among other uses (Landecker 2). That is, matter such as cells and their chemical bases 1) can be made to "live" outside their normal settings and ecosystems—the human form—in laboratories; or 2) function as metonyms for the entire individual or even community in terms of being proxy bodies. It therefore becomes difficult, for instance, to ask where the *individual* Henrietta Lacks ends and the *population* that is the Lacks-line (HeLa) begins. This argument works for xenotransplantation, genetic crossovers, and hybridisation as well, where the borders between bodies become increasingly blurred, and the blurring involves the relocation of cellular, chemical, living, *and* non-living matter.

Fourth, and related to the point above, the emergence of an "immunitary bioeconomy" (Brown et al.) around, say, Cord Blood (CB) banks as a part of what Catherine Waldby and Robert Mitchell identified as the "tissue economy", and thereby expanding the role of tissues and their features—immunity-generation—in the life story of individuals, families, and even the human race at large. Thus, the banking of CB by families or for commercial purposes means that certain kinds of matter sourced from human bodies begin to acquire the status of currency itself. As Nik Brown et al. put it:

> immunity itself has become a corporeal resource and currency for community. CB banks provide a form of immunologically based protection or exemption for those fortunate enough to benefit from

participation in the blood markets of advanced industrial bureau-cratic economies. Whether private or public, such banks are immu-nitary ventures, stockpiles of immunity.

(1116)

In other words, the evaluation of an individual's life and its worth may require attention to the immunitary bioeconomy in which her/his cells and Cord Blood are situated and marketed: because this matter alone *matters*. Just as once we studied auto/biography in terms of class, gender, race, and the market, we may know how to reposition the human cellular matter—an individual's auto/biography, as we have seen above—within emerging markets around certain kinds of matter (see Rajan on the bio-economy market). If we think of immunity as the expression and man-ifestation, in specific conditions, of *matter* in combination, then auto/biography, especially of the genomic variety, will need to address the immunitary and tissue bioeconomy.

## The Genomic *Bildungsroman*

Autobiogenography, such as Gessen's, Skloot's, or Wexler's (but also exemplified in sci-fi scenarios such as those by Octavia Butler, Kazuo Ishiguro, or Margaret Atwood), may be read as a genomic *bildungsro-man*, a subgenre of the *bildungsroman*, whose principal genre is the growing up *novel*. The classical *bildungsroman*, Franco Moretti argues, is marked by a tension between self-determination and social integration. The full and proper citizen is one who has been convinced that his (the dominant gender of the genre is male) internal development ties in with social requirements. In the case of autobiogenography, we can see two strains of the traditional model.

In texts like Gessen's or Wexler's, the very idea of individual devel-opment and growth over the years is read through the perspective of gene expression. Whereas in the conventional *bildungsroman* educa-tion, family, property-acquisition, and cultural training (including reli-gion) are constitutive conditions for the individual's growth, the genomic *bildungsroman* maps the centrality of genetic material in this process. Thus, "growth" or "aging" is mediated through the possibilities of the genetic mutation *finally* expressing itself. Wexler, for instance, is intensely aware of her own body's aging as she recalls the exact moments when *her* mother first started exhibiting symptoms of Huntington's disease.

In the second strain, seen in contemporary reworkings of the genre, such as Ishiguro's *Never Let Me Go*, organ transplants alter the relation of the body to the community (through donations). Michael Eatough argues:

For the clones of Ishiguro's tale, physical adulthood merely indicates that their organs contain an optimum amount of time. In contrast to organ recipients, whose failing organs no longer possess sufficient time, the students' organs contain the abundant time of "full" adulthood that is direly needed by "normals."

(143; see also Levy)

In examining the *bildungsroman* genre, Ursula Heise argues that the "victim's gradually deepening realization of the danger to which she or he is exposed' " is part of the growing up and self-realisation processes (139). I suggest, merging Heise and Eatough here, that autobiogenographies such as Wexler's and Gessen's invariably document their discovery of the corporeal time-bomb they carry. Coming into middle age means recognising that the time of their organs, functions, personhood—especially in the case of Wexler, who understands that once Huntington's symptoms appear in her, her personality is likely to change—and the quality of their life is different from that of the normative humans in the social–familial circle they occupy. The mutated gene eventually *separates* the individual from the normative human race, a reversal of the traditional *bildungsroman's* sequence, and more on the lines of Joseph Slaughter's "dissensual bildungsroman" (2007), where (inherent, immanent) conditions *obstruct* the individual's full growth and integration.

The new subject in life writing studies is read, literally, from the molecular level upward. While there exists a certain worry over the biological determinism of this genetic turn in the field, with increasing memoir writing and forms of biosociality (for example, in the case of online sites such as PatientsLikeMe) being built around genetic conditions (called "genetic citizenship", Heath et al.), we need to conceive of the subject, in addition to the traditional ways of emotions, rationality, agency, among others, as a collection of material chemicals whose intra-molecular interactions *constitute* the subject's self. Bionarratives and disease narratives have to be taken seriously by life writing scholars because they reference the *material* foundations of a host of subject-characteristics, in the form of syndromes, conditions, features, and embodied behaviour.

## Works Cited

Angrist, Misha. *Here Is a Human Being: At the Dawn of Personal Genomics.* New York, NY: HarperCollins, 2010.

Annas, George J. et al. "Protecting the Endangered Human: Toward an International Treaty Prohibiting Cloning and Inheritable Alterations." *American Journal of Law and Medicine*, vol. 28, no. 2, 2002, pp. 151–178.

Brown, Nik et al. "Immunitary Bioeconomy: The Economisation of Life in the International Cord Blood Market." *Social Science & Medicine*, vol. 72, 2011, pp. 1115–1122.

Coole, Diana, and Samantha Frost. "Introducing the New Materialisms." *New Materialisms: Ontology, Agency and Politics*, edited by Diana Coole and Samantha Frost. Durham, NC and London: Duke UP, 2010, pp. 1–43.

Couser, G. Thomas. *Vulnerable Subjects: Ethics and Life Writing.* Ithaca, NY: Cornell UP, 2004.

Eatough, Michael. "The Time that Remains: Organ Donation, Temporal Duration, and *Bildung* in Kazuo Ishiguro's *Never Let Me Go.*" *Literature and Medicine*, vol. 29, no. 1, 2011, pp. 132–160.

Gessen, Masha. *Blood Matters: From BRCA1 to Designer Babies, How the World and I Found Ourselves in the Future of the Gene.* Boston, MA: Mariner, 2009.

Grosz, Elizabeth. "Feminism, Materialism, and Freedom." *New Materialisms: Ontology, Agency and Politics*, edited by Diana Coole and Samantha Frost. Durham, NC and London: Duke UP, 2010, pp. 139–157.

Harris, Anna et al. "Autobiologies on YouTube: Narratives of Direct-to-Consumer Genetic Testing." *New Genetics and Society*, vol. 33, no. 1, 2014, pp. 60–78.

Heath, Deborah et al. "Genetic Citizenship." *A Companion to the Anthropology of Politics*, edited by David Nugent and Joan Vincent. Malden, MA: Blackwell, 2004, pp. 152–167.

Heise, Ursula K. *Sense of Place and Sense of Planet: The Environmental Imagination of the Global.* Oxford: Oxford UP, 2008.

Hoskins, Janet. "Agency, Biography and Objects." *Handbook of Material Culture*, edited by Christopher Tilley et al. London: SAGE, 2006.

Landecker, Hannah. *Culturing Life: How Cells Became Technologies.* Cambridge, MA: Harvard UP, 2007.

Levy, Titus. "Human Rights Storytelling and Trauma Narrative in Kazuo Ishiguro's *Never Let Me Go.*" *Journal of Human Rights*, vol. 10, 2011, pp. 1–16.

Moretti, Franco. *The Way of the World: The Bildungsroman in European Culture.* London: Verso, 2000.

Nayar, Pramod K. "Autobiogenography: Genomes and Lifewriting'." *a/b: Auto/Biography Studies*, vol. 31, no. 3, 2016, pp. 509–525.

———. "Genomes, or the Book of Life Itself." *a/b: Auto/Biography Studies*, vol. 32, no. 2, 2017, pp. 217–219.

Pinker, Steven. "My Genome, My Self." *New York Times*, 7 June 2009. Web. 9 Apr. 2016.

Skloot, Rebecca. *The Immortal Life of Henrietta Lacks.* New York: Pan, 2010.

Slaughter, Joseph. *Human Rights, Inc.: The World Novel, Narrative Form, and International Law.* New York: Fordham UP, 2007.

Sunder Rajan, Kaushik, editor. *Lively Capital: Biotechnologies, Ethics, and Governance in Global Markets.* Durham, NC and London: Duke UP, 2012.

Waldby, Catherine, and Robert Mitchell. *Tissue Economies: Blood, Organs and Cell Lines in Late Capitalism.* London: Duke UP, 2006.

Wexler, Alice. *Mapping Fate: A Memoir of Family, Risk, and Genetic Research.* New York: Random House, 1995.

# 23 Doing Disability Autobiography

## Introducing Reading Group Methodology as Feminist Disability Praxis

*Ally Day*

When I first met T, I asked her why she was interested in getting involved with my research project about HIV memoir. "I want to write my own memoir someday", she tells me, "and I thought this might help" (23 August 2012). T contacted me in response to a flyer I disseminated through my local AIDS Service Organization. I was looking for (self-identified) women living with HIV to be a part of a reading group that would meet weekly to discuss HIV memoirs.

Early in my PhD work, I began seeking out published memoirs written by women living with HIV in the United States; I was interested in how women's voices had been left out of the larger national HIV story centred on the experience of cisgendered white gay men in the 1980s.[1] I was also seeking voices who could speak to living with a chronic illness that were not from a racially and class-privileged perspective, an observation made by G. Thomas Couser (190).[2] Couser writes about how there is a new wave of disability memoir that aligns with other kinds of activist memoirs, focusing on disability as an empowered identity; at the same time that he produces an insightful analysis of recent disability memoirs in the early 2000s, he misses an opportunity to engage with memoirs written by working-class people and women of colour (165–190). I began to wonder if perhaps Couser's understanding of "disability" itself was too limited; that a broader interpretation of what "counts" as disabled would expand our ideas about reading and writing disability. As a queer woman, I had been doing work within the HIV movement for years; as a woman with a chronic illness in a rural state, it was gay men living with HIV who first taught me how to negotiate with the medical industrial complex. The more I engaged with disability studies and its growing critiques of life writing, the more I thought about those of us left out of the narrative—people of colour, queer people, people with chronic illness. HIV life writing seemed like one way to engage some of these voices.

At the time I was seeking out these HIV memoirs written by women, African American women were the fastest growing population of new HIV diagnosis.[3] By 2010, there were five published memoirs written by US women; they spanned publication dates from 1996 to 2010; they crossed class and racial divides, and types of publication presses.[4] These memoirs had not been written about by life writing or other academic scholars; they were also not well known even among AIDS Service workers and activists. Writing about and theorising from the perspective of these memoirs became necessary work for me.

But I was not someone living with HIV. And if, as a feminist disability studies scholar, I was going to truly live by the imperative "Nothing About Us Without Us",[5] I did not want to provide just one more subgenre of disability life writing to be taxonomised on a shelf, added to a list of represented diagnosis (Couser; Smith and Watson; Rak)[6] that would fade in and out of public interest. I wanted to know how our understanding of life writing changes if we theorise together and unpack themes, narrative structure, and even paratextual context. Life writing, understood in this way, is not a static entity to be taxonomised but a negotiated product interpreted differentially through embodied reading practices. In this chapter, I propose that doing disability autobiography begins with this fundamental understanding. This includes recognising intersectional experiences of power and privilege (gender, race, class, sexuality, dis/ability, religion, citizenship) in both the authors and the readers; this includes understanding that the experience of dis/ability shape-shifts in relation to power and cannot be disentangled from other experiences of privilege and oppression. Doing disability autobiography does not mean simply reading and interpreting memoirs about disability; it means investigating how these memoirs are transformed through multiple processes of reading and how our own embodied experiences affect our temporal interpretations.

Doing disability autobiography is first and foremost a close reading of narrative—both published written narrative and oral or informal narrative that often remains invisible because of barriers of access to publication and multimedia production. This follows contemporary theories in feminist autobiographical studies in recognising that autobiography itself is an open-ended history of embodiment. As Susannah Mintz writes, "disability is an inconstant experience, its significance to the story of self requiring multiple retellings, repeated narrative shaping" (4). While I believe the narratives I analyse about HIV share themes of disabled embodiment, intersectional oppression, and an ongoing negotiation of medical power relations with other disability narratives, particularly those narratives that address chronic illness, there is also a way in which this research highlights the particular and not the universal. Doing disability autobiography is always about embracing the particular.

Doing disability autobiography does not mean that one's research is meant to speak for all people living with a particular condition like HIV or all medical practitioners working with people living with HIV. The project of theorising through and alongside narrative is intended to bring to the forefront marginalised experiences while maintaining keen attention to the power relations that shape those experiences. Feminist theorist Sara Ahmed asks us to question how some texts become considered theory and others not and how systems of power play into those demarcations (8–10). Ahmed writes that "we use the particulars to challenge the universal" (10), and indeed, doing disability autobiography is doing just that; in the work I discuss in this chapter, the broadest particular is the experience of HIV in the United States as understood through published life writing and my own ethnographic work with reading HIV and disability memoir with women living with HIV. These forms of life story, in the retellings and contradictions, are embodied theory about identity, self, and illness.

## Nothing About Us Without Us: Methodological Nuts and Bolts

I began this project by reading every HIV memoir written by women in the United States, compiling a reading list (with brief summary notes) for my field research; I then applied for Institutional Review Board approval (the university-based ethical review boards that, by federal law, review human subject research in the United States) and small grants to pay for books and food, and collaborated with local AIDS Service Organizations (with whom I had pre-existing relationships) to secure a private meeting space and recruit participants. Prior to our first group meeting, I interviewed each participant, asking about their reading habits, their interest in engaging in the project, and any information about their background they wanted to share. I shared with them my own HIV negative status, my experience with chronic illness, my research interests. At the conclusion of our initial interview, I asked each participant to look at the reading list and circle three HIV memoirs that interested them.

After interviews, I coordinated a weekly meeting time, and for six months, I met with women over coffee and brownies to discuss our books; often women skipped weeks and often we were on different chapters, sometimes even different books, when we came together. This dynamic was helpful in reminding me that I was not leading a literature class—that I was not teaching but listening. Each week I asked open-ended questions about themes and characters, likes and dislikes. Often, a scene or a moment in a memoir inspired conversations among my participants about their personal experiences. I audio recorded each meeting and transcribed and coded transcripts. At the end of our time together, I conducted follow-up interviews, asking many of the same questions I had six months earlier.

The themes and disclosures of medical discrimination in particular inspired me, more than a year later and in a city a few hours away, to host a reading group with AIDS Service workers. I followed the same methodology with one-on-one initial interviews, regular meetings, and follow-up interviews, comparing and contrasting transcripts. This process allowed me to deepen my understandings of how doing disability autobiography involves multiple readings and how textual interpretation is always an embodied practice.

## Tale of Two Cities/Two Groups

Each of my reading groups chose their reading selections from the same list; as such, there is overlap in selections that provides me with opportunities to compare responses to memoirs. One such memoir is Catherine Wyatt-Morley's *Journal of an HIV Positive Mother* published by Kumarian Press, a small African American press in 1997.[7] Wyatt-Morley's memoir is the first book-length account of living with HIV written and published by a woman in the United States. *Journal of an HIV Positive Mother* is primarily in the style of a journal, tracing her experience from her diagnosis after a hysterectomy and the later divorce from her husband (who contracted the virus through infidelity and then infected Wyatt-Morley), through her experience founding a HIV activist and support group for women. Throughout the memoir, Wyatt-Morley traces her experience as an African American mother of three and factory worker, emphasising how HIV diagnosis has complicated her experience as a single mother.

In the context of our discussion of this memoir in my group with women living with HIV, and the many experiences of medical and workplace discrimination Wyatt-Morley shared with her readers, reading group participants began sharing their own stories of medical discrimination, some even from just the week preceding our conversations. It became clear in our discussions that for women living with HIV, because of their experiences of medical discrimination, it still feels very much like the early days of the HIV crisis. In contrast, in the group of AIDS Service workers, the response to this memoir was overwhelmingly negative, one participant saying, "We just don't have patients like this anymore. This is historical but not relevant". Another worker lamented, "I have minority fatigue—I mean, what happened to the voices of white gay men?" How is a black woman living with HIV supposed to receive adequate services when her psychiatric nurse practitioner refers to her experience with overlapping systems of oppression as causing him minority fatigue? This is one of the theoretical questions that emerged as central to my larger project.

My two reading groups often had disparate receptions of memoirs. In another example, each group read Regan Hoffman's *I Have Something to Tell You*. Published in 2009, Hoffman was already known to the HIV community as an editor of *POZ*, a magazine of HIV news and feature stories distributed for free through AIDS Service Organizations. Hoffman writes of her surprise of diagnosis as a wealthy young white woman—a strategy that perhaps emphasises all people's vulnerability but also works to distance herself from women of colour and gay men. However, she spends the second half of her memoir writing about HIV globally, situating herself and her intersectional privilege as part of a diverse, global, and vulnerable community.

The members of my AIDS Service worker reading group overwhelmingly chose this book as their favourite among the memoirs we read, saying it was the one that was most articulate and inspirational. In contrast, the women living with HIV in my first reading group overwhelmingly disliked this book, many not even finishing it because, as T said, "I couldn't get past her and her damn horse" (17 January 2013). The cover of Hoffman's memoir is a photograph of a thin white woman on a horse, long hair shielding her face. This difference in reception highlights the importance of how a memoir is marketed; Hoffman's publisher is an international New York-based publisher, which is reflected in the overall production value. What is inspirational to one group (AIDS Service workers), is unpalatable to another (women living with HIV). While both groups could identify as peers of Hoffman, since she is both a woman living with HIV and an AIDS Service worker, only one group feels this affinity. Unpacking these dynamics is essential for doing disability autobiography and became another central objective of my larger research project.

These are just two examples of how the field research guided the kinds of questions about HIV life writing that became central objects of investigation. My reading groups set the parameters and exposed me to questions that emerge through embodied reading practices.

## Notes

1. Jacquelyn Foertsch argues that many of the first HIV memoirs written by white gay men can be understood through the rhetoric of invasion and containment (22–24); similarly, Priscilla Wald outlines how HIV was constructed through the Patient 0 narrative as foreign invader. As I have written about elsewhere, when women begin writing about their own experience with HIV, particularly in relation to diagnosis during pregnancy, this narrative of foreign invasion becomes much too simplistic.
2. Couser explores the various rhetoric imposed on disability life writing (33). Common rhetoric includes triumph over adversity (Couser 2009, 33–34), the gothic rhetoric of horror (34–35), the closely linked medical rhetoric (34–35), the rhetoric of spiritual compensation (36–37), and the rhetoric of nostalgia (38–39). Couser writes of an "upsurge" during the late twentieth century of life writing about bodily experience, what he calls auto/somatography (164). What makes this new upsurge unique is the memoir's "disability consciousness"; in other words, the rhetorical move itself of focusing on the disability versus the impairment (165). This upsurge in disability life writing puts a distinct emphasis on the social; Couser compares this writing to other kinds of activist autobiographies (165). The story in these new memoirs is not about the triumph over impairment, which has been a central feature of the disability narrative, but about how individual bodies are circulating in socially constructed environments and claiming a political identity (167). While Couser

makes broad claims about disability life writing, he also laments that the disability memoir as a whole still represents a primarily white, middle-class authorship (190).

3. At the time of writing this chapter, new HIV diagnosis among African American women has had a 40% decrease; black women, however, are still fifteen times more likely than white women to contract the virus. For more about recent statistics and demographic trends in HIV diagnosis, please see "Black Americans and HIV/AIDS: The Basics" published by The Henry J Kaiser Foundation, 6 February 2018. www.kff.org/hivaids/fact-sheet/black-americans-and-hivaids-the-basics/ Accessed 18 July 2018.

4. Marvelyn Brown. *The Naked Truth: Young, Beautiful, and (HIV) Positive.* New York: Harper Collins, 2008; Regan Hoffman. *I Have Something to Tell You.* New York: Atria Books, 2009; Paula Peterson. *Penitent, With Roses: An HIV+ Mother Reflects.* Middlebury, VT: Middlebury College P, 2001; Paige Rawl. *Positive: Surviving My Bullies, Finding Hope, and Changing the World.* New York: Harper Collins, 2014; Catherine Wyatt-Morley. *AIDS Memoir: Journal of an HIV Positive Mother.* Bloomfield, CT: Kumarian P, 1997; Catherine Wyatt-Morley. *My Life with AIDS: From Tragedy to Triumph.* Westport, CT: Four Pillars Media Group, 2012.

5. "Nothing About Us Without Us" became a slogan for the Disability Rights Movement, resisting the idea that any policy that affects people with disability can be made without the input and perspective of disabled people; this is written about in detail by James Charlton in his book *Nothing About Us Without Us: Disability Oppression and Empowerment.*

6. G. Thomas Couser, Julia Watson, and Sidonie Smith all offer careful taxonomies of life writing; in reviewing the work of these scholars, Rak suggests that life writing has been taxonomised into more than sixty categories but asks us to think beyond coming up with new categories, writing, "It makes more sense to understand what the publishing industry, the bookselling industry, and the public think that memoir means than to coin little used terms for the types of content that appear in its examples" (24).

7. In 2012, Wyatt-Morley published another memoir, *My Life With AIDS: From Tragedy to Triumph*, which tells many of the same details as her first memoir (now out of print) but with a different format. This is another way in which life experience is retold and temporally and narratively adapted.

## Works Cited

Ahmed, Sara. *Living a Feminist Life.* Durham, NC: Duke UP, 2017.

Brown, Marvelyn. *The Naked Truth: Young, Beautiful, and (HIV) Positive.* New York: Harper Collins, 2008.

Charlton, James I. *Nothing About Us Without Us: Disability Oppression and Empowerment.* Berkeley, CA: U California P, 2000.

Couser, G. Thomas. *Signifying Bodies: Disability in Contemporary Life Writing.* Ann Arbor, MI: U of Michigan P, 2009.

Day, Ally. "Embodied Triumph and Political Mobilization: Reading Marvelyn Brown's The Naked Truth: Young, Beautiful and (HIV) Positive." *Auto/Biography Studies*, vol. 28, no. 1, 2013, pp. 112–125.

———. "Postfeminist Motherhood? Reading a Differential Deployment of Identity in American Women's HIV Narratives." *Disabling Domesticity*, edited by Michael Rembis. New York: Palgrave Macmillan, 2017.

Foertsch, Jacquelyn. *Enemies Within: The Cold War and the AIDS Crisis in Literature, Film and Culture.* Urbana, IL: U of Illinois P, 2001. Print.

Hoffman, Regan. *I Have Something to Tell You.* New York: Atria Books, 2009.

Martin, Emily. *Flexible Bodies: The Role of Immunity in American Culture From the Days of Polio to the Age of AIDS.* Boston, MA: Beacon P, 1994.

Mintz, Susannah B. *Unruly Bodies: Life Writing by Women With Disabilities.* U of North Carolina P, 2007.

Mollow, Anna. " 'When Black Women Go on Prozac': The Politics of Race, Gender and Emotional Distress in Meri Nana-Ama Danquah's *Willow Weep for Me.*" *The Disability Studies Reader.* 2nd ed., edited by Lennard Davis. New York: Routledge P, 2006, pp. 283–299.

Peterson, Paula. *Penitent, With Roses: An HIV+ Mother Reflects.* Middlebury, VT: Middlebury College P, 2001.

Rak, Julie. *Boom! Manufacturing Memoir for the Popular Market.* Ontario, Canada: Wilfred Laurier UP, 2013.

Rawl, Paige. *Positive: Surviving My Bullies, Finding Hope, and Changing the World.* New York: Harper Collins, 2014.

Smith, Sidonie, and Julia Watson. *Reading Autobiography: A Guide for Interpreting Life Narratives.* 2nd ed. Minneapolis, MN: U of Minnesota, 2010.

Wald, Patricia. *Contagious: Cultures, Carriers, and Outbreak Narrative.* Durham, NC: Duke UP, 2008. Print.

Wyatt-Morley, Catherine. *AIDS Memoir: Journal of an HIV Positive Mother.* Bloomfield, CT: Kumarian P, 1997.

———. *My Life With AIDS: From Tragedy to Triumph.* Westport, CT: Four Pillars Media Group, 2012.

# 24 Sanctioning Subjectivity

## Navigating Low-Risk Human Ethics Approval

*Phillip Kavanagh and Kate Douglas*

Phillip Kavanagh recently returned from a field trip to the United States to conduct interviews with a research subject. These interviews took place over two months, lasting several hours at a time, up to three times a week. Two weeks into this interview process, the subject turned to Kavanagh. "Do you have anything specific you wanted to ask me?" Kavanagh did not.

This field trip was for Kavanagh's doctoral thesis—a memoir artefact and exegesis—for which Kate Douglas is the primary supervisor. The impetus for the project was an uncanny coincidence—Phillip Kavanagh is a gay 30-year-old comedy playwright, born in 1988, with a deep sense of irony and a habit of finding himself in farcical situations. The interview subject is the American writer Joe Keenan, who created a fictional version of himself across a trilogy of novels: a gay comedy playwright with a deep sense of irony and a habit of finding himself in farcical situations, first published in 1988, aged 29 in the third novel, and named Philip Cavanaugh.

While Phil and Joe agreed that the coincidence was worthy of further investigation, they also both felt that a work of life narrative exploring the relationship between Joe Keenan and Phillip Kavanagh would require more than the eighteen months of email exchanges they had accumulated. The two of them needed to meet. And so began the conversation that occurs between many a new PhD student and their supervisor: "You'll need to apply for ethics approval".

As Sidonie Smith and Julia Watson note, "questions of ethical representation are at the heart of autobiographical studies today" (221). And Douglas argues that

> ethical scholarship is about academic integrity—research that fulfils the requirements of institutions and disciplines, and is appropriate for circulating among peers and students and within the community . . . scholarly disciplines and the intellectual communities within them have their own set of expectations regarding research, which go beyond the legal and institutional toward the

moral, contextual, and often shifting mores that govern how we proceed with research. Such scholarly ethics consider the social and political responsibilities that accompany research. Going beyond the question of liability, they include considerations of harm, benefits, and power dynamics.

(272)

Each university has its own guidelines for how they process human ethics approvals. This chapter is a case study that ties some peculiarities that have arisen during Phillip's process of applying for human ethics and undergoing field research (in this instance, conducting interviews). We outline some of the specific challenges we have faced in negotiating the low-risk human ethics approval process at our university—Flinders University (South Australia)—such as how to conduct interviews that are ethical but flexible, as well as the process of navigating ongoing consent.

The initial application that we lodged was fairly straightforward—Kavanagh was planning to travel to the USA to meet with Keenan, and he would conduct interviews that would form the basis of his PhD's creative artefact: a comedic, meta-textual memoir. The tone of the work, the subject, the existing (albeit online) relationship between Kavanagh and Keenan, and the enthusiasm of both parties all contributed to this project being classed as low risk. However, this initial application was still met with suggestions for revision. As G. Thomas Couser argues, "the closer the relationship between writer and subject, and the greater the vulnerability or dependency of the subject, the higher the ethical stakes, and the more urgent the need for ethical scrutiny" (*Vulnerable Subjects* xiii). Ethics questions and offers some formality and protection, or indeed mindfulness, to what might otherwise be seen as an organic, mutually beneficial professional relationship.

We anticipate that navigating both formal and informal ethical standards is a challenge shared by other life narrative practitioners (perhaps, in particular, graduate students) within university contexts. Our aim is to provide a useful case study for life writing practitioners as they work with these structures at their own institutions.

## Experiencing and Remembering as Data Collection

Couser explores the complex, indeed sometimes contradictory, ethical demands placed on memoir. He writes,

> to require too much in the way of factual accuracy is to cramp memoirist's style and unduly limit the genre as art. At the same time, not to insist on some adherence to fact in serious memoir is to undermine the genre's power and interfere with its work. We need to strike a

medium between legalistic insistence on "just the facts" and indifference to veracity.

(Couser, Memoir 80)

We were mindful, from the outset, of building a methodology from within these principles. In the first instance, Kavanagh had proposed that the interviews with Keenan would not be recorded. There were several reasons for this suggestion. First, the project was not intended to be a biographical study of Keenan, but rather an autobiographical retelling of the interactions between Kavanagh and Keenan. So, while "interviews" is a term that makes sense for an ethics application, it is not entirely accurate; "rapport building" might be a more appropriate, if nebulous, term. The presence of a recording device formalises the relationship in a way that establishes very clear roles—the interviewer and the interviewee. The data Kavanagh desired wasn't any specific piece of information he could request from Keenan through a series of questions, but rather an unfolding and strengthening of the relationship they had begun eighteen months prior through email correspondence. As such, the presence of technology that formalised these roles was undesirable and could prove detrimental to the project. However, when the suggestion was raised that ethical protocol required audio recordings, we challenged this by providing an ethical rationale for our decision.

## Research Results as Literature

One of the quirks of a low-risk ethics panel is it is likely to be made up of fewer people than one for higher risk projects. It is sometimes just one person conducting approvals executively. So, while there may be cross-disciplinary representation in the make-up of the larger panels, these smaller panels are likely to have a narrower expertise base, while still examining a diverse range of projects. This means that the methods of data collection for life writing practitioners may end up being held to the same standards as projects whose eventual research output is a scientific study. When the data collected via fieldwork is the researcher's memories, and the eventual research project privileges the subjectivity of the researcher, an ethics assessor may be thrown. However, the memoir is not striving for an objective record of events, and will involve some degree of paraphrasing and shuffling of details, in line with the (re)constructed nature of memory and the stylised tone and needs of the narrative. Because this is what memoirs "do"; this is what is expected of memoirs from readers (see Couser's earlier point). The ethics panel, taking this into account, conceded that notes taken after the "interviews" would suffice as data collection. This shows that there is a willingness on the part of these panels to expand their understanding of ethical practice for creative life writing projects.

On a side note, when Kavanagh and Keenan did meet for the first time, Kavanagh had a moment of panic that perhaps he should record their conversations to refer back to, and asked if Keenan wouldn't mind him recording their chats on his iPhone. As it turns out, Keenan preferred Kavanagh simply remember what they said, and told him to put the phone away. This goes to show that even the expected default for ethical practice, with a view to protecting participants, needs to be open to review for participants who prefer other means of documentation to audio recording. Responding to research subjects and making sure they are happy is at the heart of ethical research.

## Consent

Collaborations are intended to be "mutually beneficial" (Couser, *Memoir* 94). While Keenan's initial consent was a necessary element of the project being sanctioned, we recognised that how this consent is continually negotiated is even more important. As Smith and Watson note, writing collaboratively requires an ongoing commitment to ethical practice; someone will be giving "thematic shape to life writing by virtue of decisions about what is included or excluded" (68). As Kavanagh progresses from notes and journals into a crafted memoir, he will bring Keenan into this process. Because their interviews were informal, it is unclear what was on and what was off the record, so allowing Keenan to have an active role in this construction, and to express what elements of his representation he is happy to include, offers us an ethical framework for this project. Robert McGill puts forward a similar methodological process as best practice for authors of autobiographical fiction in *The Treacherous Imagination*.

This may mean Kavanagh finds he has to make aesthetic compromises down the line, if interesting material he had assumed was on the record was very much off the record. But we feel these compromises will be worth making to maintain the ethical integrity of the work. Keenan was generous enough to allow Kavanagh access to his life, and Kavanagh has no desire to see that generosity disabused. This process is what Couser describes as "transactional transparency" (Couser, *Memoir* 99): "Prefatory notes can explain how the subject and author came together . . . how the narrative was produced . . . whether the subject had a chance to vet the manuscript" (Couser, *Memoir* 99). The text must "satisfy readers that the narrative [. . .] has been ethically produced" (Couser, *Memoir* 99).

## The Necessity of Uncertainty

There are inherent risks involved in this semi-biographical memoir. The ethics application process can be viewed in part as a form of risk mitigation, and a life writing practitioner setting out to build upon a new relationship for the purpose of writing about it runs the risk that the relationship will not be fruitful. At worst, it may become toxic or even exploitative (see Janet Malcolm's *The Journalist and the Murderer* for an examination of the soured relationship between Joe McGinniss and Jeffrey R. MacDonald). Despite two years of email correspondence between Keenan and Kavanagh before the field trip took place, there was still every chance that the relationship between the two would not be productive, that they might clash, dislike one another, or simply fail to form any kind of rapport. It is sheer good fortune, then, that Kavanagh and Keenan genuinely enjoyed one another's company, respected each other, and ended the trip on good terms. But that does not mean the trip was without unforeseen problems. In fact, the relationship that Kavanagh is now most conflicted about the ethics of documenting is not with a person at all, but with a dog.

This dog was first owned by a Hollywood actress best known for her work a popular 1990s teen drama, and he was caught up in a complex gossip story in 2014 that saw him the primary subject of multiple paparazzi articles, complete with candid snapshots. As such, he is already something of a public figure, with a digital archive of life writing dedicated to his backstory and his brush with death. The questions of how Kavanagh navigates the representation of this animal—who he was cohabitating with and helping to care for, whom he formed a close bond with which was later severed when the dog attacked Kavanagh on multiple occasions—is fraught with many issues and remains an ongoing concern.

Perhaps more so than any other figure represented in this memoir, this dog fits Couser's typology of a "vulnerable subject", not simply because he is incapable of shaping his own representation, but also because he is deaf, and a breed that is banned in certain countries, which also positions him as belonging to multiple "socially or culturally disadvantaged minorities" (Couser, *Vulnerable Subjects* xiii). Given that such breeds of dog are already subject to strict legislation, individual narratives of violence and aggression perpetuate a collective narrative that such breeds are "dangerous". This is before Kavanagh even touches on the implications of representing the dog's owner. In such instances, Couser argues,

> the justice of the portrayal has to do with whether the text represents its subject in the way the subject would like to be represented, with whether the portrayal is in the subject's best interest, with the control the subject has over it, and with the degree and kind of any harm or wrong done by misrepresentation.
>
> (Vulnerable Subjects 42)

Paul John Eakin similarly asks us to consider: "What is the good of life writing, and how, exactly, can it do harm?" (1). How this all plays out remains to be seen and will be the basis of further analysis through Kavanagh's PhD exegesis, and perhaps the memoir itself. It also points to the inevitable complications of this kind of field research.

## Unexpected Subjects

The ethics panel was not blind to a large gap between the proposed research project as a whole and the very narrow limits of the proposed ethics approval application. We sought approval for Kavanagh to meet and correspond with Keenan, but inevitably Kavanagh would meet other potential subjects on his travels. Eakin reminds us that "life writing is experiential. Because we live our lives in relation to others, our privacies are largely shared, making it hard to demarcate the boundary where one life leaves off and another begins" (8). As the ethics panel pointed out, even waiters in the restaurants where Kavanagh and Keenan met would be implicated in the narrative of Kavanagh's trip. At the time, we stressed that only Keenan would need to be identified, and all other subjects could be described without identifying features, or with these changed to protect their anonymity. However, during the field trip, Kavanagh met many people whose lives became entangled with his own. To write about his life during these two months will be to write about theirs. One way of mitigating against a breach of their trust was to be entirely transparent about the motives for his trip. Kavanagh told every person he met that he was planning to write a book about his travels. For some potential subjects, this helped as a shorthand for the knowledge that they might be represented by Kavanagh in the future. One new friend would constantly point out which of his statements was on the record and which off. In general, Kavanagh will only be certain who he wishes to write about as he now begins this process of shaping the memoir. Which may lead us back to that very same ethics approval process.

## Retrospective Ethics Approval

The conventional wisdom with regards to applying for ethics approval retrospectively is "don't do it". University-based life writing practitioners are urged to plan for contingencies that may occur before embarking upon field research, and to receive ethics approval to cover them. In practice, the most interesting events are likely to be unforeseeable, and walking around with a bundle of consent forms is a sure-fire way of scaring off potential friends. For some events, approaching the memoir the way we suggested we would with that hypothetical waiter may prove the simplest option—removing identifying markers and allowing them to float into this work of non-fiction as an ostensibly fictional character. For other subjects, these identifying markers are indelibly linked to their role in this narrative. Those who are willing to be identified, and who Kavanagh can enter into a similarly collaborative relationship about their ongoing representation, as he has agreed to with Keenan, should be able to feature. However, this will likely mean an ethics amendment, shaped around allowing Kavanagh to use data collected during an official field trip with subjects who, at the time, were not identified as such. This process has implications for life writers who seek to use their own past as the raw material for their work, as approval would not have been sought prior to gathering their lived experience outside the confines of a university. This is new territory for Flinders, and we hope that this next step in testing the nature of ethical practice for life writers will have benefits for future researchers embarking upon similar projects, confident that embracing uncertainty will pay dividends that can be negotiated after the fact.

## Conclusion

The points we have covered here are just a few that have arisen as we have negotiated the complexities of creating a work of life writing for the artefact of a PhD thesis. While specific to Kavanagh's project, we hope that they will give future scholars an idea of some of the kinds of issues that may arise with this kind of creative research. We want to stress, however, that these limitations need not be static, and need not be seen as wholly problematic. University ethics committees are forever updating their ideas of ethical practice, and students and practitioners should be encouraged to do the same. The complexities of university ethics approval can be a chance for researchers to interrogate and formalise their own ideas of what constitutes ethical practice. It offers a framework that can be outlined to potential subjects as they arise during field research. It can be revisited and revised as the changing ethical concerns of the project present themselves. And it offers the project not only a way of regulating and mitigating the potential harms that can be caused through life writing, but also a resource of critical self-reflexion that can be presented as methodological research.

## Works Cited

Couser, G. Thomas. *Memoir: An Introduction*. Oxford: Oxford UP, 2012.

Couser, G. Thomas. *Vulnerable Subjects: Ethics and Life Writing*. Ithaca, NY: Cornell UP, 2004.

Douglas, Kate. "Ethical Dialogues: Youth, Memoir and Trauma." *a/b: Auto/ Biography Studies*, vol. 30, no. 2, 2015, pp. 271–288.

Eakin, Paul John. *The Ethics of Life Writing*. Ithaca, NY: Cornell UP, 2004.

McGill, Robert. *The Treacherous Imagination: Intimacy, Ethics, and Autobiographical Fiction*. Columbus, OH: Ohio State UP, 2013.

Malcolm, Janet. *The Journalist and the Murderer*. New York: Vintage Books, 1990.

Smith, Sidonie, and Julia Watson. *Reading Autobiography: A Guide for Interpreting Life Narratives*. Minnesota, MN: U of Minnesota P, 2010.

# 25 Girls' Auto/Biographical Media

## The Importance of Audience Reception in Studying Undervalued Life Narrative

*Emma Maguire*

Sidonie Smith and Julia Watson have enjoyed long careers theorising and interpreting life writing, and they point out that as readers, and as scholars, we "have notions about whose life is important, whose life might be of interest to a broader public, and what experiences 'count' as significant. In these expectations we imply a set of questions about life narratives" (*Reading* 237). When studying the auto/biographical media of girls and young women, I have discovered that—for some scholars— the lives and experiences of these young creators are not often regarded as important. But they do offer rich opportunities for studying key concerns for life narrative scholars, such as the construction of subjectivity, the performance and consumption of identities, the marketability of particular lives and stories, the channels of circulation for life narrative, and the differing cultural value of auto/biographical modes and genres. A problem with getting scholars to recognise this rich potential is that girls' digital texts—beauty blogs, fangirl Twitter threads, ephemeral activist Tumblr blogs, for example—are not always recognised as worthy or rich objects for literary study. Although feminist and media scholars like Jessalynn Keller, Emily Hund, Brooke Erin Duffy, Mary Celeste Kearney, Angela McRobbie, Anita Harris, Sarah Banet-Weiser, and Dawn Kelly, among others, have done important work on analysing gender and identity in girls' cultural production, my methodology draws on this rich body of research and incorporates it within a framework of literary and auto/biography studies. Attending to evidence of how audience reception shapes self-presentation is an important element of my methodology when it comes to reading these undervalued auto/biographical texts, because they reveal the vital role of community norms, values, meanings, and cultural pressures in creating the self that young women present to their audiences.

One way that life writing scholars have approached marginal life writing is to assert that publishing such stories and voices in the privileged form of the book raises the status of these stories and permits them to circulate in the mainstream, finding readers who can engage empathically with lives different from their own (Gilmore; Smith and Watson *Reading*;

Whitlock). This has often been the case with memoir. But with digital life narrative texts like tweets, Snapchat snaps, YouTube videos, and online diaries, these forms are neither culturally privileged nor—for most of them—likely to reach a wide audience. How, then, do we read undervalued, marginal, or fleeting forms of auto/biographical engagement in media that do not necessarily accommodate traditional tools of literary scholarship such as close reading or appraisal of literary aesthetics, while still finding value in them *as texts*, i.e., as creative products that mediate lives and selves?

In this chapter, I use my experiences of studying digital auto/biography by girls and young women to suggest the value of adopting a methodology attentive to surface reading and audience reception—one that also considers the mechanics of self-presentation and life narration in multiple media forms. This approach adapts some of the tools of reading life writing to new forms of digital media, and it is useful in a field where the objects that we study are not always books but, increasingly, a range of digital media authored by subjects that may not have always had access to traditional forms of publishing their life stories (Arthur 313; McNeill and Zuern v–vi; Poletti and Rak 5).

First, the question of value. The autobiographical media of young women is undervalued in three ways. The kinds of media they produce—YouTube videos, Instagram accounts, fangirl Twitter threads—are not often studied as literary objects. Often, these texts are taken as raw data that reveal something true about girls as a demographic group, or as insubstantial entertainment, for example in the case of beauty bloggers that I discuss below. It is not that this media is considered to be "low art" but rather that it is not always considered to be a product of creativity at all. In addition, even as English syllabi and the range of texts we choose to research increasingly expand to include material authored by creators that are not only white, or male, or dead, it is still relatively rare to see texts authored by young women as studied in academic contexts for their textual strategies and innovations (the literary works of Helen Oyeyemi, Zadie Smith, and Hannah Kent are some notable exceptions). Auto/biographical writing is often positioned as non-literary, or not-as-literary as fiction or poetry—and digital media that is auto/biographical in nature can seem to be an inappropriate fit for literary study. It is also the case that, in public discourse, the voices of girls and young women are often interpreted as naïve, trivial, shallow, or uninformed (Maguire 4). Despite the low cultural value attached to girls' auto/biographical media, the texts that I study present rich opportunities to examine how young producers are innovating, contributing to, and shaping forms, strategies, and methods for representing lives online. These texts, which may not appear to have much substance, in fact reveal important things about subjectivity, self-presentation, and "what it actually means to *be* online and to have an online life" (Poletti and Rak 4).

One method of extracting such value from these texts is by factoring in audience reception as a key textual element. As Smith and Watson explain, "online venues assume, invite, and depend on audiences, [. . .] How a site appeals to an audience and the kind of response it solicits is worthy of attention" ("Virtually" 74). In terms of audience reception, young women's self-presentations occupy contested space in online contexts and thus provide rich sites for examination. On the one hand, the recent wave of online feminism has certainly raised the value of young women's voices, particularly when they are telling stories about gendered inequality, for example the success of the blog and subsequent memoir of Pakistani activist Malala Yousafzai. On the other hand, girls and young women are so often the targets of online abuse in the forms of bullying, doxing, rape and death threats, and revenge pornography. A prominent example is the extreme and ongoing harassment of feminist media critic and blogger Anita Sarkeesian in the #gamergate controversy of 2014. Such practices threaten to curb the space that young women are able or willing to claim online (Sobieraj 1700). But young women are persistent media producers, and they navigate the pressures and perils of online media networks with resilience and innovation. The media objects that they create about themselves and their lives demonstrate awareness of the context for circulation and, when read attentively, reveal strategies for negotiating access to online space and an audience that employ technological skill, negotiation of their position within matrices of power and cultural discourses, and facility with modes of address and language. They also reveal how constructions of youthful femininity are shaped discursively. One way of investigating audience reception is to read comments sections such as those afforded by platforms like YouTube and Instagram. But it is also possible to read strategies of self-presentation inside the text for evidence of how the anticipation of audience reception is shaping the self that the author creates.

A good example is the anticipation of and attempt to avoid negative audience feedback in the case of YouTubers who work in the beauty and lifestyle genre. These vloggers use their self-presentations to market both their personal brand as well as partner brands, sponsors, and products, and so they must be keenly attentive to how audiences perceive them. Often, I have noticed that these vloggers will make statements that anticipate negative reactions from their audience. For example, one of Australia's most prominent beauty vloggers, Lauren Curtis, has been building her brand and making videos on YouTube since 2010, and she often uses this strategy to negotiate negative audience reactions. One early video begins with Curtis looking polished and presentable but with no make-up on, and she addresses her audience by making disclaimers for several elements of her appearance: "A few things to apologise for quickly: my roots are terrible at the moment, getting it done on Monday, just been a busy girl; tee-shirt is not ironed" ("In-Depth"). Pointing out these elements of her appearance that she thinks might be perceived by view-ers as imperfections is a strategy to avoid receiving comments pointing out such flaws. The comments sections of YouTube videos are often per-ceived as one of the worst spaces for online abuse, most often directed at the subject/s of the video (Tait), and comments sections on beauty blog-gers' videos often contain audience criticism of their appearance.

I have been following Curtis and her beauty blogging business since 2012, when I began my PhD on girls' autobiography, and I have noticed "the dis-claimer" as a persistent element of her self-narration across her YouTube videos, Snapchat stories, and Instagram posts. Curtis will often explicitly state that her advice is her "opinion" rather than an objective truth; that she is aware that people will disagree with her or adopt different methods or techniques; she does not intend to offend anyone ("MAKEUP DO'S"). Her fake tanning routine is a frequent subject of conversation among her community of followers and she has done several videos about it. Each time she demonstrates how she applies fake tan she states her reasons—she has very fair skin and "personally" feels more confident when her skin appears tanned ("In-Depth", "My Fake", "My Updated"). She also explains that it is okay to have fair skin but she just prefers for her own skin to be tanned, and that "it doesn't mean I think that being pale is ugly" ("In-Depth"); that "girls with very light skin are just as beautiful as girls with very dark skin" ("My Updated"); and that she has "nothing against people with pale skin, I do not find it undesirable or unattractive" ("My Fake"). She reiterates that she is not advocating for fake tan as a beauty standard but that "it's just personal preference, I just like the look of being tanned" ("My Updated"), and "I prefer how I look with a tan as opposed to how I look when I am at my palest" ("My Fake"). This anticipates accusations from her audience that she is negatively representing pale skin, that people who have fair skin should do something to improve their complexion, or that she is uphold-ing a beauty standard of tanned skin: in short, that she is "shaming" those viewers who have fair complexions.

This may sound incredibly trivial. However, it demonstrates a com-plex negotiation between the life narrator and her audience, authenticity and authority in the autobiographical voice. In reducing her discourse to the personal (as opposed to claiming expertise), Curtis signals a relin-quishing of authority. The subtext is, I am only speaking for myself, I do not speak for you, I am not an authority. In giving up the authority to speak on a subject, this rhetorical manoeuvre paradoxically frees Curtis to dispense whatever advice or opinion she wants. The adoption of the position of amateur, in which her knowledge is based on her own per-sonal preferences, is a way to negotiate lenience from a shifting body of audience members that can be fickle, sensitive, and aggressive in their response to content that offends them. Noticing and analysing strategies like this one that aim to manage audience reception can reveal a number of things useful for researchers, such as: the community norms that shape self-presentation; the expectations that an autobiographical subject feels they must negotiate in order to find and hold an audience's attention; how and in what ways participatory audienceship shapes user-created media; the tensions at play between creators and audiences; and how creators respond to such tensions.

This example also speaks to a very real concern for many young people who choose to present their lives to audiences via social media platforms like Twitter, Instagram, and Snapchat. Not only is there the pressure to appear beautiful and to present a desirable lifestyle through an aesthetically cohesive and rhetorically engaging mediated self; but functions like comments, direct messages, tagging, and the ability to share and edit the posts of others via Instagram stories, for example (or any photo editing app), also mean that these young producers are keenly aware of audience feedback and how their self-presentations might be received. The possibilities for reception, here, form part of the self-presentations of these media producers, not only in implicit ways but also explicitly, punctuating the text in strategic places. These interjections are visible traces that demonstrate several important elements of how the anticipated receptions of the text shape the text itself as well as the narrating subjects' awareness of the crucial role of audiences in the success or failure of each video, photo, post, or story.

Ümit Kennedy has argued that contemporary digital auto/biographical texts "are created in and by specific online communities" ("The Vulnerability" 410), and that the networked, multimedia nature of such autobiography is in fact *collaboratively* created among these communities when members share, comment on, participate in, and in other ways shape the self-presentations of one another (Kennedy "These Vlogs"). Reading for reception, then, becomes a crucial part of understanding and analysing the autobiographical strategies and practices of digital media users, particularly those for whom taking up space online often means opening themselves up to antagonistic or abusive feedback from audiences.

One benefit of studying voices, texts, and lives that have been silenced or undervalued is the potential for empathic engagement. Kate Douglas and Laurie McNeill note in their introduction to a special issue of *a/b: Auto/Biography Studies* on pedagogy and life writing that

> auto/biography courses can invite students into productive encounters with those they might not know about or may even consider abject. When we study narrated lives, we can humanize the Other in multiple ways, which creates sustained engagement with our students and the lives of Others.
>
> (6)

In the same issue, Jennifer Drake argues that "to teach life narrative is to teach empathetic practice" (67). While there is certainly value in this approach, what I want to emphasise here is that empathy with the lives of others is not the only benefit in studying and teaching life narrative texts. Indeed, it can be a fraught process, as Gillian Whitlock makes clear in *Soft Weapons*, where she problematises the function of life narrative texts as sites for engendering empathy in readers by bringing the texts and stories of marginal Others to the centre. I am not claiming that beauty bloggers are abject or in need of humanisation in the same way that, for example, refugees or demonised ethnicities have been, but rather that beauty blogs—and many other forms of digital life narrative that girls and young women use to narrate their lives and present a subjectivity—are undervalued both in terms of the subjectivities that they construct and the (gendered) devaluing of their subject matter: makeup, beauty, and lifestyle concerns are easy to dismiss as the frivolous concerns of affluent and shallow millennial women. I have tried, in my scholarship, to develop a methodology that positions young women's automedia not only as sources for engaging readers' empathy but also for the valuable contribution they make to innovating and progressing modes of and strategies for digital life narrative.

By recognising in such online engagement the complex negotiations of reader expectations and community norms for self-mediation, the sophisticated textual manoeuvres that young women execute in order to take up space online, we are able to see the value in examining such literary or media objects for what they can tell us about selfhood, identity, self-presentation, and the cultures from which they emerge and in which they circulate.

Our job as life narrative scholars is to read, interpret, and theorise life writing and, increasingly, auto/biographical media. But as the scope for what counts as an appropriate object for the study of life narrative broadens, this gives us new methodological challenges and prompts us to consider new problems and ways of studying such texts. Analysing instances where autobiographical subjects engage with and anticipate audience reception—either directly or indirectly—has the potential to reveal much about the deeply relational nature of online auto/biography.

Examining these auto/biographical practices and traces for what we can learn about them formally, technologically, and culturally emphasises the creative practice that these modes of self-narration require. As media for self-presentation become increasingly networked and social, and as the lines between producers and consumers of media continue to blur and shift away from a unidirectional flow of production and consumption, the role of audiences in shaping, reading, and even collaborating on these forms of digital auto/biography should form an increasing part of our methods of reading and researching autobiography.

## Works Cited

Arthur, Paul. "Coda: Data Generation." *Biography*, vol. 38, no. 2, 2015, pp. 312–320.

Curtis, Lauren. "-ALLCAPMAKEUP DO'S + DON'TS-ALLCAP!" *YouTube*, uploaded by Lauren Curtis, 22 Oct. 2013. www.youtube.com/watch?v= gkELwnplEmE.

———. "In-Depth Makeup Tutorial for PALE SKIN!" *YouTube*, uploaded by Lauren Curtis, 27 May 2013. www.youtube.com/watch?v=9ErevB_KNVc.

———. "My Fake Tanning Routine!" *YouTube*, uploaded by Lauren Curtis, 4 Sept. 2013. www.youtube.com/watch?v=iWqFA_lOpWw.

———. "My Updated -ALLCAPFAKE TANNING-ALLCAP Routine!" *You-Tube*, uploaded by Lauren Curtis, 12 Nov. 2014. www.youtube.com/ watch?v=3mF_f6V4ZsQ&t=72s.

Douglas, Kate, and Laurie McNeill. "Heavy Lifting: The Pedagogical Work of Life Narratives." *a/b: Auto/Biography Studies*, vol. 32, no. 1, 2017, pp. 5–14.

Drake, Jennifer. "Embracing the Surface: How to Read a Life Narrative." *a/b: Auto/Biography Studies*, vol. 32, no. 1, 2017, pp. 67–74.

Gilmore, Leigh. *The Limits of Autobiography: Trauma and Testimony.* Cornell UP, 2001.

Kennedy, Ümit. "These Vlogs Aren't Real: Memory Making and Authenticity in Family Vlogging on YouTube." *Life Narrative in Troubled Times: 2017 IABA Asia-Pacific Conference*, Central Queensland U, Noosa, 23 June 2017.

———. "The Vulnerability of Contemporary Digital Autobiography." *a/b: Auto/ Biography Studies*, vol. 31, no. 2, 2017, pp. 409–410.

Maguire, Emma. *Girls, Autobiography, Media: Gender and Self-Mediation in Digital Economies.* Palgrave Macmillan, 2018.

McNeill, Laurie, and John Zuern. "Online Lives 2.0: Introduction." *Biography*, vol. 38, no. 2, 2015, pp. v–xlvi.

Poletti, Anna, and Julie Rak. "Introduction: Digital Dialogues." *Identity Technologies: Constructing the Self Online*, edited by Anna Poletti and Julie Rak. U of Wisconsin P, 2014, pp. 3–22.

Smith, Sidonie, and Julia Watson. *Reading Autobiography: A Guide for Interpreting Life Narratives.* U of Minnesota P, 2010.

———. "Virtually Me." *Identity Technologies: Constructing the Self Online*, edited by Anna Poletti and Julie Rak. U of Wisconsin P, 2014, pp. 70–95.

Sobieraj, Sarah. "Bitch, Slut, Skank, Cunt: Patterned Resistance to Women's Visibility in Digital Publics." *Information, Communication & Society*, vol. 21, no. 11, 2018, pp. 1700–1714.

Tait, Amelia. "Why Are YouTube Comments the Worst on the Internet?" *New Statesman*, 26 Oct. 2016. www.newstatesman.com/science-tech/ internet/2016/10/why-are-youtube-comments-worst-internet.

Whitlock, Gillian. *Soft Weapons: Autobiography in Transit.* U of Chicago P, 2007.

# 26 Locating Diasporic Lives
## Beyond Textual Boundaries

*Ricia A. Chansky*

Diasporic lives can be difficult to locate, engage with, and analyse, even when studying them in more anticipated modes of self-narration, such as printed and bound memoirs. Lives that are lived across borders, in between conflicting constructs of national identities, and within diasporic communities built to a certain extent on the simulacra of home-nations are challenging to situate as they move between real and imagined spaces. These lives are in motion and are mutable, making it rather complicated for us to trace and study them. Since diasporic lives are on the move and are unable to be located within set boundaries and borders, diasporic life stories are correspondingly difficult to trace within traditional textual boundaries. Despite these challenges, considering the constructs of lives on the move is becoming increasingly relevant as numerous mass-migrations take place on a global level. Our twenty-first-century world is in a constant state of flux, and reading diasporic lives is one way to comprehend this instability. In this chapter, I suggest two ways of reading diasporic lives outside of traditional textual boundaries as a means of beginning to rethink our methodological approaches to locating diasporic lives.

Born of movement and the complexities of migration and resettlement, lived or inherited, diasporic lives exist in the in-between-ness of two or more delineations for constructing national or socio-cultural identities, making them difficult to situate as static or fixed. This lack of stability in national identity contributes to an emphasised need to belong both within the home-nation and the new nation, although this impetus may vary greatly depending upon the time and mitigating circumstances of experience. After a disaster or tragedy, for instance, a diasporic subject may perceive a new or revitalised need to identify with a home-nation.

While category five Hurricane María ravaged Puerto Rico in 2017, for example, the Diasporican creator of the Broadway musical *Hamilton*, Lin-Manuel Miranda, was writing song lyrics. In an interview with Jimmy Fallon on *The Tonight Show*, Miranda describes composing while waiting for news from the island. The resultant song, "Almost Like Praying"—which was recorded and released as a fundraiser for relief efforts within two weeks of the storm—lists the names of the seventy-eight towns of Puerto Rico, something that Miranda says was important for him to do because "there are a lot of towns that don't feel heard". In the unnerving silence after the hurricane, when communication systems were wiped out for days, the naming in "Almost Like Praying" served multiple purposes. The prayer the song offers up is first and foremost for the survival of the towns and the people in them, and then a plea for recognition, visibility, and witnessing of the devastation that María wrought.

The Fallon interview, however, continues with a humorous story about Miranda's 3-year-old son, a known harsh critic of *Hamilton*. Miranda reports that when he played "Almost Like Praying" for his son for the first time, the little boy ran around the house shouting, "I am Puerto Rico! You are Puerto Rico! We are Puerto Rico!" Through this work, Miranda, who was not born in Puerto Rico and has never lived in Puerto Rico, creates a diasporic bridge between the island and the United States that both establishes and initiates a sense of belonging to Boricua *identidad*: one exemplified by his son's response. The project becomes Miranda's declaration of affiliation with Puerto Rico to both himself and his audience.

The song and video of "Almost Like Praying" feature several other Diasporican performers—including Jennifer Lopez, Marc Anthony, Gloria Estefan, Gina Rodriguez, Fat Joe, and John Leguizamo, among others—who sing the names of the towns and repeat again and again, "Puerto Rico, Puerto Rico, Puerto Rico". This aural resonance has certainly achieved its intended goal of bringing attention to Puerto Rico, its individual towns, and its people; "Almost Like Praying" has contributed significantly to the millions of dollars Miranda has raised for hurricane relief in partnership with the Hispanic Federation. For our purposes as auto/biography scholars, though, the song serves as an example of auto/biographical acts committed within diasporic communities that demonstrate in-group affiliation through the positioning the self as connected to home-communities. Whether born in Puerto Rico or not, whether residing on-island or not, Miranda's penning of the lyrics, his organising of the participating celebrities to sing with him, the editing of the resultant video, and his promotion of the project to raise funds for hurricane relief efforts, become a pronouncement of identity. This song—both its lyrics and function as a transmission on behalf of a location struck by a natural disaster and an incompetent governmental response—mirrors his son's declaration of a Puerto Rican identity.

The video for "Almost Like Praying" shows multiple other Diasporicans who perform in different musical styles—rap, salsa, pop music, musical theatre, to name a few—working together to record the song.[1] In certain scenes, Miranda reviews lyrics with some of these performers, while in others he hugs them. Split screens are often used in the video: in one segment, the screen is divided into four equal parts, each with a different person singing the same words; in other scenes, the screen splits in two to depict performers singing together. Miranda shares the screen with legendary performer Rita Moreno; he samples music from *West Side Story*, and there is even a recording of the beloved Puerto Rican singing frog—*el coquí*—intertwined with the background music: all of which further establish his affiliation with both the Diasporican community and home-nation.

The video-recording and its visual and aural editing further portray Diasporican musicians as connected to each other and to Miranda's framing of identity. Together they follow his lead of naming the seventy-eight towns as a mantra of protection and connection. Furthermore, these spliced scenes and the visual effect of collaboration portrayed in them convey that the participants are working together to craft this plea to draw attention to and raise funds for hurricane relief; the assembled are united as Diasporicans for Puerto Rico. Miranda's linking of different genres, generations, and geographies in the song and resultant video demonstrate relationality, community, and communal identity constructions, and an emphasised need for belonging to the home-nation, especially visible in a time of crisis. In other words, Miranda's noted sense of helplessness during Hurricane María caused an emphasised need to affiliate as demonstrated by the multifaceted aspects of "Almost Like Praying", including the penning of the lyrics, the editing of the music and video, the organisation of and collaboration with other Puerto Rican and diasporic musicians, use of Puerto Rican and Diasporican cultural identity markers, and the fundraising aspects carried out in conjunction with the Hispanic Federation.

My methodological approach to "Almost Like Praying" includes an interview on a late-night television program, a child's statement of self-identification,[2] song lyrics, a music video, the webpage for a charitable trust, a popular Broadway musical and its Hollywood film remake, and a naturalist's recording of a beloved singing frog that has become a well-known identity marker in Puerto Rico. What this reflection on "Almost Like Praying" and my means of reading it as an auto/biographical act offer, then, is an understanding that the work of locating diasporic lives can supersede traditional textual boundaries. Lives that exist in the in-between are difficult to locate and map, but doing so— especially when they exist beyond geographic, national, and cultural boundaries—provides necessary insights into the identity constructions of the multitudinous peoples who are currently participating in mass-migrations and shifting global communities.

One of the tropes of diasporic narratives that seems particularly necessary to our understanding of such texts is an enhanced need to belong to or to affiliate with both the home-nation and the new nation, an impetus that varies dependent upon time, place, and experience. Just as "Almost Like Praying" is a situation-specific diasporic affiliation with home-nation that arose after a natural disaster, differing circumstances shape a diasporic subject's sense of belonging or need to associate. Multiple other diasporic narratives demonstrate discordant responses regarding national identity and home-country affiliation that shift based upon circumstantial elements. Jamaica Kincaid's two travel narratives—*A Small Place* and *Among Flowers: A Walk in the Himalayas*—show, for example, a marked transformation in how the author self-identifies.[3]

In *A Small Place*, Kincaid's 1988 postcolonial critique of tourism and colonialism in Antigua, the author states, "Antiguan . . . for I am one" (8). Kincaid makes this assertion regarding her national identity after approximately nineteen years working abroad in the United States, a period during which she did not make a return trip to her Caribbean home-nation. Witnessing the "pastrylike-fleshed" (13) tourists running rampant on her island, Kincaid wishes to distance herself from the stream of visitors pouring through V.C. Bird International Airport who are rushed into cars filled with the wrong gas and driven by unlicensed drivers across unpaved roads to one of the all-inclusive, walled, and gated resorts that populate Antigua (6–7). Melanie A. Murray suggests that, contrary to Kincaid's avowal of national affiliation, the almost two decades of separation from her home-nation positions Kincaid more securely in the tourist class than that of the native (79). Witnessing the neo-colonialism of US and European tourists to her home-nation causes Kincaid to reassert her national identity as she affiliates with Antigua rather than with her physical home in the US. In this case, the diasporic subject who exists between two or more nations has a circumstances-based need to declare belonging. In other words, Kincaid's revulsion over the tourist class and fear of being included in the category of the "outsider" cause her to repeatedly declare her affiliation with Antigua as a means of rejecting this identity construct and accentuating in-group status.

In *Among Flowers*, however, Kincaid states that she "would never have dreamt of calling myself anything other than American" (73). In this 2005 travelogue, one that chronicles her National Geographic Society-funded seed-hunting trip in the Himalayan Mountains of Nepal, the author's positionality slips from the self-identified native of *A Small Place* to the role of the tourist as she realigns her affiliation with the United States. It would be easy for readers to be dismissive of this shift or even assume—as some of my own students are eager to do—that Kincaid is now a traitor to the postcolonial project. Philippe Lejeune's "autobiographical pact" also comes to mind at this juncture. If, as Lejeune asserts, the correlation between the name on the cover of an auto/biographical text and the name of the main character align, are there not certain promises made between reader and writer concerning truth values? What happens when a diasporic author produces multiple auto/biographical texts with differing declarations of what is truth in relation to their self?

The primary context in *Among Flowers* that produces Kincaid's declaration of Americanness is certainly the Nepalese Maoist guerrilla insurgency that causes her party to worry about their physical safety. In fear, she clings to a US identity that signifies to her comfort and safety. However, there are multiple other events woven into the narrative that reaffirm her conceptualisation of the self as transitioning from Antiguan to US citizen. Kincaid admits in *Among Flowers* that she has "never been so uncomfortable, so out of my own skin in my entire life" (27). She misses "her house with its convenient and fantastic plumbing" (24). She and her friends rechristen the expedition's assistant cook, "Table", as "he carried the table and four chairs on which we sat for breakfast and dinner" (26) and "we could not pronounce or even remember this man's name" (30). Their party begins to see "children [that] had hair that had lost its natural pigmentation . . . a sign that some essential nutrient was missing from their diet", something that they observe while eating a lunch of "fresh vegetables and tinned fish" (51) with local people looking upon them and their meal. The list of disquieting scenes of out-of-place tourists on holiday continues throughout the narrative, culminating in Kincaid becoming so drunk on the trek that she "had a hangover that made me feel I was dying" (176). The perceived strangeness of her surroundings and the situationally located threats to her physical being and identity construction push Kincaid to reify connections to the US: a place where, as she continually reminds readers, she enjoys a very comfortable life.

When read together, these travel narratives reveal the instability of national identity constructs in diasporic subjects and the benefits of reading for patterns in and across serial narratives. Kincaid is not necessarily undermining the autobiographical pact by presenting unreliable truth value to her readers. She is not—cannot be—*either* Antiguan or of the US. As a diasporic subject, she is simultaneously both and neither to varying degrees based upon time, location, and situation. The truth value of her auto/biographical narratives is not so much found in pinpointing a finite national-identity marker, but rather in following the meandering trails that diasporic subjects chart when their national identities are comprised of more than one geographic location and multiple interpretations of "home".

Leigh Gilmore maintains that while "writing *another* autobiography is more than slightly suspicious . . . [w]riting beyond the limit of one autobiography is a way to resist the little death that ending an autobiography represents" (96–97). For the diasporic life writer, the self is always figuratively dying and being reborn in some ways as the self is continually shifting between identifying with home-nation and new nation. Tracing the self through serial narratives—a space in which Gilmore articulates that "a subject-in-process is constructed" (97)—is a means for both reader and writer to locate the self as it dies, is born, and is reborn again in relation to the spaces and places it occupies. Kincaid's two travel narratives and the other texts in her oeuvre—whether labelled non-fiction or not—constitute a record of a life in motion, one that is mutable.

Diasporic lives are hard to trace: they exist in Bhabhian third spaces between geographies, cultures, customs, and fluctuating ideas of what constitute national identities, gender constructions, and personhood. Often times they are formed between two or more languages. While diasporic movement emphasises the need to affiliate, the multiplicities of such lives cause the diasporic subject to shift between sites of belonging, between the home-nation and the new nation. The variability of diasporic lives pushes readers to consider both innovative sites for investigating auto/biographical acts and alternate methodologies for exploring traditional forms of self-narration, often times moving beyond what we tend to conceptualise as textual boundaries. The reward of such work, however, is a deeper understanding of these early years of the twenty-first century that are marked by mass-migrations and their impacts upon individuals and the communities they inhabit.

## Notes

1. While there are additional Latinx recording artists involved in this performance—including other places in the Spanish-speaking Caribbean—and the argument could certainly be made that this inclusion fosters Miranda's association with a larger community, for the space of this chapter, I focus only on the Diasporican aspects of this affiliation.
2. At the time, Miranda's son, Sebastian, could not pronounce the letter "r", so he was actually shouting "Puerto Lico".
3. For a larger discussion of Kincaid's two travel narratives in conversation with each other, see "Between Selves: An Intertextual Approach to Jamaica Kincaid's *Among Flowers*." *Biography: An Interdisciplinary Quarterly*, vol. 37, no. 4, 2015, pp. 135–151.

## Works Cited

Gilmore, Leigh. *The Limits of Autobiography: Trauma and Testimony*. Cornell UP, 2001.
Kincaid, Jamaica. *Among Flowers: A Walk in the Himalaya*. National Geographic Society, 2005.
———. *A Small Place*. Farrar, Straus and Giroux, 2000.
Lin-Manuel Miranda interview with Jimmy Fallon on *The Tonight Show Starring Jimmy Fallon*, 24 Oct. 2017.
Murray, Melanie A. *Island Paradise: The Myth an Examination of Contemporary Caribbean and Sri Lankan Writing*. Rodopi, 2009.

# 27 The Diary as a Life Story
## Working With Documents of Family and Migration

*Anne Heimo*

My father Pauli (b. 1930) loves talking about his years at sea and sharing the stories behind his three tattoos from Japan, Canada, and Hong Kong. In 2005, my father gave me a two-volume diary he had kept from September 1957 to December 1960. It was only after reading the diary that I realised, that I was not a sailor's daughter, as I had always imagined. And almost none of the stories I had been hearing all my life were mentioned in the diary. Only after reading his diary did I realise that my image of him was in fact based on a myth, an intriguing and strong narrative rooted in reality, which gives substance to the family lineage (Smart 542) and is a necessary feature of all life stories (Samuel and Thompson 1–22).

Personal narratives, including oral histories, memoirs, letters, and diaries, provide access to intimate pasts otherwise difficult to grasp. For scholars interested in family memories or migration, diaries offer a more direct and rawer glimpse into the author's past than memoirs and oral histories, which are written retrospectively, or letters, which are addressed to a specific reader or readers (Summerfield 22, 50). In this chapter, I examine Pauli's diary as one version of my father's life story. The stories he tells (orally, conversationally) about his life represent another version of Pauli's life story. Although the diary is a chronological and detailed account of his journey to Australia, the events and experiences he has chosen to write about express something about him, just like the stories he entertains people with (Abrams 40–41; Summerfield 6). Though this chapter focuses on a particular individual, my father, and his unique experiences, it also tells a more or less typical story of a young working-class (Finnish) man with little formal education migrating to Australia. The diary can be used as a historical source to examine experiences of migration or gender, class or ethnicity, or to explore the author's subjective views on these (Summerfield 50–51, 71–72), or as a reference point to his current life story.

Personal narratives can be used for various reasons: to entertain, to argue, to justify, to engage, and to remember, among other purposes. In order to better understand the reasons for Pauli to write his diary, I have used narrative analysis. Narrative analysis refers to a set of analytical methods that offer tools to examine how a narrator tells his or her narrative and expresses meaning—in other words, what is being said, to whom, and for what purpose and how does the speaker or writer do this? (Riessman 8–11). My first reading of Pauli's diary was quite intense and not very analytical. This reading was driven by my need as Pauli's daughter and as a researcher of memories of migration. Only after indulging my curiosity was I able to read the diary more analytically. During my second reading, I paid close attention to *what*, which topics and recurring themes, he wrote about. At this point, I did not yet focus on *how* or *why* he wrote about these themes. After this thematic analysis of the diary, I commenced the close reading of the text and analysed the entries, carefully looking at the structure of the diary and his choice of words and expressions. I also pondered what he possibly had left unmentioned and why, and compared his diary entries to the stories I had grown up listening to. Had some of the events mentioned in the diary lost their significance in the course of time and some other incidents gained meaning, and why had this happened?

## Pauli's Diary: In Search of a Better Life

The first volume of Pauli's diary (September 1957–November 1959) tells of Pauli's four-week-long journey on the migrant liner M/S *Skaubryn* to Australia, his time at Bonegilla Migration Reception and Training Centre in Albury, Victoria, and his efforts to find a decent job and earn money despite his poor language skills. He travels around Australia doing odd jobs on various construction sites in Melbourne, Canberra, and Sydney and spending his free time taking English classes and hanging out with his friends at bars. Like thousands of other immigrants, he also works at the hydro-electric power plant known as the Snowy Mountains Scheme and cuts sugar cane in North Queensland on farms owned by Finns. All this time, Pauli has been saving money to take back home with him, but in July 1959 he finally gives in to his long-time urge and buys a car, stating "that it is better to invest your money in a car than beer and whiskey". The volume ends in Mt. Isa, where there was at the time one of Australia's largest Finnish communities.

The second volume of Pauli's diary (November 1959–December 1960) has a very different character to it. It is more of an adventure narrative. It begins in Mt. Isa, where Pauli tries to get a job as a mine worker but is once again turned down because of his poor language skills. Frustrated with the situation, he returns to South Australia, first to Adelaide and Melbourne, then to Sydney, where he enlists on a freight ship, the S/S *Arneta*, heading for Japan.

After only a few days at sea, Pauli is ready to abandon ship, because he finds the work boring and the salary low. However, his mind changes

upon arrival in Tokyo, where he is immediately captivated by the pleasures of the city and writes that Japan is "a paradise for single men".
From Japan, the S/S *Arneta* continues its journey to Canada and Sydney.
A few months later, Pauli is back in Japan and this time fulfils his plan,
abandons ship, and ends up in jail for three days. After having "the time
of his life" in Japan, Pauli travels to Hong Kong for a few weeks and
then leaves on the S/S *Fukien* back to Australia, as the only passenger on
board.

In late November, Pauli is back in Australia and travels once again to
Canberra. On Boxing Day 1960, a little over three years after his arrival
in Australia, he writes his last entry. In it, he mentions that his financial
situation is still quite poor, that he has sent postcards to his girlfriends
in Japan, and that he is a bit concerned about how things are at home.
He also mentions meeting "L.M.", whom he anticipates meeting again
and writes in English: "I think it not finish yet". Time proved that he was
right; Pauli's and L.M.'s story did continue. L.M. became his first wife—
and my mother—with whom he moved back to Finland six months later
in July 1961.

## The Construction of the Diary

Pauli's diary is typical in many aspects (Summerfield 50–51). He writes
daily, but sometimes retrospectively, days or even weeks afterwards.
Except for some sports results, he rarely mentions public events and
world news. The entries are usually quite long, from half a page to several pages long. He writes in detail, but without much background information and sometimes so tersely that the entries resemble code. He keeps
a record of all the photos he has taken, the books he has read, the films he
has seen as well as his correspondence with family members and friends.
He lists people he has met and places he has been to, for instance the bars
he has been to in Tokyo and Osaka: "Europe ban, Rose ban, Windmill,
Union, Fuji, Seven Sea Mickey, Logos, Hollywood, Sherry Port, Oslo,
Metro etc. etc., 27 to 28 altogether" (16 May 1960). He also keeps count
of his earnings and savings as well as his purchases, e.g., a radio, carpen-
ter tools, a camera, a car, a watch, and presents for his family members.

Diaries are rarely as spontaneous or sincere as the impression they give.
Neither are they so private as often assumed (Fothergill 27). He does not
address anyone in his diary nor does he mention any particular reason
for writing it. Pauli writes his first entry onboard the ship from Turku,
Finland, to Stockholm, Sweden, unsure—as he has later mentioned—if
he will ever see his home country again. However, the fact that he begins
the diary the very day he commences on his journey and writes in detail
about his observations indicates that he felt it important to keep a record
of his once-in-a-lifetime journey. As a keen reader of novels and memoirs, he probably had models of travel writing in mind to follow.

Although Pauli's diary seems a faithful record of his daily life, it is in many parts a careful construction (Heimo 162). He is clearly quite conscious about what and how he writes about certain matters. He only hints about hanging out in bars and nightclubs, drinking, gambling, and romances; in the remote company town of Cabramurra he mentions: "The Hungarian girl is here making money. Very good business" (4 April 1959), and in Canada he writes: "the scenery is wonderful here and people have nice houses, but for a sailor this is a dull place" (16 June 1960). After his language skills improve, he begins to use English when speaking of these topics, e.g., "A little sick, you know", "Typical Australian girl, you know", and "Good time with Nobuko, you know". This co-existing censoring and confessing and his choices of expression suggest that he anticipated that others than himself might also read the diary and challenge the public/private divide often related to diaries (Summerfield 67, 72).

## Reflections

Though Pauli's diary is quite laconic and focuses more on external happenings than on his inner life, he frequently discusses different matters with himself, like his motives for leaving Finland and if he has achieved his goals or not. Sometimes he scolds himself for spending too much money or seeing several girls at a time. There are also numerous references to his feelings: boredom, fatigue, anger, laziness, sorrow, frustration, eagerness, joy, hope, longing, etc. He is disappointed about the employment situation in Australia and that because of his poor language skills he cannot get a decent job and is forced to do heavy menial work on a low salary, although "there is no reason for him to suffer", that "he deserves better". Only in Japan does he express overwhelming joy:

> 16.5.1960. Monday. Now one phase is over again and only longing memories left and a slight yearn. I used a lot of money but had also the best two weeks ever—I haven't counted, but I think I spent at least the front wheels of a Volkswagen or maybe more 80.000 yens.—Now everything seems dull. I guess things will soon be better. I guess I'm also a bit lovesick. If everything goes well, I think I'll lift my luggage on the wharf in Canada—

> Tuesday evening 11.10.60—I cashed checks and exchanged money for 114 thousand today. So it has happened, that I have lost my Volkswagen [car] on this trip, but it is easier to get a new Volkswagen than this holiday in the Far East. I am totally satisfied with the way things are. No one knows what tomorrow will bring—

Despite the fact that he complains about his work continuously, Pauli sees his own critique as more justified than most of his fellow citizens.

He rarely comments on his fellow Finns, but when he does, it is usually something critical concerning their personality, their lifestyle, or their attitude towards work or Australia:

> 5.12.[1957]—Last night there was an eager conversation, comparison of Finland and Australia. It felt that some were ready to return to Finland. That sort of chaps, who are never happy wherever they are. I say farewell to them. Though I think they do not need them in Finland either.

> 13.12.[1959]—I really do not care to work with our lot, because some don't take work seriously and are idle. Yesterday Frank gave one guy notice. I cannot understand that some have problems with what to do with their free time. I never have enough free time.

Though most of his friends and acquaintances are Finnish, Pauli works and spends time with many different nationalities. Every now and then, he remarks on ethnic traits, but does not express open prejudice towards any specific group of people, only their attitude towards work: "The Italians are not very hard-working. The Swede is" or "I don't think the Italian will stay. He seems different from the others".

Although Pauli expresses discontent throughout his diary, he still presents himself as a content man, who makes his own choices and is in control of his life. The stereotypical (male) Finnish migrant is presented as hard-working, trustworthy, honest, brave, clean, socially awkward, and quiet, but also a heavy drinker (see e.g., Lammervo 101–136; Latvalehto 36, 194–195). Pauli's portrayal of himself resembles this image to some degree, but it does not give the impression of him being socially reserved, and although he spends much of his free time in clubs and bars, he doesn't indicate having a drinking problem. Furthermore, his diary seems to be an exception among diaries of Finnish men, who usually write about their lives as continuous hardship without any joy or alternatives, of lost opportunities, melancholy, solitude, and depression (Siimes 7–10)—to the extent that is has been argued that those Finnish men who are happy and content with their lives do not even feel a need to write about their lives (Peltonen and Roos 8–9) or are too busy to write (Hyvärinen 38–39). However, it appears that as time passed Pauli found the image of the brave, strong, and fearless sailor who drinks, fights, and is a ladies' man (Kirby and Hinkkanen 231; Karjalainen 115) more to his liking and began to highlight his experiences at sea.

## Conclusions

In this chapter, I examined Pauli's diary as one version of his life story, in other words, how he represented himself as a young Finnish working-class man during his once-in-a-lifetime journey. Because of the recession in Finland and supported migration, Australia particularly attracted working-class, single men like Pauli who wanted to better their income in the late 1950s. Furthermore, it offered him a safe and easy way to fulfil his desire for adventure and curiosity to see the world. Like so many other Finnish migrants, he travelled around Australia and overseas after work and returned to Finland several times before eventually settling down in Australia, where he continues to live.

I first began reading my Finnish-Australian father's diaries as his account of migrating to Australia and his experiences at sea as a sailor, but to my astonishment found out that instead of "years" he had actually been at sea only for six months. Neither had he spent "months" in jail in Japan or worked on a ship delivering post to exotic and remote places like Surabaya. There is no mention in his diary of those stories that belong to his oral repertoire and that he presents to enforce his image of a heroic sailor: the several accidents which he miraculously survived without any injuries and all the remarkable coincidences that saved him from a tough situation or led to new and exciting undertakings. Only after analysing the diary did I understand that it had not been written by a Finnish-Australian migrant or a sailor, but rather by an ordinary 27-year-old Finnish man, one who preferred life in seaports to life at sea but later altered his life story to make it more attractive to his listeners and, concurrently, created a family myth.

## Works Cited

Abrams, Lynn. *Oral History Theory*. Oxon and New York: Routledge, 2010.
Fothergill, Robert A. *Private Chronicles: A Study of English Diaries*. London: Oxford UP, 1974.
Heimo, Anne. "The Use of Eyewitness Testimony in Constructing Local History: What Really Happened During the 1918 Finnish Civil War in Sammatti?" *Oral History: Critical Concepts in Historical Studies*, edited by Graham Smith. Oxon and New York: Routledge, pp. 146–166.
Hyvärinen, Matti. "Miehen lajityypit." *Miehen elämää: Kirjoituksia miesten omaelämäkerroista*, edited by J.P. Roos and Eeva Peltonen. Helsinki: Finnish Literature Society, 1994, pp. 7–11.
Karjalainen, Mira. *In the Shadow of Freedom: Life on Board the Oil Tanker*. The Finnish Helsinki: Society of Sciences and Letters, 2007.
Kirby, David, and Merja-Liisa Hinkkanen. *The Baltic and the North Seas*. New York: Routledge, 2000.
Lammervo, Tiina. *Significance of Cultural Heritage, Language and Identity to Second and Third Generation Migrants: The Case of Finns in Australia*. Turku: Institute of Migration, 2009.
Latvalehto, Kai. *Finnish Blood, Swedish Heart? Examining Second-Generation Sweden-Finnishness*. Åbo: Åbo Akademi UP, 2018. http://urn.fi/URN:ISBN:978-951-765-906-2.

Riessman, Catherine Kohler. *Narrative Methods for the Human Sciences*. Los Angeles, CA and London: Sage Publications, 2008.

Roos, J.P., and Eeva Peltonen. "Esipuhe." *Miehen elämää: Kirjoituksia miesten omaelämäkerroista*, edited by J.P. Roos and Eeva Peltonen. Helsinki: Finnish Literature Society, 1994, pp. 37–67.

Samuel, Raphael, and Paul Thompson. "Introduction." *The Myths We Live By*, edited by Raphael Samuel and Paul Thompson. London and New York: Routledge, 1990, pp. 1–22.

Siimes, Mika. "Lukijalle." *Eläköön mies: Mieselämäkertoja*, edited by Mika Siimes. Helsinki: Finnish Literature Society, 1994, pp. 7–10.

Smart, Carol. "Families, Secrets and Memories." *Sociology*, vol. 45, no. 4, pp. 539–553. doi:10.1177/0038038511406585.

Summerfield, Penny. *Histories of the Self: Personal Narratives and Historical Practice*. Oxon and New York: Routledge, 2019.

Weckström, Lotta. *Representations of Finnishness in Sweden*. Helsinki: Finnish Literature Society, 2011.

# 28 Between Forced Confession and Ethnic Autobiography

*Y-Dang Troeung*

In 1978, Michel Foucault wrote that in the West, the confession was "one of the main rituals we rely on for the production of truth" (*The History of Sexuality Vol 1* 58). Contrasting with this form of confession were modes of writing the self—writing that addressed the nuances of life and mood, intensifying and widening "the experience of oneself" (*Technologies of the Self* 28). Writing the self appears similar to *testimonio* writing in Latin America, or Gramsci's notion of taking a historical inventory to broaden our relations to others, or, as we will argue, the traditional ethnic novel. As these terms show, the power to shift frames from confessional writing to writings of the self lies in the hands of not only the author but also the critic and their power to uncover the radical upsets of autobiographic writing that makes the violence of the narrative palpable to contemporary contexts, creating new "truth-effects", as Foucault called them. Without this intervention by the critic, even radical autobiographical texts that speak truth to power are susceptible to re-establishing and legitimising power relations by being recast into confessional forms. Through thorough research and understanding of the contexts that push the writer to make their past transparent for a wide audience, critics can both reveal and re-frame the political motivations that involve the creation of these works.

This chapter will explore methods for reading diasporic literature in relation to genres of life writing such as ethnic autobiography and confession. I turn specifically to two contemporary fictional texts, Madeleine Thien's *Dogs at the Perimeter* (2011) and Viet Thanh Nguyen's *The Sympathizer* (2015), as works by diasporic authors that implicitly compare the genres of autobiography characteristic of Asian American texts with the forced confessions characteristic of communist regimes in the former Indochina. This comparison reveals the biases and compromises forced upon the artist herself, who is pushed into ethnic autobiography as a genre, asking the writer to "confess" the parts of themselves that create sympathy and appear tolerable while hiding those deemed queer, perverse, traumatic, or outside the binds of their given ethnic identity.

## Forced Confessions

Forced confessions are statements, made by a prisoner in the context of an interrogation or torture, in which an individual implicates themselves in a crime. Elicited through coercion, forced confessions often reflect the prisoner's fabrication of details in order to satisfy the interrogator and to put an end to immediate suffering. In Madeleine Thien's novel *Dogs at the Perimeter*, about the traumatic history of the Cambodian genocide and its afterlife, the protagonist Janie painfully reflects on the role life narratives played in the genocidal apparatus of the Khmer Rouge regime from 1975 to 1979:

> Angkar had been obsessed with recording biographies. Every person, no matter their status with the Khmer Rouge, had to dictate their life story or write it down. We had to sign our names to these biographies, and we did this over and over, naming family and friends, illuminating the past.
>
> (25)

Thien's novel offers a fictional meditation on the history of the Khmer Rouge regime's use of biography to uncover and persecute designated "enemies of the people". Like in China during Mao Zedong's Cultural Revolution and in neighbouring Vietnam following the end of the Vietnam War, Cambodian people during the era of Democratic Kampuchea learned to distrust their own biographies. To tell the wrong life story was to risk not only self-destruction but also the destruction of all one's loved ones.

Thien's metaphor of an "obsession" with recording biographies is apt, for Pol Pot's communist regime elicited and documented the life stories of people on an unprecedented scale. The archive of hundreds of thousands of forced confessions recorded at the Tuol Sleng S-21 Prison, an archive now held at the Documentation Center of Cambodia, attests to the regime's brutal methods of generating biographies through physical and psychological torture. Today, these forced confessions form the foundation of the prosecution's case against senior Khmer Rouge leaders on trial at the U.N.-backed tribunal in Cambodia, a tribunal that has been mired in complications since the court was established. In order to survive the genocide, Cambodians had to find ways to circumvent the forced confession: teachers reinvented themselves as farmers, city people as rural people, scholars as labourers, artists as beggars. People took on multiple aliases, invented elaborate life narratives of "pure" and "uncontaminated" origins in order to persuade the regime of their loyalty to the state. They did this to protect themselves and their dearest kin.

After four years of self-erasure under the dictates of the regime—of forgetting names, parents, children, siblings, lovers, hometowns, pastimes—many Cambodians struggled to return to, or sometimes even to remember, their former selves. In Thien's novel, a character named James, a Japanese Canadian Red Cross doctor who survives imprisonment and torture by the Khmer Rouge, emerges at the end of war with a new identity, a new alias, and chooses never to return to his past. *Dogs at the Perimeter* employs fictional licence to bear witness to the difficult, sometimes impossible, process of living in the afterlife of trauma, of holding an unresolved, excruciating grief inside one's psyche while the world outside remains silent about this past. As the narrator comments in the opening pages, "many of the missing . . . no longer wish to be themselves, to be associated with their abandoned identity. They go to these great lengths in the hope that they will never be found" (2). A profound literary treatment of the enduring psychological fragmentation engendered by war, genocide, and displacement, Thien's novel complements the vast archive of testimonial life narratives by Cambodian and Cambodian diasporic writers and filmmakers such as Rithy Panh, Vaddey Ratner, Luong Ung, Sotho Kulikar, Anida Yoeu Ali, Alice Pung, Davy Chou, and others. The ongoing absence of justice and reconciliation for Cambodians, one scholar notes, "provides one explanation for why there has been more life writing by or about Cambodians than by or about any other ethnic cohort in the United States during the past several decades" (Yamada 147). It is impossible to understand the proliferation of Cambodian life narratives outside of the contemporary context of failed international justice, widespread historical silence about the Khmer Rouge era, and a deep sense of unreconciled wounds among survivors.

## Ethnic Autobiography

At first, the comparisons between forced confessions and ethnic autobiographies seem absurd—one produces an alternative self at the imminent threat of violence and even death, while the other celebrates and rewards the exposure of the authentic self. Yet this binary division between these two forms also erases the mask-wearing and self-making of ethnic autobiographies that emerge as a direct response to liberal audiences seeking a tolerable and transparent ethnic figure worthy of sympathy and available to educate the reader on their culture. As Betsy Huang has pointed out, Asian American literature is often read within an "autobiographic imperative" that sees marginalised voices as always within a form of life writing (7). In turn, such texts are marketed as authentic gateways to a homogenised ethnic subject or autoethnography, which is invested in telling white audiences "something about another culture in a truthful manner" (Lai 56). The demand for transparency and truth of the ethnic autobiography is subjected to the whims of a literary audience, the reader or editor who diligently edits the minority subjects' story so that it appears legible to a normative and white mainstream, incorporating authors into post-racial notions of immigrant progress. In response, scholars like Stephen Hong Sohn have pushed for "reading practices that move away from an autobiographical or autoethnographic impulse attuned to authorial ancestry" (3), as such reading practices can reinforce the ghettoisation of ethnic literature and restrict race narratives to particular times, histories, and spaces that seem to "illuminate only Asian American social contexts" (209).[1]

Within the generic binds of ethnic autobiography, Thien's *Dogs at the Perimeter* might strike the reader as an anomaly. Rather than tie the narrative to a single character with a single backstory, the story leaps through the disjointed and trauma-scorched labyrinth of memories affected by war. Indeed, as Guy Beauregard has argued, many critics who responded negatively to Thien's novel faulted the book for its seeming lack of coherence, assuming that "the difficult histories represented in Thien's novel could or should be told straightforwardly" (170). Beauregard, however, finds that if one reads the novel outside these presumptions, the book "opens up space for us to rethink the critical language we need to read difficult histories across the North and the South, even as such a language remains persistently out of reach" (169).

Agreeing with Beauregard's argument concerning Thien's desire to form a critical language of histories of war, I also find that the negative reviews of *Dogs at the Perimeter* cannot be fully understood without considering the novel's racial politics as a novel written by a non-Cambodian author. First, *Dogs at the Perimeter* follows Thien's book of short stories, *Simple Recipes*, and her first novel, *Certainty*, both of which spotlighted Chinese-Malaysian diasporic experiences. Though the language in *Dogs at the Perimeter* is self-consciously more opaque than the minimalism of *Simple Recipes*, it is also comparable to *Certainty* in many ways, as well as her latest novel, *Do Not Say We Have Nothing*, which was nominated for the Man Booker Prize and also featured a large cast of characters with shifting memories and fissured narratives. As the diasporic routes of the characters in *Simple Recipes*, *Certainty*, and *Do Not Say We Have Nothing* seem to align more closely with the author's biography as a person of Chinese-Malaysian ancestry, reviewers have not generally read these novels through the lens of appropriation. By writing about Cambodia, Thien's *Dogs at the Perimeter* seems to be held to a different standard. A 2018 review of *Dogs at the Perimeter* by Anjan Sundaram encapsulates the presumptions of reading an "outsider" narrative[2] rather than one packaged with the aura of ethnic authenticity. Sundaram writes that the intellectual pursuit of the novel "appears to be Thien's more than Janie's". Sundaram is at his most abrasive when he faults the novel for being written by an outsider: "In writing the story of another person or community, a writer can feel empathy for them and imagine their lives. This is possible, to a degree, from the outside. But to transcend Janie's memory of the Khmer Rouge, Thien would have to walk beside Janie through that experience, through the frightening abyss. This requires a real authority with that experience: the authority of having lived it. Anything less than that is only imagination. It is to imagine that one's dreams are imaginary. . . . Thien's novel seems to appropriate survivors' stories."

Sundaram's condemnation of the novel and accusation of appropriation never considers the novel's vigorous research process, Thien's own participation with the lives of survivors in Cambodia and the Cambodian diaspora, or the fact that white writers are routinely praised for writing the stories of Asians who have survived wartime traumas, such as Adam Johnson, with his Pulitzer prize winning novel *The Orphan Master's Son* (2012) about North Koreans. Whereas Thien's use of imagination can only be seen as a derogatory fault lacking "the authority of having lived it", writers like Johnson are praised for their imagination. This rush to evaluate and often condemn texts on the basis of the author's failure to inhabit an ethnic identity that finds pure authentic symmetry with the author's subject matter fails to taken into account asymmetric alignments based on shared, but not identical, lived or inherited experiences or communities of solidarity, as well the "truth-effects" of the texts that can emerge through the complexity of narrative content and form itself. As scholars of life writing, we need to move beyond uncomplicated paradigms of authorial ethnic authenticity in the assessment of literary works to look deeply at the works themselves. This method of deep reading, as opposed to apolitical or ahistorical methods of surface reading or close reading, should also entail thorough research into historical, social, and collaborative contexts of their creation.

## The Ventriloquist Author

At the same time that I advocate for a method of reading that complicates oversimplified readings of diasporic writing through a lens of authorial ethnic authenticity, I am also attuned to the way in which the confessional mode shapes and constrains diasporic writing. The bulk of Viet Thanh Nguyen's 2015 Pulitzer Prize winning novel, *The Sympathizer*, self-consciously stages this tension between the confessional mode and diasporic writing. *The Sympathizer* is written as a confessional forced out of the novel's anonymous narrator by a communist cadre in the aftermath of the Vietnam War. The forced confession, to the narrator's surprise, offers him a chance to be truthful, after living a life as a spy, double agent, and trickster. As the narrator writes:

> I suspect, my dear Commandant, that this confession is not what you are most likely used to reading. I cannot blame you for the unusual qualities of my confession—only me. I am guilty of honesty, which was rarely the case in my adult life.
>
> (70)

Throughout the text, the narrator remains appreciative for this opportunity to confess, even when confession determines his destiny (death, torture, incarceration, or freedom). The reader only discovers, in the last section of the novel, that the narrator's confessional has been overseen by an "eminently reasonable" looking Commandant, who "was a diligent editor, always ready to note my many errata and digressions and always urging me to delete, excise, reword, or add" (296). Such "editing" includes changing the narrator's words from seeing himself as a "prisoner" to a "guest" to a "patient" (297).

By the novel's end, even this placative confessional has not gotten to the bare truth of the narrator's participation in the Vietnam War. Instead, his story has been a catalogue of memory without blame, confession without self-reflection, transparency without truth, or what Nguyen in his scholarly book *Nothing Ever Dies* calls "the firepower of memory that defines and redefines that war's identity" (13). The irony of Nguyen's confessional form is that, besides the occasional notes of direct address ("my dear Commandant", "comrade"), the narrator's forced confession looks nearly identical to an autobiographical immigrant narrative that has remained ubiquitous throughout the history of Asian American literature. Conscious of the problems of the immigrant narrative, Nguyen insists that he is a refugee, not an immigrant, and that "*The Sympathizer* is a war novel rather than an immigrant story" (Goyal 378), hinting that the novel's appearance as an immigrant story is a ruse, even as it meets the expectations of the Asian American ethnic autobiography genre (a first-person narrative, a story of displacement, a character who has the same race and diasporic homeland as the author). Nguyen's novel uses fiction to self-consciously raise a series of questions: what are the similarities between the forced confession and the ethnic autobiography? Can they easily be separated into "ideological" and "resistant", or even "forced" and "free?"

The normalising of the ethnic autobiography in American ethnic literature comes from a history of exclusion, wartime violence, and colonisation. As Nguyen writes, this context created an "urge for self-representation and self-determination" that was embedded into ethnic literature, from slave narratives to today, so that now "if 'ethnic' means anything in relation to literature, it is the sign of the ethnic speaking of and for the ethnic population" (*Nothing Ever Dies* 209). At the same time, this presumption that the ethnic writer must speak for his or her presumed population provides a fantasy of authenticity and allows us to forget that even the deepest forays into one's backstory are often written through the American arts of compromise and self-invention.

As Nguyen's novel *The Sympathizer* suggests, transparency is not the same as truth, confession not quite self-criticism. Indeed, the seeds of Nguyen's criticism of autoethnography can be found rooted in his first book, *Race and Resistance*, which he credits as both helping him become aware of "the complications of literary speech from, for, and by members of a minority group" but was also a book "marked by the conventions of academic discourse, muscle-bound with theory and jargon in the kind of display that academics like to flaunt and like to look at" ("Dislocation Is My Location" 429). This affective self-flagellation again returns to the subject of form and genre, where authorship of a piece meant to appear truthful and transparent is often a negotiation between the author's view of herself and the gaze of a white North American audience, or as Nguyen puts it in *Race and Resistance*, "the racialized and sexualized gaze of colonial and majority authority" (39). For the ethnic author to continue telling stories that matter, the stories they are compelled to tell, Nguyen advises, "they must do so aware of the fact that all literature is an act of ventriloquism" (*Nothing Ever Dies* 211).

Though the risks of the forced confession are absent, the comparison between these two politicised genres remains crucial and reveals how the ethnic writer too must take on acts of performance in order to be seen by the colonising authority. This authority may not be the "dear Commandant" of *The Sympathizer*, or even the academic audience of *Race and Resistance*, but is rather the white literary publishing industry of agents, editors, and publishers, of whom 79% identify as white (Low), and an audience demanding self-criticism, authenticity, and transparency. But do these demands get us any closer to the truth, or do they merely tell artists which mask to wear, and how they must package the self they are seeking to sell? The literary works of Madeleine Thien and Viet Thanh Nguyen unsettle our firm division between confessions and "writing the self", pushing critics to better navigate the fraught ethical space of autobiography by attending to the erasures of history and the political projects that autobiographical "truth" can benefit or harm.

## Notes

1. For more on the demands of ethnic autobiography, see Christopher Patterson's *Transitive Cultures: Anglophone Literature of the Transpacific*, p. 166.
2. For more on "outsider novels" about the subject of the Cambodian genocide, see Y-Dang Troeung. "Witnessing Cambodia's Disappeared." *University of Toronto Quarterly*, vol. 82, no. 2, 2013, p. 152.

## Works Cited

Beauregard, Guy. "Interwoven Temporalities: Reading Madeleine Thien's Dogs at the Perimeter." *Studies in Canadian Literature/Études en littérature canadienne*, vol. 39, no. 2, 2014.

Foucault, Michel. *The History of Sexuality: An Introduction*. Vol. 1. New York: Vintage, 1978.

———. *Technologies of the Self: A Seminar With Michel Foucault*. U of Massachusetts P, 1988.

Goyal, Yogita. "Un-American: Refugees and the Vietnam War." *PMLA*, vol. 133, no. 2, 2018, pp. 378–383.

Huang, Betsy. *Contesting Genres in Contemporary Asian American Fiction.* Springer, 2010.

Lai, Paul. "Autoethnography Otherwise." *Asian Canadian Writing Beyond Autoethnography*, 2008, pp. 55–70.

Low, Jason. "Where Is the Diversity in Publishing? The 2015 Diversity Baseline Survey Results." *The Open Book*, 26 Jan. 2016.

Nguyen, Viet Thanh. "Dislocation Is My Location." *PMLA*, vol. 133, no. 2, 2018, pp. 428–436.

———. *Nothing Ever Dies.* Harvard UP, 2016.

———. *Race and Resistance: Literature and politics in Asian America.* Oxford UP, 2002.

———. *The Sympathizer: A Novel (Pulitzer Prize for Fiction).* Grove/Atlantic, Inc., 2015.

Patterson, Christopher B. *Transitive Cultures: Anglophone Literature of the Transpacific.* Rutgers UP, 2018.

Sohn, Stephen Hong. *Racial Asymmetries: Asian American Fictional Worlds.* NYU P, 2014.

Sundaram, Anjan. "Survivor Stories." *Mekong Review*, vol. 11, May 2018.

Thien, Madeleine. *Dogs at the Perimeter: A Novel.* WW Norton & Company, 2017.

Troeung, Y-Dang. "Witnessing Cambodia's Disappeared." *University of Toronto Quarterly*, vol. 82, no. 2, 2013, pp. 150–167.

Yamada, Teri Shaffer. "Cambodian American Autobiography: Testimonial Discourse." *Form and Transformation in Asian American Literature*, edited by Zhou Xiaojing and Samina Najmi. Seattle and London: U of Washington P, 2005, pp. 144–167.

# 29 Autobiographical Research With Children

*Maria da Conceição Passeggi and Ecleide Cunico Furlanetto*

## Introduction

One of the challenges of autobiographical research is finding the most appropriate methods for data gathering and analysis. When working with vulnerable populations such as children, these questions often become more pressing. What are the risks and benefits of choosing certain methods of data collection over others? How can researchers ensure that the research is child-centred and that it protects (indeed, elevates) the interests and rights of the child participants?

We work in the discipline of education; our research assumes that life narratives have significant value as qualitative research data and can inform various disciplines about humans' perceptions of their own life experiences. Our previous research has found that life narration is something that most subjects approach willingly, and while their narration of their experiences does not change the narrated events, it may change their interpretation of their life experiences (Bruner; Delory-Momberger; Passeggi),

We have been conducting research with adults for more than fifteen years, analysing the oral and written life narratives of adults to study their perceptions of their life experiences. More recently, however, we turned these methods to research with children as subjects for the purpose of studying their ways of seeing the world and themselves. For example, children's narratives about their experiences in schools and hospitals is currently under-researched, but such qualitative life narrative data could inform knowledge and practice in disciplines such as health science, education, and life narrative studies.

Two main questions informed our research. First, since autobiographical research with adults can help us understand the heuristic potential of self-referential narratives and autobiographical reflexivity processes (Dilthey; Ricoeur; Bruner; Passeggi), can we consider children's accounts with such conviction? Second, to what extent can children's accounts be considered "stable enough" for educational research? Our aim was to research the way children give meaning to their life experiences, map the way autobiographical reflection is evident in their accounts, consider how this knowledge could help us to understand the relationship children have with their surroundings, and, therefore, inform research and practice in this field. This chapter presents three epistemological approaches that foreground the instructive value of some of the challenges we faced in working with children's life narratives in educational contexts.

## Research With Children: Three Epistemological Approaches

We acknowledge that studies of autobiographical narratives in the discipline of education already offer significant theoretical and conceptual grounding for understanding how autobiographical narratives might be used (in a variety of settings) as a methodology for understanding how humans interpret their lives and experiences (Brockmeier and Harré; Bruner; Delory-Momberger and Jorge Larrosa). Our challenge lies in the methodological spaces between research with adults and research with children.

From an epistemological point of view, we identified three essential approaches to working with children and their autobiographical narratives. The first one is an *epistemopolitical* approach. This neologism, promoted by Gaston Pineau and Jean-Louis Le Grand, does not segregate epistemological principles from a political approach. This integrated approach allowed us to consider children as subjects with rights and to acknowledge the legitimacy of their discourses, as opposed to the selective standards of scientific research, which may only acknowledge the rights of "literate adults" and only recognise the value of adults' autobiographical reflections. Trying to research children while ignoring their critical perspectives and the knowledge produced by them denies children's citizenship and human rights. In our research, we adopted Paulo Freire's vision to look into children's worlds, and, like Freire, we aimed to acknowledge that underestimating the knowledge produced from children's sociocultural experiences would be a scientific mistake and result in adult-centric knowledge and values being reproduced in the research.

Our second approach is informed by postcolonial perspectives. According to Boaventura de Sousa Santos, modern science has established human beings as epistemic subjects—abstract, rational, objective—rather than empiric subjects—concrete, flesh and blood, emotional, historic (81). Such approaches partly explain the marginalisation of certain subjects—for instance, children, people who are illiterate, or women—from research. In other words, much scientific research has historically been adult-centric, androcentric, ethnocentric, and euro-centric. Jerome Bruner addresses this dichotomy by proposing two ways to build a different approach: the paradigmatic mode—logical-scientific—and the narrative mode—hermeneutic-interpretative (27). While the paradigmatic mode strives to reach the ideal of a formal explanatory system, the narrative mode focuses on human experience, adopting the subject's point of view, to question what occurs in the field of action (in the external "objective" world) and what occurs in the field of self-consciousness (within the subject's perceptions). In our research, we aimed to link both (paradigmatic and narrative) modes in the ways proposed by Santos: between a "Northern (colonial) epistemology" and a "Southern (postcolonial) epistemology". The autobiographical research, based on the narrative mode, would join the Southern epistemology, creating opportunities to include and recognise multiple voices, including those of children.

Our third approach is post-disciplinary. According to Franco Ferrarotti, the biographical method in social sciences is not multidisciplinary, interdisciplinary, or transdisciplinary but rather post-disciplinary (25). Ferrarotti argue that "heuristic and methodological instruments are to be gathered where they can be found: in social history, philosophy, social and cultural anthropology, ethnography, psychology and psychanalysis, and also in literature and poetry" (25).

These three approaches (epistemopolitical, postcolonial, post-disciplinary) helped us develop child-centred methodologies and instruments for our research. Our aim was to address children's innate inclinations to narrate, so as to "organize the experience in terms of a narrative reasoning" (Delory-Momberger 14). That is the way human beings *produce* discourses, being at the same time characters of the narrated story, objects of reflection, and reflective beings, retrospectively and prospectively analysing themselves, placing themselves between what has gone and what is next to come.

## Sourcing and Micronarrative Analysis[1]

We commenced the project once we had a protocol in place that seemed to address the ethical requirements of research with children and minimise the risks.[2] We adopted focus groups, or what we have termed "rounds of talks", where children between the ages of 4-13 and participated. We held these sessions in a range of different socio-economic contexts: a rural school in which thirty-four children participated; an inner-city school in which fourteen children participated; a school in a community comprised of the descendants of enslaved peoples in which forty-two children participated; and a well-known prestigious school in which sixty-five children participated. In addition to these school settings, we worked with nine children who were hospitalised with chronic diseases.

The protocol[3] that we used was drawn from previous work by Martine Lani-Bayle and Passeggi; Passeggi et al.; and Passeggi, Nascimento, and Oliveira. We chose this approach because it focuses on four characteristics of the culture of childhood: interactivity, playfulness, fantasy, and reiteration (Manuel Jacinto Sarmento). The children were invited to take part in an organised playtime of "make-believe". While showing the children a small stuffed "alien" doll,[4] the researcher said:

> Pretend that this is a little alien, who comes from a planet where there are no schools (or no hospitals). And he is very curious to know what the school is like (or what the hospital is like), what it is for, what we do here, how make friends [and so on].

As we stated in a previous article (Passeggi; Rocha; De Conti 32):

> The extraterrestrial doll facilitated make-believe, collaborating to create zones of proximal development: "through play, a lot of action in the imaginative sphere occurs in this situation of make-believe, such as the creation of voluntary intentions and the formation of real-life plans, constituting thus the highest level of development" (Vygotsky 117).

Therefore, the presence of the extraterrestrial in conversation circles helps create the space of mediation and creation of zones of proximal development through playful situations.

From a methodological perspective, the little extraterrestrial doll becomes a mediator between the child and the researcher, reality and imagination, allowing for an intergenerational dialogue (with the researcher), an intra-generational dialogue (between peers), and an intercultural dialogue (with the alien). The invention of a *make-believe* universe proved appropriate for building a positive and productive relationship between participants, making the talks a place to share likes and dislikes experienced in schools and hospitals. It is important to emphasise that the talks were audio recorded, and along with the research team, we analysed both child and researcher participation in the talks, which allowed us to identify mistakes to be avoided and successes to be strengthened in the next talks.

The rounds of talks were organised in three moments: *opening*, symbolically the invitation to *take part in the talk*. At this moment, the alien is introduced to the children, who were shy at first, but soon played along. Older children (8–13) had fun in the talks. Once this initial barrier is broken, the second step begins: the *talk* itself, the interaction among the participants, including the alien who they talk to, though sometimes the children asked the researcher to tell the doll what they wanted it to know. Due to ethical guidelines, the talk could not exceed one hour. The last step of data collection was the *closing*, symbolising the alien's goodbye, as he returns to his planet. The children did not always want to let him go, due to their engagement in the play. If this happened, we asked children to draw or write a letter for the doll to take to his friends. In these drawings, they expressed their ways of seeing the distant planet, suggesting how the hospital or school should be in their own planet. Sometimes, they asked to keep the doll with them as a present.

The results of the research so far have revealed particular themes pertinent to children's experience of their school life and relationship to school: fear of violence, worry about the future, concerns about sickness, fear of abandonment, and a desire for solidarity. These are the subjects that arise most frequently in the children's narratives. According to Bruner, the child learns to construct elaborate narratives when 3 years old. They narrate not in order to solve "personal matters" but to understand what happens to him/her, watching what happens to the world around him/her. In that sense, autobiographical narratives are not just representations of the world but instruments to build reality and subjectivity. According to Mikhail Bakhtin, narratives "exert a reverse effect on mental activity: they structure internal life and give it a more defined and stable expression" (118). Thus, a narrative would not be limited to a group of abstract linguistic sequences, isolated from body and emotions. As stated by Jean-Paul Bronckart, through the effort of interpretation of "narrative discourses, human psychic functioning expands, nourishes and restructures itself perpetually" (62). Thus, in proposing a research methodology whereby children tell what happens in school, in the hospital, in their communities, we recognise the potential of the child's act of narrating, sustaining the possibility for the narrative to enrich and restructure ways of thinking, as Bronckart suggests. We used this argument when representing the project to the ethics committee, considering this reflection as an eventual benefit to the child who participates in the research.

## Polyphonic Narratives

The transcriptions of the talks revealed that children narrate their experiences with sentences that are short but full of meaning. It was important to find new narrative methods for interpreting these texts that considered the particular narrative styles and themes of the children's narratives. It is vital to emphasise that the team dedicated many months to the transcribed data from the talks, in search of referrals that allowed us to expand what we had proposed in our adults' narrative analysis. We could not use the conventional structure of beginning, middle, and end. We adopted, like Barthes, the principle that every (affirmative or negative) sentence represents a draft of a short narrative. We integrated the "minimalist conception of life account", proposed by Bertaux, admitting that the description of part of a life experience may be considered a short narrative. This less structuralist understanding allowed us to take a quantum leap in the analysis. We observed, during the transposition process from speech to writing, that children were collectively building narrative sequences about what happened in school, in the community, and in the hospital. This insight provided a significant theoretical-methodological advantage, which allowed the analysis of collective micronarratives that we designed as polyphonic, harmonically made up of different voices of children participating in the round talks. The following excerpt by three children, on the possibility of the lack of rural schools, represents an example: "It would be very bad. One would not be able to read and study. And thus, in the absence of school, we would not be able to find a job either". In this transcription, we avoided orality features, as Pierre Bourdieu (711) suggests in *A miséria do mundo*: "transcribing is necessarily to write, in the sense of rewriting", which enables to lighten "the text from parasite development", "confusing phrases", "verbal or speech tics redundancies" ("well", "right"). This option pointed out by Bourdieu seemed better "to speak to the sensitiveness [of the reader], not lending to sensationalism" (711).[5]

## Transitory Conclusions

One of our chief concerns in our research with children was to reduce the risks of symbolic violence, understood as forms of pressure, of interpreting distortion, naively explained on behalf of a scientific or moral reason. Intentionally reducing these risks does not mean we have eliminated them during source analysis or during the processes of gathering data, interpretation, and publication. Noting what Pierre Bourdieu suggests, in those different stages our ethical practices translated into the following precautions: when gathering sources, we intended to promote the benefits of the child's autobiographical reflection by adopting a dialogical and horizontal approach, and avoiding eventual prejudices, interruptions, and omissions. When transcribing speeches, we deleted orality features, but without omitting or changing words. What we adopted with ethical care was avoiding the child being eventually seen as having low cultural capital; in the analysis, we always avoided hierarchising points of view, so as to "transmit to the reader the means to convey to the declarations [of children] that vision which justifies and reinstates the needs and reason to be of the research subject", as suggested by Bourdieu (712). Finally, in the publication process we aimed to adopt the "democratization of the hermeneutic approach" suggested by Bourdieu, so that the reader may grant to "ordinary narratives [of the child] the enthusiastic reception that some reading traditions reserve to the finest forms of poetry or philosophy" (712).

The analysis illuminates a common axis: the autobiographical reflective capacity of children and the significance of school over their lives in the different contexts analysed. Their narratives indicate that, in and out of school, sociohistorical structures are reflected over the construction of the children's views on the meaning of school in their lives and how they belong to the world. Rural children's chief concerns, for example, relate to their learning. For children living on the outskirts of the city, school violence was the most prevalent concern in the narratives: trivial conflicts, aggressive attitudes, concerns about friendships, abandonment, and safety. For children in between regular and hospital classes, continuity in regular school and the return to normal life was the main concern expressed.

If we agree with Bruner (75) that "self-creation is a narrative art", then why not consider how that creation occurs in childhood? What subjects feature in the internal and external landscapes of children in different socio-economic and geographical contexts? And what meanings do children ascribe to them? Children's narratives, their voices, perceptions, and knowledge, are under-represented in qualitative autobiographical research. Thus, the task of autobiographical research is to devise and practice more appropriate theoretical-conceptual instruments and methods, and to consider how epistemopolitical, post-disciplinary and postcolonial matters can open paths leading to new horizons.

## Notes

1. This discussion builds on our reflections in a previous essay (Passeggi; De Conti; Rocha 27–38), for the special edition of *Auto/Biography Studies*, edited by Laurie McNeill and Kate Douglas.
2. The protocol was used by our team's researchers in three regions of Brazil: North, Northeast, and Southeast (Passeggi et al.).
3. The National Commission for Ethics in Research (CONEP) of the Ministry of Health, which considers ethical issues regarding risks and benefits for research participants in the defence of their dignity, freedom, and autonomy, previously approved our project and emitted a Certificate (the CAAE 06433412.3.0000.5292, Opinion: 168.818); 23 November 2012.
4. With children in hospital, we used one of the *Toy Story* dolls because it was possible to sterilise it.
5. There is no space here to discuss these narrative analysis procedures, so we present a recently published text: Passeggi et al.

## Works Cited

Bakhtin, Mikhail. *Marxismo e Filosofia da Linguagem*. Translated by M. Lahud and Y. Vieira. São Paulo: Hucitec, 1985. Print.
Barthes, Roland. "Introduction à L'Analyse Structurale des Récits." *Communications*, vol. 8, 1966, pp. 1–27. Print.
Bertaux, Daniel. *Le Récit de Vie*. Paris: Armand Colin, 2005. Print.
Bourdieu, Pierre. "Compreender." *A Miséria do Mundo*. Petrópolis, RJ: Vozes, 2003, pp. 693–732. Print.
Brockmeier, Jens, and Harré, Rom. "Narrativa: problemas e promessas de um paradigma alternativo." *Psicologia: Reflexão e Crítica*, vol. 16, no. 3, 2003, pp. 525–535. Print.
Bronckart, Jean-Paul. *Activité Langagière, Textes et Discours*. Delachaux et Niestlé: Paris-Lausanne, 1996. Print.
Bruner, Jerome. *Atos de Significação*. Porto Alegre: Artmed, 1997. Print.

————. *Culture et Modes de Pensée: L'esprit Humain dans ses œuvres.* Paris: Retz, 2000. Print.

————. *Pourquoi Nous Racontons-Nous des Histoires?* Paris-Retz, 2005. Print.

Delory-Momberger, Christine. *Histoire de Vie et Recherche Biographique en Éducation.* Paris: Anthropos, 2005. Print.

Dilthey, Wilhem. *L'Édification du monde historique dans les sciences de l'esprit.* Translated by Sylvie Mesure. Paris: Editions du Cerf, 1988. Print.

Ferrarotti, Franco. "Partager les Savoirs, Socialiser les Pouvoirs." *Le Sujet dans la Cité*, vol. 4, 2013, pp. 19–27. Print.

Freire, Paulo. *Educação como Prática da Liberdade.* São Paulo: Paz e Terra, 2003. Print.

Lani-Bayle, Martine, and Maria Passeggi, editors. *Raconter l'École: à l'Écoute des Vécus Scolaires en Europe et au Brésil.* Paris: L'Harmattan, 2014. Print.

Larrosa, Jorge. "Notas sobre a experiência e o saber de experiência." *Revista Brasileira de Educação*, no. 19, 2002, pp. 20–28. Print.

Passeggi, Maria. "A experiência em formação." *Educação*, Porto Alegre, vol. 34, no. 2, 2011, pp. 147–156, maio/ago. Print.

Passeggi, Maria et al. "Autobiographical Narratives: Pedagogical Practice as a Lifeline for Hospitalized Children." *a/b: Auto/Biography Studies*, vol. 32, 2017, pp. 27–38.

————. "As Narrativas Autobiográficas como Fonte e Método de Pesquisa Qualitativa em Educação." *Revista Lusófona de Educação*, vol. 33, no. 33, 2016, pp. 111–125. Print.

————. "Narrativas da Infância: o que Contam as Crianças sobre a Escola e os Professores sobre a Infância." MCTI-CNPq-14, 2014 (n. 462119/2014-9). Print.

————. "Narrativas de Crianças Sobre as Escolas da Infância." *Educação*, vol. 39, no. 1, 2014, pp. 85–104. Printed.

————. "Narrativas Infantis. O que Contam as Crianças sobre a Escola da Infância?" MCTI-CNPq | MEC-CAPES N° 07, 2011 (n. 401519/2011-2). Print.

————. "Pesquisa (Auto) Biográfica com Criança: Olhares da Infância e Sobre a Infância." MCTI-CNPq, 2016 (Processo n. 310582/2016-4). Print.

Pineau, Gaston, and Jean-Louis Le Grand. *Les Histoire de Vie.* Paris: PUF, 2007. Print.

Ricoeur, Paul. *Soi-même comme un autre.* Paris: Seuil, 1990. Print.

Santos, Boaventura de Sousa. *A Crítica da Razão Indolente: Contra o Desperdício da Experiência.* São Paulo: Cortez, 2002. Print.

Sarmento, M. Jacinto. "Cultura da Infância nas Encruzilhadas da 2ª Modernidade." 2015. Web. 10 Dez. 2015. http://proferlaotrabalhosalunos.pbworks.com/f/AS+CULTURAS+DA+INFANCIA+NA+ENCRUZILHADA+DA+SEGUNDA+MODERNIDADE.pdf.

# 30 Ecocriticism and Life Narrative

*Alfred Hornung*

The common basis of ecocriticism and life narrative is a concern for nature and survival. The critical engagement with ecology and the sustainability of the environment correspond to the implicit motive of all life writing for a continuation of life after death. Both represent human endeavours that seek to mediate between the fundamental elements of nature and the changing conditions of culture over time. Although most ecocritics and life writers are based in concrete geographical locations within national boundaries, they recognise and thematise the transcultural and transnational reaches of their subjects in critical theories and narratives of life. More often than not, life narratives combine these human endeavours and become media of ecocritical concerns and propositions of environmental activism. As such, life narratives complement and augment the goals of a global ecological movement and advocate the genre's capability to correlate aspects of nature and culture for a sound biosphere.[1]

It is not surprising that this combination of life writing and ecocriticism emerges in areas and at times where and when nature and human life are endangered by the course of social developments or man-made interferences with natural conditions. The universal appeal of this joint endeavour in the preservation of life and the environment makes the genre of life writing a privileged medium of expression for all people of different stations of life and different disciplines. Although auto/biographical narratives in the past were mostly located and studied in the field of literature and culture, the subject of ecology transcends the literary frame both in the composition and interpretation of such narratives. The long-held bias of literary scholars in dealing with forms of autobiography as a minor genre of literature has changed in view of the newly discovered potential of life writing to give minority positions a voice and the genre's availability to non-literary authors who seek to account for their professional goals using forms of life writing. I will exemplify this change in the conception and practice of ecocritical life writing with reference to historical and contemporary models that stand for the range of possibilities in practical and critical applications by writers and natural scientists: the American transcendentalist Henry David Thoreau, the

Harvard myrmecologist E.O. Wilson, the Japanese Canadian zoologist David Suzuki, and the ecofeminist scholar Terry Tempest Williams. These examples show the cross-disciplinary and all-inclusive range of the genre of life writing and reveal the way in which the authors transform the genre by including scientific ideas and methods and transform their professional lives in the process of writing their lives. Both aspects of the generic and professional transformation also apply to the reception of these changed forms of life writing, calling for new cross-disciplinary and transnational methods in their evaluation and in teaching. This new reading of humanistic and scientific visions will hopefully also lead to changed attitudes in life toward the environment.

Henry David Thoreau encapsulates in his series of autobiographical essays, *Walden; Or Life in the Woods* (1854), all areas of ecological concerns and stipulates the transcultural and transnational dimension of ecological life narratives. Thoreau's resistance against the materialism of his time and his country's political position at home and abroad motivated him to leave society and lead an independent life in nature on Walden Pond, not far from Concord, Massachusetts, where the American Revolution began. In his return to a simple and self-sufficient existence, he adjusted his life to the rhythms of nature, recognising and appreciating the common biosphere with flora and fauna. In this "primitive" lifestyle, he feels supported by his occasional encounters with Native Americans and by his readings in Asian philosophy. When the transcendentalist author turns the actual experience of two years and two months (1845–1847) into a life narrative, he condenses it into one year and coordinates it with the cycle of the seasons. Thoreau's *Walden* begins with the erection of his cabin in the summer, proceeds through autumn and winter and ends with the renewal of nature in spring. The natural cycle of the seasons serves as an analogy for the regeneration of life achieved poetically in the narrative. Thoreau combines Romantic ideas of a cyclical concept of time and Daoist beliefs in a contemplative attitude and recognises in nature an uninterrupted "poem of creation" whose qualities he repeats in *Walden*, his own poem of creation.

> I love a broad margin to my life. Sometimes, in a summer morning, having taken my accustomed bath, I sat in my sunny doorway from sunrise till noon, rapt in a revery, amidst the pines and hickories and sumachs, in undisturbed solitude and stillness, while the birds sang around or flitted noiseless through the house, until by the sun falling in at my west window, or the noise of some traveller's wagon on the distant highway, I was reminded of the lapse of time. I grew in those seasons like corn in the night, and they were far better than any work of the hands would have been. They were not time subtracted from my life, but so much over and above my usual allowance. I realized what the Orientals mean by contemplation and

the forsaking of works. For the most part, I minded not how the hours went. The day advanced as if to light some work of mine; it was morning, and lo, now it is evening, and nothing memorable is accomplished. Instead of singing like the birds, I silently smiled at my incessant good fortune.

(111–112)

A correlative feature of Thoreau's life writing is the political aspect of a patriotic self who moves into the cabin on the fourth of July to mark his own declaration of independence. This imaginative romantic design allows Thoreau to transcend the realistic details of concrete experiences and to expand his local horizon of Walden Pond to a transcultural/transnational context. In the "Conclusion" of his life narrative, he refers to Africa, South America, and China only to advise his reader to be "a Columbus to whole new continents and worlds within" one's self imaginatively and to "be an Expert in home-cosmography" (320–321). For Lawrence Buell, *Walden* constitutes an "ecoglobalist" project of life writing advocating a planetary scale (Buell).

Henry David Thoreau's concern for evolutionary processes in nature recreated poetically in his practice of life writing coincides with Charles Darwin's evolutionary biology, developed in his *Origin of Species* (1859), and the embracement of this theory by the German zoologist Ernst Haeckel, who created the term ecology in 1866 for the description of the environment of living beings and forms of housekeeping (Haeckel 1866). Thoreau's first chapter, "Economy", as the philosophy of living wisely, reveals common concerns of the humanities and natural sciences in his time to emphasise the importance of a natural environment shared by all living creatures, visible in the Greek root "oikos" of both terms. This close interconnection of evolutionary biology and ecology extends to other areas of research and lends itself to the genre of life writing. Thus, Bernhard Kuhn maintains that the Victorian biologist Herbert Spencer, who extended Darwin's evolutionary theory to Social Darwinism, used his *Autobiography* (1904) "to demonstrate the applicability of Darwinian theory to the life of the individual" (Kuhn 9). Two contemporary examples of this biological interrelation are the autobiographies of the Harvard myrmecologist E.O. Wilson and the Japanese Canadian zoologist David Suzuki. They both reflect in life writing the dangerous components of scientific theories, such as Social Darwinism and sociobiology, that have led to racist discrimination, disastrous eugenic programs, and the threat of nuclear destruction. This critical perspective of revising harmful scientific ideas in narrating one's professional life becomes the basis for self-critical evaluations in scholarship and teaching.

E.O. Wilson, the Alabama-born scientist, derives his academic interest from nature experiences in his childhood as the basis of his cross-disciplinary methods of inquiry into natural sciences, social sciences, and the humanities. Over and above his more than twenty scientific books, his autobiography *Naturalist* (1994) and his autobiographical fiction *Anthill* (2010) represent a synergy of his research and life dedicated to the study of ants. A fervent defender of evolutionary biology, he extends the scientific laws derived from insects to the whole biosphere, believing that the genetic rules that govern ant organisms also govern human populations. While he tries in his life writing to reconcile his juvenile experiences in the natural environment of Alabama with the research environment of his scientific career, he also uses *Naturalist* to address the criticism of his concept of "sociobiology". Thus, he reconfirms his analogy of evolutionary biology in animal behaviour and ecology, but also accepts the criticism of the unacceptable similarity of the genetic determinism of human nature and its racist implications (*Naturalist* 307–353). In the final chapter, "Biodiversity, Biophilia", Wilson relates the way in which the discussion of his theories about life and critical engagement in the political reality of his time engendered new areas of his life sciences and turned him into an environmental activist. The increasing destruction of the rain forests on a global scale, which for him "are of crucial importance as reservoirs of diversity", seriously imperil the biosphere (*Naturalist* 357). Ultimately, he trusts in the capacity of "biophilia", "the inborn affinity human beings have for other forms of life, an affiliation evoked, according to circumstance, by pleasure, or a sense of security, or awe, or even fascination blended with revulsion" (*Naturalist* 360). In the final analysis, his narrative journey is a powerful reinstatement of a harmonious interaction of all organic life in the biosphere and a call for an active engagement in the preservation of the environment, also prefigured in the role of the courageous protagonist of *The Anthill* as a lawyer of environmental justice.

David Suzuki shares Wilson's ideas of evolutionary biology, but he clearly rejects biological determinism and its racist implications, which he as a second-generation immigrant and his family experienced during World War II in Canada. In two consecutive autobiographies, *Metamorphosis* (1987) and *The Autobiography of David Suzuki* (2006), he reconstructs the analogy between animals and human lives and eventually invites his readers to participate in his environmental activism. The analogy is based on his first object of study, the fruit fly *Drosophila melanogaster*, in which he recognises the common biological traits of all organic life and which he sees as "a perfect genetic organism" (*Metamorphosis* 135–137) in its analogy to human life cycles:

> Fruitflies have been a passion in my life for three decades. In reflecting on their heredity, behaviour and life cycle, I've come to see that in many ways, the changes in our lives parallel those remarkable stages that take place in a fly's life. All life forms receive a genetic legacy

> from their ancestors in the form of DNA, the chemical blueprint that
> shapes the way we are.
>
> (*Metamorphosis* 7)

It is the contact with a First Nations family, his father's long-time friends,
on a mushroom-hunting trip in British Columbia that leads to his recognition of "our shared genetic heritage" and the acquaintance with Asian
worship of nature (*Autobiography* 11). The experience of his family's
discrimination, which includes their relocation and the grandparents'
repatriation to Japan, and his perception of man-made ecological disas-
ters combine to his decision in 1979 to leave his professorship at the University of British Columbia and to become the host of an acclaimed TV
program of CBC called *The Nature of Things*, covering a wide range of
scientific and philosophical matters. This change from an academic to a
media personality also prepares his transformation into an environmental activist who discovers the transnational dimension and global impact
of destructive effects of human interventions on planet earth. Thirteen
out of eighteen chapters of his second autobiography are descriptions
of ecological projects, which range from environmental work with First
Nations people on the Islands of British Columbia, Indigenous people in
the Brazilian rain forest and Papua New Guinea (see Huggan and Tiffin). As part of his engagement he coordinates their ecological concerns,
presents them in his TV show, and brings them to the attention of fellow
activists at the Rio Earth Summit and the Kyoto conference on climate
change. The ecological program launched in his foundation with a "Declaration of Interdependence" encapsulates his environmentalist credo:

> At this Turning Point in our relationship with Earth, we work for
> an evolution from dominance to partnership, from fragmentation to
> connection, from insecurity to interdependence.
>
> (*Autobiography* 277)

For Suzuki, the interdependence of human societies and the natural
world, which is endangered by toxic pollution and global warming,
requires a planetary consciousness and the restoration or realisation of
"the sacred balance", an ethical program pursued by the proponents of
deep ecology.

> Many worldviews endow human beings with an even more awe-
> some task: they are the caretakers of the entire system, respon-
> sible for keeping the stars on their courses and the living world
> intact. In this way, many early people who created worldviews
> constructed a way of life that was truly ecologically sustainable,
> fulfilling and just.
>
> (Suzuki and McConnell 12)

The sustainability of the planet earth and its inhabitants is contingent on a healthy environment. The careless destruction of nature, as visible in the uncontrolled logging of the rain forest exposed in Suzuki's feature *The Nature of Things*, endangers the health of all organic life. This is the subject of the ecofeminist Terry Tempest Williams.

Terry Tempest Williams' autobiography, *Refuge: An Unnatural History of Family and Place* (1991), is based on a belief in and the impact of the disruption of the balance between nature and culture. Imbalances created by natural or human-made catastrophes result in disturbance and destruction. As a scholar of environmental humanities at the University of Utah and ecofeminist activist, she observes the changes to the water level of the Great Salt Lake and its influence on life. Thus, the flood of the 1980s had destroyed the Bear River Migratory Bird Refuge, and Williams deplores the loss of burrowing owls, which for her are "birds you gauge your life by" (Williams 8). A more disastrous interference with the shared natural history is the destructive exploitation of nature in the course of the "above ground atomic testing in Nevada [. . .] from January 27, 1951 through July 11, 1962" (Williams 283). Williams sees an analogy between the loss of the birds due to rising lake levels and the rate of cancer diseases caused by the nuclear testing. In the Prologue and the Epilogue, "The Clan of One-Breasted Women", she records and grieves the deaths of seven members of her family who died of cancer, including her mother, grandmothers, and her brother. These losses also motivate her to emerge from the traditional background of an obedient Mormon woman and to participate in an illegal walk-in of ten ecofeminists on the testing ground, "taking their cues from coyote, kit fox, antelope squirrel, and quail" (Williams 288). In this "act of civil disobedience" and in unison with animals, they are supported by the "voices of their [Native American] sisters across the mesa" (Williams 289).

This form of environmental activism becomes part of a healing process. Although the human losses cannot be undone, concrete measures can counteract the human destruction of the environment, similar to the restoration of the natural habitat of the migrating birds.

> Volunteers are beginning to reconstruct the marshes just as I am trying to reconstruct my life. I sit on the floor of my study with journals all around me. I open them and feathers fall from their pages, sand cracks their spines, and sprigs of sage pressed between passages of plain heighten my sense of smell—and I remember the country I come from and how it informs my life. [. . .] I am telling this story in an attempt to heal myself.
>
> (Williams 3–4)

The close interconnection of the repair work to restore the natural habitat for the birds and the return to a healthy life in union with nature is the purpose of Williams' life writing. This literature emerging from the interrelation of nature and culture represents a form of "cultural ecology" and promises a sustainable future (see Zapf 2016).

These examples of the interrelation of ecology and life narratives corroborate the common goal of humanists and natural scientists. Their concerns for the preservation of nature and human lives is part of the shared destiny of all humankind on a global scale. The resort to the medium of life narratives by different authors of different disciplines opens up the space of life writing scholarship beyond the conventional literary practice. The resort to life writing for the representation of ecological issues turns out to be a new approach to the discussion of personal concerns similar for all people on earth. The writer Henry David Thoreau leaves his literary home in Concord to become a naturalist encountering new areas of life in the experience of nature, Native Americans, and Asian wisdom. The naturalist and biologist E.O. Wilson turns into a writer of his life and of fiction, in which he revises the dangerous implications of his scientific theory of sociobiology. The zoologist and geneticist David Suzuki, who had discovered racial discrimination in Canada and the potential of nuclear destruction in the Oak Ridge National Lab in Tennessee, leaves the classroom to engage in practical work as an environmental activist, the subject of his autobiographies. The ecofeminist scholar Terry Tempest Williams uses her life writing as a new form of scholarship in which her personal case becomes the overall intention of healing nature and all its inhabitants. Their common message of an activist engagement in the sustainability of our biosphere and the planet earth invites us to join their example in theory and practice.

## Note

1. This contribution is based on my earlier publications: *Ecology and Life Writing* (2013) and "Ecology and Life Writing in Transnational and Transcultural Perspective" (2016).

## Works Cited

Buell, Lawrence. "Ecoglobalist Affects: The Emergence of U.S. Environmental Imagination on a Planetary Scale." *Shades of the Planet: American Literature as World Literature*, edited by Wai Chee Dimock and Lawrence Buell. Princeton, NJ: Princeton UP, 2007, pp. 227–248.
Haeckel, Ernst. *Generelle Morphologie der Organismen: Allgemeine Grundzüge der organischen Formen-Wissenschaft, mechanisch begründet durch die von Charles Darwin reformirte Descendenz-Theorie.* Berlin: Georg Reimer Verlag, 1866.
Hornung, Alfred. "Ecology and Life Writing." *Handbook of Ecocriticism and Cultural Ecology*, edited by Hubert Zapf. Berlin: De Gruyter, 2016, pp. 334–348.

————. "Life Sciences and Life Writing." *Anglia*, vol. 133, no. 1, 2015, pp. 37–52.

Hornung, Alfred, and Zhao Baisheng, editors. *Ecology and Life Writing*. Heidelberg: Universitätsverlag Winter, 2013. Chinese Translation: 生态学与生命写作 [*Shengtaixue Yu Shengming Xiezuo*]. Translated by Lin Jiang. Beijing: China Social Sciences P [中国社会科学出版社, Zhongguo Shehui Kexue Chubanshe], 2016.

Huggan, Graham, and Helen Tiffin. *Postcolonial Ecocriticism: Literature, Animals, Environment*. London: Routledge, 2010.

Kuhn, Bernhard. *Autobiography and Natural Science in the Age of Romanticism: Rousseau, Goethe, Thoreau*. Farnham: Ashgate, 2009.

Suzuki, David. *The Autobiography*. Vancouver: Greystone, 2007 [2006].

————. *Metamorphosis: Stages in a Life*. Toronto: General, 1988 [1987].

Suzuki, David, and Amanda McConnell. *The Sacred Balance: Recovering Our Place in Nature*. Vancouver: Greystone, 1999 [1997].

Thoreau, Henry David. *Walden*. Edited by J. Lyndon Shanley. Princeton, NJ: Princeton UP, 1971 [1854].

Williams, Terry Tempest. *Refuge: An Unnatural History of Family and Place*. New York: Vintage Books, 2001 [1991].

Wilson, Edward Osborne. *Anthill: A Novel*. New York: W.W. Norton & Company, 2011 [2010].

————. *Naturalist*. Washington, DC: Island P, 2006 [1994].

Zapf, Hubert. *Literature as Cultural Ecology: Sustainable Texts*. London: Bloomsbury, 2016.

# Afterword

# 31 The Box in the Attic
## Memoir, Methodology, and Family Archives

*G. Thomas Couser*

I was flattered to be invited to contribute to this volume, but also a bit surprised, as I never considered methodology my forte. My academic work did not focus on the methodology of life writing, with the significant exception of my concern with its ethics, particularly when it involved "vulnerable subjects"—those who may not be able to represent themselves or to participate in, or even consent to, their representation by others. And my scholarly methodology was quite straightforward, a matter of reading secondary sources about my chosen life writing texts, beginning with autobiography, in my dissertation, and ending with memoirs of disability. So, during most of my career, I had been concerned almost exclusively with published, book-length life narratives, ignoring most other forms of life writing.

That changed, however, when I began to research and write *Letter to My Father: A Memoir*. Doing so changed my perspective on the memoir, from that of critic to that of creator; it also required me to engage with new genres in ways that touch upon matters of methodology. It thus opened my eyes to the richness and complexity of that common, but under-theorised, life writing resource: the family archive.

In reading through the table of contents for this collection, I was interested to discover how many of the topics listed there my memoir touches upon in some way: family histories/life writing; the diary; reading diasporas; disability and life writing; childhood/youth; death narratives; migration; biography; trauma narratives; ethics; letters; writing memoir; and archives. It also touched upon gay life writing, which does not have an entry of its own. I will italicise these topics when they appear in what follows.

\*

*Letter to My Father* was prompted by a crisis in my relationship with my father: in 1969, shortly after returning from a year of graduate work at Oxford, I discovered that my father, whom I had never seen even mildly intoxicated, had been secretly binge drinking to a degree that threatened his employment, his marriage, and even his life. That fall, I wrote him a *letter* intended to function as an intervention. In it, I reviewed our relationship—never very close—and the effect that my discovery of his drinking had on my sense of him. I intended the letter to open a dialogue, but he found it "devastating" (according to my mother) and was never willing to discuss it with me. Our relationship deteriorated further, as did his mental health. And I came to think of my letter as toxic to him.

In 1974, my mother died of ovarian cancer; a mere eight months later, my grief-stricken father died of depression and drink. When he died, I found a cache of personal documents in his closet. Among them, to my surprise, was my own letter, which I was unequipped emotionally to read at the time. I boxed the documents and stored them, unread, for thirty years. In my early sixties, the age at which my father spiralled into a clinical depression and began to self-medicate with alcohol, I felt my biographical clock ticking. So I retrieved the box from the attic and delved into the contents at last.

Dad's archive included substantial sets of correspondence, mostly from his premarital life: letters he wrote home from Aleppo, Syria, where he'd spent the early 1930s teaching English to students, almost all of whom were survivors of the Armenian genocide (and thus part of the *diaspora*: several migrated to the US and became lifelong friends); letters from a woman who had been in love with him for over a decade (but whom he did not marry); letters to and from three close male friends, all of whom were apparently gay; and letters to my mother from the South Pacific, where he served in the US Navy during World War II. Over the following decade, I traced and recreated my father's early life using these documents, supplemented by some archival and internet research.

The resulting memoir is constructed of two quite different parts. One, "The Father I Never Knew, but Now Know", traces his life from his birth in (what is now Northern) Ireland in 1906 to my birth immediately after World War II. This section is necessarily *biographical*. It's a memoir, because I knew him, but it's biographical, because I didn't know him *then*. I was extraordinarily lucky to inherit the documents that permitted me to reconstruct so much of his early life. The earliest ones (his birth certificates, his parents' marriage certificate, and so on) had to do with his emigration to the US in 1910, as a child of four. His father Isaac used his expertise in jacquard linen weaving as his ticket to a new life in America. At least, that was the apparent impulse behind the family's emigration; the archive revealed that Isaac and Maria had lost two infant children to illness within a single month in 1908.

I came to believe that this double tragedy may have been the real driver of their emigration. His parents were comfortable economically in Ireland and both came from large families; their departure obviously must have been wrenching for them and for those who stayed behind. The archive included a touching letter from Isaac's mother, expressing her grief over his departure and her desire to see him again: "You said when you went away you would come to see me in two years. Many a time I wonder will I ever live to see you again" (she did not). This letter brought home to me the psychic toll of *migration*, even under what seemed favourable circumstances. And the discovery of the deaths of my father's two siblings when he was 2 years old led me to consider him the victim of a *childhood trauma*, one that he was indeed too young to absorb or even to register in a way that made it accessible to him for later therapy. I came to the conclusion that this childhood trauma might explain his otherwise mysterious depression in late middle age. None of his younger siblings, who were born after this tragic event, most of them in the US, developed depression or abused alcohol. Indeed, they all lived at least twenty years longer than he did.

The bulk of the archive consisted of letters, however, and I learned that my father lived a good deal of his early life through that life writing genre. I had previously not paid much attention to letters, but nearing the end of my career I discovered the value of the epistle. Personal correspondence connects parties known to each other—friends, relatives, lovers. Most of the archived letters were intensely personal. Not task oriented, they express emotion rather than convey factual information about his life. Rather than containing "evidence" of his whereabouts and actions, they implicitly—and sometimes explicitly—characterise the correspondents' relationships—how they are understood, how much is invested in them. In letters—especially among male friends—correspondents may express feelings they are less likely to communicate when present to one another. I came to think of Dad's letters as the substance of his life, rather than epiphenomena. In my sixties, I finally "got" letters.

In my entire academic career, I had never done any archival research. But my research into my father's teaching at Aleppo College, which was founded by the American Board of Commissioners for Foreign Missions (which also established Robert College in Istanbul and the American University of Beirut), led me to the archives of the Yale Divinity School. There I found documents composed and printed by students at the school, some of which had never been opened; from them, I was able to learn a good deal about the school's progressive curriculum and ethos. I suddenly understood the appeal of leafing through old documents like a sleuth. And handling them, I felt a frisson of contact with their creators.

The letters to and from Dad's three close male friends during his time in Aleppo are startling in their frank emotionality: most of them are undeniably love letters. They were all the more intriguing in view of his friends' apparent homosexuality. Understanding them involved a bit of research in *gay* history and culture. I came to understand these homosocial relationships as what social historians call "romantic friendships", which were more common in the Victorian era than the early twentieth century. This reinforced my sense that love letters are not just the occasional verbal distillate of relationships between the parties. Rather, for the duration of Dad's time in Aleppo, they were the medium through which his friendships were sustained and developed. For that period at least, they *constituted* the relationships.

The other part of *Letter*, "The Father I (Thought I) Knew", is memoir in the conventional (etymological) sense; it is derived from memory and personal experience. Even there, however, I found my family archive useful. My mother's documentary legacy was very different from my father's. Although she was a prodigious letter-writer, she left no correspondence behind, sadly, nor any documents that revealed anything new about her premarital life. But, in contrast to my father, she left copious records of our life as a family. Every Christmas for decades, one of us would give her an engagement calendar. Each week would feature a picture on the verso page (scenes of New England or, when Jane and I were at university, of our campuses). The recto page would be divided into wide stacked rectangles, one for each day of the week. In those boxes, my mother recorded—and sometimes tersely annotated—significant events: doctor's appointments, social engagements, trips, and so on. Her gift to us, then, was to create, and eventually leave behind, a substantial *family history*. With these documents, my sister and I can learn where each of us was on nearly a daily basis from childhood through and beyond our years at university.

Though seemingly utterly mundane, the engagement calendar deserves more attention as a life writing genre. In theory, it may be gender-neutral (I keep a datebook myself), but in my mother's case, there is a strong gender inflection: she is not so much the protagonist of her life as she is the annalist of our collective life as a family unit. Engagement calendars are quite unlike diaries. For one thing, they are not private. My mother's would lie open on her desk, available to all for inspection. And whereas diary entries are retrospective, engagement calendar entries are prospective: they anticipate future events. Finally, diaries are typically focused on the author's experience and emotions; they may be intensely personal. My mother's engagement calendars were focused on the family, not herself, and they were generally factual, not expressive, entries.

At times they moved toward *diary*, however, in their retrospective annotations of events. More interestingly, what appeared to be a family chronicle also served her surreptitiously as a diary. Given the circumstances of my father's death, my review of his life took on a forensic dimension. And when I was using Mum's calendar to reconstruct our life, I was alert to any signs of distress in the marriage and/or depression in my father. Scrutiny revealed that after Jane and I left home for university my mother had kept a coded account of Dad's drinking: she marked days on which he'd been drunk with small red D's. And as she became progressively more frustrated with him, she began to record conflicts between them. The engagement calendar proved an invaluable source for my memoir in ways I hadn't expected. In doing so, it suggested the fluidity of genre, as well: her calendar was functioning also as a pathography. Because of my mother's successive cancers (breast cancer in her fifties, which she survived, and ovarian in her sixties, which she did not) and my father's depression, my memoir incorporates *narratives of illness and disability* (auto/pathography).

My attempt to fathom my father's depression led me to acquire and examine his medical records for a four-month stay at McLean Hospital in Belmont, Massachusetts (the same facility Susanna Kaysen depicted in her memoir, *Girl, Interrupted*). Here again, the supposedly memory-based part of my memoir is in effect biographical. I function here as a kind of medical detective and/or psychoanalyst. As it happened, I found his medical chart more revealing of the limits of psychiatric diagnoses than of my father's psyche. But his medical records confirmed my sense that his distress was a delayed response to his childhood trauma, triggered by his own children's leaving home.

As the author of *Vulnerable Subject: Ethics and Life Writing*, I was acutely aware that I was treading on dangerous *ethical* ground in revealing details of my father's depression and alcoholism, which was unknown even to some of his siblings while he was alive. Depressed and distressed, my father was certainly a vulnerable subject. And by my own account, his being dead did not render him invulnerable. (In Chapter 8 of *Signifying Bodies*, "Lucy Grealy and the Some Body Obituary", I take the position that dead subjects can be harmed.) Furthermore, I am sure that he would not have wanted those aspects of his life exposed. And yet, his suffering was also at times my suffering, and that of his wife. I felt I had a right to tell his story insofar as it was also our story. Perhaps more to the point, I considered the process of writing the memoir an act of affiliation and reconciliation.

My main concern was that I might damage his image and his reputation, among surviving family members and his former students at Melrose High School, where he taught English in the 1950s, 1960s, and 1970s. I felt, though, that while I was exposing unsavoury episodes, my account was sympathetic to his plight and in fact memorialised him in an honourable way. And the responses I've received from readers who knew him have confirmed that belief. There was nothing shameful about his depression and death. The shame was that I was ashamed at the time. Writing the memoir helped me move beyond that initial response.

Now in my seventies, with friends losing their longer-lived parents and inheriting archives of their own, I see my case as a microcosm of a larger one. Having published my memoir and given book talks, I am approached by friends and relatives who are dealing with their own archives. And among them, I am surprised to discover new life writing formats. For example, my wife, Barbara Zabel, discovered a diary of her mother's in a format I'd never seen, a "five-year" diary. Each page was divided like that of an engagement calendar—a stack of horizontal boxes—but each box was devoted to the same day in five successive years. So, at the end of the first year, the diarist returns to page one, where she is encouraged to register each day in relation to its counterpart the previous year, for four more years. It's literally a recursive form, one that encourages a sense of perspective not built into the conventional diary. Here the diary moves toward memoir by encouraging reflection and a longer perspective.

At a family reunion, a cousin of mine brought along several volumes of his scrapbook—another life writing genre that I'd never given any serious consideration. Two things struck me about it. First, it was begun not by him, but by his doting mother: she began to collect and arrange his dossier for him when he was too young to do it himself. At some point, when he was in secondary school, I think, having been trained in the format, he took it over: so his scrapbook, begun as biography, became autobiography. As a whole, then, it is co-authored. There's another sense in which the scrapbook is not solely self-authored. For the most part, it gathers and arranges materials created by others: report cards, letters of recommendation, news clippings, and so on. It's a collection of data, a collage of print and graphic materials, a proto-biography more than an autobiography.

Less private genres found in such archives also illustrate the pervasiveness of life writing. In the US, at least, graduating classes in secondary schools and universities are memorialised in yearbooks. (Incoming classes may also be surveyed in what are termed "facebooks"; Harvard's was the inspiration for the now global social medium.) Typically, such books chronicle the collective life of a cohort of students for the duration of their education by means of verbal and visual records of memorable campus (and sometimes historical) events. At the back of the book, each member of the class is represented by a standardised headshot and a brief profile: activities engaged in, offices held, teams joined, and perhaps a personal phrase or two. These documents amount to auto-prosopographies: collective images of a distinct demographic group composed by its members. The individual entries are thumbnail sketches of the members of the cohort. These are sometimes composed by their subjects, sometimes by the yearbook staff. (I was amused, but also a bit embarrassed, to discover that in my father's 1927 Wesleyan College yearbook, he was remembered for his loud snoring in a music class.)

*

My experience composing my memoir—itself an addition to the family archive—demonstrates how complex family archives can be, how many distinct life writing genres they may involve. Sally Mann's memoir, *Hold Still*, begins with a meditation on the family archive. She writes:

> We all have them: those boxes in storage, detritus left to us by our forebears. . . . Cutting the string on the first family carton, my

mother's, I wondered what I would find, what layers of unknown family story. . . . What ghosts of long-dead, unknown family members were in them, keeping what secrets?

(ix, xiv)

And her prologue likens this "detritus" of our lives, the impress of our presence on earth, to the mark an animal's body makes in grass when bedding down, a meuse.

*Pace Mann*, we *don't* all have these archives. In any case, they will become less common as many of these forms of life documentation I have discussed here become obsolete—if they haven't already—in the era of electronic social media. Of course, this makes those that exist all the more precious. And for lucky life writing scholars, like me, there is ample material to examine right under their noses (or over their heads). With our professional expertise, we should be prepared to advise amateurs as they inherit and try to sort through their dossiers. Doing so should enhance our appreciation of the ubiquity of life writing and augment our current methodologies.

## Works Cited

Couser, G. Thomas. *Letter to My Father: A Memoir*. Lanham, MD: Hamilton Books, 2017. Print.

———. *Signifying Bodies: Disability in Contemporary Life Writing*. Ann Arbor, MI: U of Michigan P, 2009. Print.

———. *Vulnerable Subjects: Ethics and Life Writing*. Ithaca, NY: Cornell UP, 2004. Print.

Mann, Sally. *Hold Still: A Memoir With Photographs*. Boston, MA: Little, Brown, 2015. Print.

# Index

*a/b: Auto/Biography Studies* 4
affordances 39, 43, 44, 51, 54, 93, 134, 136, 138
algorithm: identity construction 117–118, 136
ancestry.com 76, 119
anecdote; and Indigenous Australian life writing 125; use of, in scholarly writing 98–99
archival research 20–23
archives 19–24, 37; access 20; family 247–253; letters 84; queer 54; zines 26, 31
Arendt, H. 23, 38
Asian American writing 220–226
asylum seekers 36–39; diary 93; interpreting objects relating to 37–38
audience 133, 162: diaries 92, 94; expectations of ethnic autobiography 222–223, 226; music 208; reception of digital texts 200–205
autobiogenography 179–184
autobiography: ante- 145; and comedy 14; diasporic selves in 211; digital 51, 133, 136, 204, 205; ecological concerns in 240–241; and genetics 179–180; ideal subject 171; individualism of 129; "limit cases" 70; photographs 80; scrapbook as 252; as social recognition 171, 236; *see also* disability, memoir; ethnic autobiography; memoir; trans* autobiography; visual auto/biography
autoethnography 96–102, 222–223, 225–226; democratising potential of 100; as life writing in research practice 96–97; questions to guide 98–99; relational aspects of 100–101; risks of 97, 99; use of literary technique in 101
autographics 68
automedia 50, 90, 205
auto/pathography 251

big data 116–120
biography 61–66, 103; collective 72, 119; digital 161–166; and Indigenous lives 62–66; as organising concept 63; traditional methods for studying 61–62; *see also* graphic biography
*Biography: An Interdisciplinary Quarterly* 4, 42, 61, 62–66, 132
biology: auto- 179–180; evolutionary, and life writing 238–240; *see also* autobiogenography; genetics
biopics 70–71
blogs: activist 142, 202; beauty video (vlogs) 201, 202–205; death and dying 165; feminist 202; "genie-blogs" 76; methods for selecting for research 137; mommy 43; relationship between diaries and 92, 133, 136; sex 92
body 100, 130: in creative performance 114; digital 56; in graphic biography 72–73; materiality and ethics 181–184; positivity selfies 46; refugee and asylum seeker 38, 39; regulation of the 117, 170, 175; trace of in letters 86
Boochani, B. 38–39, 93
Bourdieu, P. 103, 233
boyd, d. 117, 118, 134, 143
Butler, J. 39

Cardell, K. 14, 137
Cheney-Lippold, J. 116–117, 118
childhood 71, 140–146, 230, 234, 249
children: representation in culture 145; research with 228–234; *see also* youth; youth life narrative
close reading 44: in auto/biography studies 43; limits of for studying youth activist texts 143; as method for interpreting disability autobiography 187; of selfies 46
collaboration: in life narrative practice 39, 68, 80, 209, 240; in research practice 1, 6, 56–57, 65, 149, 155, 196, 199
collage 29, 30, 31, 55, 77, 252
confession 80, 220; and diasporic literature 224–226; forced 221–222
Couser, G.T. 8, 97, 166; disability memoir 186, 190n2; family letters 87; memoir 13, 17, 195, 196; *see also* "vulnerable subjects"
creative life writing 96, 101; doctoral thesis 193–199; Indigenous Australian lives 125–130; memoir 13–18; methodologies for human rights storytelling 150–158; zines 27–31
cultural studies 26, 70, 133, 140, 143, 147, 162

data 162, 252: archival 23; bio-, genetic, and self-tracking 119–120; collection for creative life writing projects 194–196; collection from child participants 228, 230–232; diary as a source of serial 90, 92; digital portraits and biometric 49–50; genomic 179–180; interview 105, 152; privacy and security 56; raw 201; *see also* big data
death 37, 128, 241, 248–249; and grievable lives 38, 39; narratives 161–166
De Waal, E.: *The Hare with Amber Eyes* 34–35, 78
diaries 90–94, 128, 251–252; audio 110; and engagement calendars 250–253; method for interpreting 90–94; as a method of research 90; and migration 213–217; as self-tracking technology 119
diasporic literature 210–211; implications of biographical

readings of 220–226; life writing modes in 220–226; *see also* Asian American writing; ethnic autobiography
diasporic lives 207–212, 248; challenges of researching 207, 209, 212; *see also* Latinx recording artists; travel narratives
digital humanities 120, 134
digital lives: challenges of researching 41–46, 49–50; comparative approach to reading 134; and death and memorialisation 161–166; ephemeral nature of 54, 137–138; questions of scope and selection 136–137; *see also* big data; biography, digital; blogs; girls, auto/biographical media; selfies; social media; visual auto/biography
digital research tools: data mining 134; random sampling 45; screenshots and recording 54; web clipping 54; webscraping 45, 51, 56, 57n2
disability: memoir 186–188, 190, 247, 251; studies 44, 56, 186–187
discourse analysis 2, 54
doctoral research *see* Ph. D. research
Douglas, K. 135, 193, 204

Eakin, P. J. 14, 171, 197, 198
ecocritical life writing 236–242; transcultural and transnational aspects of 237–238
ecocriticism 236
elicitation: music 106; object 78; photographs 79–80
embodiment 3; disability and 187–190; family history 79; in new media 54; research practices 21–22, 30, 96, 97, 100–101; witnessing 93; *see also* body
epistemology: *epistemopolitical* approach 229; feminist 173; relationship to methodology 135; standpoint 172–173; trans* autobiography as new knowledge 174–176
epistolary *see* letters
ethics 6, 7, 9: autoethnography 100; big data 118; consent 113, 144, 151, 196; diaries 90–94; in digital contexts 55–57, 161–166; and family history 80–81; of memoir writing 13–17, 251; in

radio and theatre production 113–114; of researching youth life narrative 140–147; social media 45; university approval 4, 8, 188, 193–199
ethnic autobiography 220, 222–226; *see also* diasporic literature
ethnography: "backyard" 134; and biography 64, 65; digital 134; and HIV memoirs 188; online 43; *see also* autoethnography

Facebook 41, 51, 136; as memorial 162, 164
family history 35, 76–81, 213–214, 250; cultural politics of 77; material culture 78; narrative techniques 81; as relational life writing 76; *see also* genealogy
family memoir 13, 34–35, 77, 80–81
feminist: black 129–130; eco- 241, 242; media studies 44, 50, 56; online activism 202; practices in performance 113–114; theory 2, 26, 27, 36, 42, 70, 114, 187, 188
fiction 196, 201: and family history 76, 80; lives and histories in literary 221–226; and memoir 13, 16; methods for reading 3, 4; writing and techniques 96, 100, 101, 129, 193
focus groups 230–232
Foucault, M.: 'biopower' and big data 117, 118; confession 220

gender: and diaries 91, 217; -diverse identities 176n1; and online self-presentation 202, 205; *see also* trans* autobiography
genealogy 76, 77–78, 180; *see also* ancestry.com; blogs, "genie-blogs"; family history
"generous reading" 7; and digital lives 133–135, 138; and youth life narrative 147
genetics 119, 179–184, 239, 240; *see also* autobiogenography
genre: diaries 90, 91, 93, 133; graphic biography 70–71; selfies 46; theory 43, 111, 133–134
Gilmore, L. 70, 80, 142, 211, 164–165
girls: auto/biographical media 200–205
Google: reverse image search 55; translate 143
graduate research *see* Ph. D. research
graphic biography 68–74

Grosz, E. 181
grounded theory 44

Haraway, D. 27, 30
Hayles, N. K. 36
Hirsch, M. 76, 77, 78, 79
HIV memoir 186–190
homosexuality: and life writing 186, 190n1, 247, 248, 249
humanism 34, 35–36, 38, 116, 117, 237, 242; *see also* new materialism; posthumanism
human rights 36–37; and uses of life storytelling 150–158

*Identity Technologies* 43, 134
illness 68, 77, 104, 180, 186–190, 241, 248–249, 251
implied reader 28–29, 164–165
Indigenous Australian: epistemologies 38; family stories 80–81, 125–130; life narratives 7; life stories and place 125, 128; lives and Western life writing genres 129; oral storytelling *vs.* documentary archives 126, 128; secrets and silences in life stories 126–130; women's lives 125–131
"informed imagination" 129–130
Instagram 42, 44, 136, 137–138; as diary 94; ethics of researching young people's selfies on 145; limits of literary analysis 134; as note-taking research tool 53–54; stories 137, 204; visual methodology 50, 51, 52
intertextual analysis 136
interviews 103–107; audio recording of 195; best practice in human rights 149, 151–155, 159; for creative life writing 193–199; life charts in 104–105; mapping methods in 105–106; music-focused methods in 106; radio documentary 110; with reading group participants 188–190; with survivors of trauma 111–112, 151–159; for theatrical production 111; transcribing and coding data from 188–189; use of creative methods in 103–107
iterative practice 149–158

Kincaid, J. 210–211
Knausgaard, K. O.: *A Death in the Family: My Struggle Book 1* 16–17

Kopytoff, I. 35, 36
Kuhn, A. 79–80

Latinx recording artists 207–209
Lefebvre, H., method of
  rhythmanalysis for archival
  research 21
Lejeune, P. 86, 120, 171;
  "autobiographical pact" 210
letters 22, 83–88; censorship 85–86;
  critical frameworks for interpreting
  87; family 83–88, 247–250;
  friendship 20, 249–250; migrant
  83–88; reading and cataloguing
  86–87
life narratives: experimental 2, 70,
  96, 98, 101; as qualitative research
  data 228
life storytelling workshops 149–158;
  exercises for 155–158
literary studies 1, 3, 26, 70, 96, 116,
  118, 133, 146, 161
Lynch, C. 145

McNeill, L. 116, 136, 147, 204
memoir 13–18; authorship and
  authority 15–16; humour as
  narrative strategy 14; publication
  boom 13; reception 190; risks of
  personal disclosure 13; writing about
  family in 15–17, 248, 250; *see also*
  disability, memoir; HIV memoir
memory work 79–80; and music 106
methodology 1, 2, 4, 5–6, 8, 26, 241,
  247; big data 45, 116, 120; child-
  centred 229–230; children and
  youth life narrative 141–147; diary
  as 91; as distinct from method 161;
  girls' auto/biographical media 201,
  205; graphic biography 69, 70,
  73; humanities 2; journaling as 29;
  reading group 188–190; social media
  44–46; trans* lives 173; visual 50;
  zine-making as research 27, 30–31
methods: books and special journal
  issues about 1–4
"mid-range reading" 134–135
migrants 213–217: and family history
  79; letters 84–85, 248–249;
  testimony 113; *see also* diasporic
  literature; diasporic lives
Miller, N. K. 76, 77, 78, 79

narrative analysis 214, 232–233
narrativity 23

narratology 70, 111
new materialism 34–35, 181–182
new media studies 43, 44, 46, 135
Nguyen, V. T.: *The Sympathizer* 220,
  224–226

obituaries: online 161–166
object: biography 36, 180; *see also*
  elicitation, object
*Offshoot: Contemporary Life Writing
  Methodologies and Practice* 2
online lives *see* digital lives
oral storytelling 2, 63, 65, 80,
  125–130, 150–158, 213, 218, 228

paratextual analysis 136
Ph. D. research 27–29, 193–199
photographs: family 54, 76, 78,
  79–80; in graphic biography 69,
  72, 73; human rights work 152;
  use of in memoir-writing 17–18; *see
  also* selfies
podcasts 2, 109, 110, 112, 114; *see
  also* radio documentary
Poletti, A. 134, 136, 140, 142, 143,
  146
postcolonial: approach to research
  with children 229–301; critique
  210
post-disciplinary: approach to
  research 230
posthumanism 34, 35–36, 117
poststructuralism 43, 46
privacy 7, 42, 100; and diaries 91–92;
  in digital lives research 56, 132,
  137–138, 163–166; in family
  history work 80; in memoir-writing
  13, 16
prosopography: school yearbooks as
  auto- 252

queer: aspects of identity in Asian
  American autobiography 220;
  digital media 56; gender 169;
  marginalisation in understandings
  of disability 186; theory 44

radio documentary 110–114
Radway, J. 31
Rak, J. 13, 50, 77, 132, 134, 135, 161
reading: contextual 142–143; deep
  224; distant 118, 120, 134;
  embodied 187; as methodology 26;
  surface 44, 201, 224; *see also* close
  reading; "generous reading"

*Reading Autobiography* 3, 42
records: census 76; medical 251;
    public *vs.* private documents 145
refugees: life storytelling projects with
    150; stories and genre expectations
    225; *see also* asylum seekers

scrapbook: as auto/biography 252
selfies: in electoral and activist
    campaigns 50; Google "art selfie"
    49–50, 53; literary reading methods
    46; youth and ethics 145
self-tracking: devices as diaries 93; as
    research method 119–120
semiotics 54, 70
situated knowledges 30, 31
Skloot, R.: *The Immortal Life of
    Henrietta Lacks* 179, 182
Smith, S. 3; and Watson, J. 51, 116,
    118, 134, 136, 142, 193, 196,
    200, 202
Snapchat 41, 137, 201, 203, 204
social media 41–46, 136, 140,
    141, 144, 147, 253; death and
    commemoration on 162; methods
    and methodologies for working
    with 44–46, 137; posts 145
sociology 7, 43–44, 137, 143; and the
    sociologist 103
Stanley, L. 2, 85, 87
Steedman, Carolyn 23, 32n5

*testimonio* 220
testimony: child and youth 142;
    diary as 93; in human rights work
    149–159; in radio and theatre
    performances 113–114; "of things"
    36–37
textual analysis 2, 134: as method for
    reading zines 26; and theoretical
    knowledge 143
theatrical production 111–114
thick description 44, 137

Thien, M.: *Dogs at the Perimeter* 220,
    221–224
thin description 43, 44, 45
trans* autobiography 169–176;
    questions of appropriation when
    researching 172
trauma: Cambodian genocide
    221–222; childhood 249, 251;
    digital biography 164–165;
    Indigenous Australian lives 80,
    126–127; and memory 52–53;
    testimony in the production of
    creative work 111–114; Vietnam
    War 224–225; young people's
    selfies at sites of 145
travel narratives 79, 145, 180,
    210–211, 214–215
Turkle, S. 34, 35
Twitter 39, 41, 50, 136, 201; as diary
    91; youth life narrative 142–143

video blogs *see* blogs
visual auto/biography 49–58; *see also*
    digital lives; selfies
vulnerability 153, 164–165, 175,
    190, 228
"vulnerable subjects" 36, 144, 194,
    197, 247, 251

Whitlock, G. 93, 132, 142, 205

youth: activists and self-representation
    142–143; girls and young women
    200–205; self-representation in the
    theatre 112
youth life narrative 140–147
YouTube: comments section as
    reception data 202–203; and
    contextual research 143; as diary
    93; researcher participation on 134

zines 26–31
Zuern, J. D. 147, 163

Printed in the United States
by Baker & Taylor Publisher Services